Suffering & Spiritual Growth

Calamities and Providence

Ebrahim Amanat, M.D
From Trauma to:
Peace, Tranquility, Sanity and Dignity

Cover and text layout and design: A.Zuccarello@gmail.com

ISBN: (10 digit) 0-9777356-9-9

ISBN: (13 digit) 978-0-9777356-9-3

This book was published in the US by:

ONE WORLD PRESS

800-250-8171

PrintMyBook@OneWorldPress.com

www.oneworldpress.com

To my beloved wife, Mahin
&
to our children
John, Ray, Frank, Sean, and Diana

About this book:

"Suffering and Spiritual Growth" is an exciting and captivating account of trauma and emotional growth. It is a metaphoric presentation of human spiritual powers. The author in this book walks a mystic path with practical feet. He brings the Buddha face to face with Freud in mindfulness meditation. Stories and metaphors presented belong to life and existential experiences, which turn the ordinary human being into a hero. When traumatized individuals decide to go inward, in the process of creating a narrative, they find a relationship between their deepest heartfelt emotions and the Ground of Being. They grow, transcend and become poets, writers, mythmakers and heroes. . Amanat has presented a wealth of information about PTSD, the current hidden epidemic around the world"

Luis Shwarz, MD,
 Distinguished Fellow of American Psychiatric Association, Clinical Associate Professor of Psychiatry, St. Louis University: School of Medicine.

"Essential reading! How did Post Traumatic Stress Disorder become such a global epidemic of our times? Learn about the fundamental causes, symptoms research findings and means of turning the letters PTSD, to Peace, Tranquility, Sanity and Dignity"

Arnold Nerenberg, Ph.D.
Author and principal investigator of "Road Rage" field, writer, lecturer, poet and author of numerous books in psychology.

Dr. Amanat wisely and compassionately conceptualizes trauma as affecting both psyche and soul, reminding the practitioner and the afflicted that Posttraumatic Stress Disorder often only begins to describe an individual's wounds. Trauma, Dr. Amanat explains, may fundamentally challenge how individuals perceive their relationships with both their "fellow man" and with God (however defined). Paralleling his Baha'i integration of the wisdom of preceding faiths, Dr. Amanat cogently integrates what science thus far reveals of brain-body alterations linked with trauma with what faith-spirituality informs of such. Both means of understanding are enlisted by Dr. Amanat in creating a therapeutic approach that particularly addresses persistent posttraumatic bitterness, rage, and alienation. He describes harnessing metaphor, aphorism, and inspirational tale as therapeutic tools, introduces the technique of Adaptive Rocking Desensitization, and, perhaps, most importantly, details a twelve-step program designed specifically for those suffering trauma-related distress. Dr. Amanat very importantly advocates progressing beyond symptom resolution to achieving posttraumatic growth. He aptly writes in step two of the twelve-step program he describes:

"Even though we often doubt that survival was better than dying, we seek meaning in our lives in order to overcome our despair. We want to be free from the nagging experiences of grief, guilt, and rage. And we want to become a privilege rather than a burden."

All of us who treat or know those suffering the "invisible wounds" of trauma concur with Dr. Amanat that we seek transforming PTSD into "Peace, Tranquility, Sanity, and Dignity."

Stuart B. Kleinman, MD,
Professor of Psychiatry, Columbia University/Presbyterian, New York.

'The mind and spirit of man advance when he is tried by suffering. The more the ground is ploughed the better the seed will grow, the better the harvest will be. Just as the plough furrows the earth deeply, purifying it of weeds and thistles, so suffering and tribulation free man from the petty affairs of this worldly life until he arrives at a state of complete detachment. His attitude in this world will be that of divine happiness. Man is, so to speak, unripe: the heat of the fire of suffering will mature him. Look back to the times past and you will find that the greatest men have suffered most.'
    'Abdu'l-Bahá.'

These passions, simple but overwhelmingly strong, have governed my life: the longing for love, the search for knowledge, and unbearable pity for the suffering of mankind. Love and knowledge, so far as they were possible, led upwards towards the heavens. But always pity brought me back to earth.
    Bertrand Russell

The battle for the world is the battle for definitions.
    Thomas Szasz

Foreword

Hope for trauma sufferers and healers

Thousands of Americans are still hurting from loss of loved ones during recent traumatic events.. Tens of thousands have been killed, uprooted or injured in recent wars and disasters such as the wars in Iraq and Afghanistan, terrorist attacks, hurricane Katrina, tornadoes, and accidents. Millions more are traumatized daily by violence, abuse, and abandonment. Most people are bombarded by media images of brutality across the planet.

Some recover quickly. Some still ask, years later: Can I ever feel whole again?

Anyone can have post-traumatic stress disorder (PTSD). If you suffer pain or trauma resulting from war, natural disaster, rape, or a violent event such as the World Trade Center attacks, this book can help you to:

- *understand the nature of trauma;*
- *know what to expect as normal;*
- *take action without pills or expensive therapies;*
- *restore a sense of faith, hope, and love;*
- *apply spiritual solutions that turn trauma into growth;*
- *help those around you do the same.*

This book will help you to see PTSD not as an illness, but as an opportunity for growth. Based on the author's extensive personal and clinical experience over the past 30 years, spiritual solutions prove to be most effective in recovery and growth.

For readers who are therapists and practitioners, I have discussed effective treatment approaches, including my own method called Adaptive Rocking Desensitization.

Stop suffering. Start reading.

Acknowledgments

Over the course of the past 30 years, my patients have shared their stories, their anguish, their strengths and their journey to recovery with me. They have been my greatest teachers and fellow-travelers. Work on this book began several years ago with loving pressure from my patients.

I am greatly indebted to my colleagues Dr. Rosalyn Shultz and Dr. Jack Steingart for their help and encouragement, to the late Susan Marchese for years of collaboration in the treatment of victims of sexual abuse, to Candace Lyles for her years of participation in 12-Step PTSD ANON groups with me, to Professor Marcia Goin of the USC Keck School of Medicine for allowing me to present seminars and lectures on PTSD to psychiatry residents, to Dr. Gary Wolf for his valuable personal help during crisis times and to Manuel Martinez for his years of collaboration at the East L.A. Vet Center.

I am deeply grateful for the special training I received through the National Center for PTSD in Palo Alto, for the opportunity given me by the LA County Department of Mental Health to work with victims of domestic violence and Katrina victims who were moved to this area, and the staff of Rio Honda clinic for referral of American Indian children who were victims of abuse and violence.

I am immensely grateful to Margaret Zambrano, Frances Pavon, and Frank Amanat for reading and commenting on parts of the text, to Nancy Ackerman of AmadeaEditing for her painstaking editing of most sections of the manuscript and numerous helpful suggestions for its improvement, and to Susan Charles for proof reading.

My deep appreciation goes to Professors Stuart Kleinman, Michael Penn and Luis Schwarz and Dr. Arnold Nerenberg for reading and commenting on the contents of this manuscript.

I like to offer warm thanks to Dr. Joel Osler Brende for allowing me to draw on his ideas and writings in setting up my version of PTSD ANON programs.

Deep gratitude goes to my brother Dr. Alex Amanat for his collaboration in the emergency treatment of victims of rape, incest, and sexual abuse.

Finally, I offer my loving thanks to my beloved wife Dr. Mahin Mashhood Amanat for her patience, support and valuable suggestions.

A Sufi Tale

Long ago, there was a beautiful and much-admired young girl, who had lost her mother and felt forlorn and sad.

Her father traveled often, leaving her lonely and grieving. One day, he decided to take her on one of his trips, to find her a husband and help her to settle down. But when they were in the middle of the sea, there was a mighty storm and the ship was wrecked. Everyone else died, except the girl, whose body was washed ashore on an island. When she regained consciousness, she cried aloud, asking God why such terrible things happen to innocent people.

A local family of weavers was deeply moved, adopted her, and taught her their language and the art of spinning and weaving colorful cloth. But before long, a band of slave-trading pirates attacked the island and captured many slaves including the young girl. They sold her to a shipbuilding family on another island, who, in turn, forced her to work making masts for their ships. She complained to God again, asking "What have I done to deserve this? Why me?"

After they completed building the great ship, her owners took to sea to sell it in a nearby port. Once again, there was a storm, the ship wrecked, and all died except the girl. For the second time, her body was washed ashore. In utter misery she asked God "What have I done to deserve these calamities?"

Just as she uttered these words, a group of people approached her and, with the utmost kindness, told her, "In our land we believe that someday a beautiful young woman will be washed ashore and if she can make a colorful tent for the king she will become queen."

Table of Contents

Early childhood and family life
Education, persecution, and terror
Compulsive repetition of trauma in revolution
Medical school
Beginning the study of PTSD

PART I: The Dilemma of PTSD in the Age of Anxiety

Vignettes of calamity and suffering
Soul Loss
Recovery from soul loss
Domestic violence: Love or hate?

Obsession with death and dying (necrophilia)
War and martial values

PART III: Spiritual Recovery and Post Traumatic Growth

Introduction

A life devoted to things is a dead life, a stump;
a God-shaped life is a flourishing tree.
             Proverbs 11:28[1]

Pain and stress related to severe trials, disasters, and calamities have been observed since antiquity and reported by historians, poets, writers, and myth makers. In two of his tragic stories, the great Iranian poet Nezami used such words as "event stricken," and "calamity stricken." Shakespeare, Keats, and other Western writers have also described the impact of trauma.

After the many reports of shell-shock and battle fatigue among veterans of earlier wars, Nazi concentration camp survivors were among the first trauma victims to undergo massive scientific scrutiny. Clinical study of these victims revealed a number of psychological reactions, embodied in the term "concentration camp syndrome," often accompanied by a variety of physical illnesses and lower life expectancy. Holocaust survivors soon became the richest source of investigation for what became known as "post-traumatic stress disorder" or PTSD. The American Psychiatric Association soon officially accepted a new terminology for these victims' suffering, calling it "gross stress reaction."

In-depth investigation of these victims revealed many new insights. It was reported that the victims "gave up easily," that they were "unable to understand the meaning of their physical sensations," or to distinguish between various emotions. Although the Korean War resulted in tremendous progress in military psychiatry, the information explosion about psychological trauma occurred after the Vietnam War.

---

1   All quotations from the Bible are taken from the New Testament of the Jerusalem Bible, Reader's Edition, 1969.

J. Robert Lifton (1967, 1972) discovered and presented 27 symptoms of PTSD in Vietnam veterans. In 1970, at the height of the Vietnam War, a group of veterans set up discussion groups to vent their suffering and raise greater awareness about the effects of the war, pressuring the U.S. government to start outreach projects with a peer counseling philosophy. Government studies soon revealed the direct relationship between war and PTSD, leading to official acceptance of this diagnosis by the American Psychiatric Association.

PTSD afflicted as many as 20 to 30 percent of the entire combat population during the Vietnam War. The prevalence stemmed from protracted traumas, POW experiences, and also exposure to betrayal, rage, prejudice, racism, the breakdown of patriotic beliefs, lack of social support, and guilt.

In his masterpiece "Stress Response Syndrome" (1986), Dr. M. Horowitz proposed an effective two-phase treatment strategy for the victims of trauma. However, experience soon revealed the elusiveness of recovery from severe trauma and its spate of physical symptoms such as seizures, insomnia, high blood pressure, chronic pain, eating disorders, sexual dysfunction, endocrine, and immune diseases. These indications, both in war veterans and in survivors of abuse, violence, or torture, redirected our attention to the body's amazing ability to record and express trauma emotions.

In the 19th century studies of hysteria, no one acknowledged the presence of violence as a routine aspect of women's daily lives. The feminist movement of the 1970s demonstrated that the most common form of PTSD appeared not among war veterans, but among ordinary women.

It took much time and consciousness-raising for women to overcome the barriers of denial, secrecy, and fear to talk openly about rape. The women's movement in America generated an avalanche of research on the topic of sexual assault. Investigation by many researchers revealed the stunning fact that one out of every three or four women had been raped, and one out of every three had been sexually abused as a child. The feminist movement redefined rape as a crime of violence and as a method of oppressing women through terror. Since the publication of initial scientific papers on rape, a flood of new research has revealed the consequences of physical, sexual, and emotional abuse, incest, battering, and family violence. The results coincide with the combat PTSD studies.

Awareness of post-traumatic stress disorder (PTSD) has dramatically increased since the September 11, 2001 attacks on the World Trade Center, due to the intense attention paid to terrorism and its consequences.

Indeed, we can easily claim our age to be the age of anxiety and terror!

Among human emotional problems PTSD is unique, having a definite point of onset and clear symptoms. Twenty-eight years has passed since PTSD was defined and included in the DSM III of the American Psychiatric Association. In the ensuing period, we have witnessed an explosion of information about its causes, symptoms, treatment, biological characteristics, and about the brain's memory and alarm systems.

In this book, I have presented a spiritual approach to the understanding and treatment of PTSD, in order to change the emphasis/focus from a disorder to a growth perspective.

PTSD is an anxiety disorder which (in 20 to 30 percent of individuals) begins acutely after exposure to major trauma and becomes a chronic illness with disabling characteristics.

Recently, we have become aware of another significant fact: the majority of traumatized individuals take a different path, called Post Traumatic Growth (PTG). Thus, I have organized the book in three sections: the first focusing on traumas which generate PTSD; the second on the remedies and therapeutic approaches to the treatment of PTSD; and the third on recovery and post-traumatic growth, or PTG.

Global research has been extensively focused on the biological aspects and pharmacological treatment of the PTSD syndrome. Only recently has a spiritual approach been gaining momentum.

Brain imaging studies using PET, SPECT, MRI, and fMRI techniques have revealed structural abnormalities in the hippocampal region of the brain and a hyperactive function of "emotion responsive" brain structures such as the amygdala, cingulate gyrus, and prefrontal areas. These are, nevertheless, neuronal substrates expressing human existential experiences and intense emotions.

Chemical-pharmacological research has demonstrated a number of neurotransmitters involved in PTSD, including serotonin, epinephrine, norepinephrin, gamma-aminobutyric acid (GABA), opioid substances, DHEA, cortisol, oxytocin, and a whole array of neurotransmitter receptors in the brain which function as sensory gates. Their actions are similar to the function of pupils which constrict in bright light, but become paralyzed when the intensity and duration of light exposure overwhelms them.

Terrifying experiences that shatter a person's sense of predictability and assumptions of safety profoundly alter the ways in which these individuals deal with emotions and the environment. Widely varying traumas such as terrorism, war, physical and sexual abuse, violence, accidents and natural or man-made disasters can lead to similar symptoms of PTSD.

As it becomes increasingly difficult to find a safe place to live anywhere in today's world, PTSD has become a hidden epidemic.

Who gets PTSD?

PTSD is quite common in the general population but particularly affects individuals with a high level of vulnerability, temperamental sensitivity, who are deprived of social support or loving bonds, or who have suffered earlier childhood traumas, or prior emotional or psychiatric problems. The role of memory and dissociation is also quite important. Since traumatized individuals cannot accept and integrate their painful memories, they charateristically engage in "splitting,"[2] and dissociation, or try to repress or bury them deep in their unconscious mind.

---

2   Splitting can be explained as thinking in dichotomous extremes, e.g., good vs. bad, powerful vs. defenseless, right vs. wrong, and so on. A two-year-old child is not sufficiently developed to be able to see a person who does something unpleasant (such as not feeding him when he is hungry), as possessing one or more bad characteristics among other good ones. The other person can only be seen as all bad at that moment in time. However, when this person gratifies the child, he or she will be perceived as all good again. Splitting was first described by Pierre Janet in his book *L'Automatisme psychologique* (1889). Splitting may become a coping mechanism later in life if a person fails to accomplish the task of integration of opposites, such as we see in borderline personalities. They are not able to integrate the good and bad images of either self or others. Splitting as a central defense mechanism enables the individual to preserve self esteem by seeing the self as purely good and others as purely bad. Splitting creates instability in relationships, when an individual can be viewed as either all good or all bad at different times, depending on whether he or she gratifies needs or frustrates them. This, and similar oscillations in the experience of the self, leads to chaotic and unstable relationship patterns, identity diffusion, and mood swings.

The longer and the more intense or repeated one's exposure to overwhelming traumas, the more intense the initial fear, helplessness, or horror, and the greater the possibility of developing PTSD.

What is trauma?

Trauma can be defined as:

- Mental, physical, sexual, and verbal abuse[3]
- Catastrophes and natural disasters
- International, domestic, and ideological terrorism
- Violence and man made disasters
- War, explosions
- Witnessing serious harm or death and threats of death to self or others Betrayal, kidnapping, etc.

Different types of PTSD

There are three types of PTSD: acute, chronic and delayed. Any one of these types can make the individual vulnerable to anxiety, panic, phobias, depression, obsessive-compulsive disorders, character defects, and even madness.

Symptoms of PTSD

These are divided into three categories, which we shall explore in detail in Chapter 3. Briefly they include the following:

- Intrusive symptoms such as flashbacks, nightmares, reliving experiences, intrusive thoughts, emotions and memories, dissociative states, insomnia, exaggerated emotional reactions, guilt feelings, etc;
- Avoidance and numbing responses, such as avoiding emotions, relations, places, events, responsibility for others, or situations which remind one of the traumatic events; depersonalization,

---

3   Child abuse is so rampant some researchers such as psycho-historian Lloyd DeMause, consider it the foundation of history (DeMause).

depression, twilight experiences, alcohol/drug abuse, and amnesia;

- Hyperarousal, such as exaggerated startle reaction, explosive outbursts, violence, hypervigilance, irritability, panic attacks, sleep problems, visual or auditory hallucinations, self victimization, etc.

The role of memory and dissociation

Since the core problem in PTSD is a failure to accept and integrate trauma experiences into one's autobiographical memory, splitting and dissociation reactions are very common. Until the details of these memories are assimilated in the individual's narrative of trauma, such dissociations continue and memory problems persist. Certain parts of the brain, such as the hippocampus and amygdale, which are related to recall, recognition and memory, are involved in this process and some researchers believe that the intensity and duration of traumatic experiences actually damage these structures. Thus, it is not surprising to notice that sufferers of PTSD have learning problems due to memory impairment. Modern memory research reveals that like a phoenix, memory continually arises from the ashes of its own destruction. Memory can be rewired and reconsolidated which makes the development of narratives extremely difficult. The flexibility of memory however has positive adaptive qualities, which helps victims of trauma update their store of knowledge.

Some of the issues discussed in this book

- Life is inherently stressful and colored by trauma or disaster.

- Stressors include developmental and health issues, such as birth, divorce, death and aging, physical disability, chronic illness; or they can include natural disasters such as earthquakes, floods, or hurricanes and man made traumas, such as rape, war, terrorism, explosions, and airplane crashes. All can threaten the physical or psychological integrity of individuals or their loved ones.

- Disasters and terrorism, in particular, cause a severe disruption in life, exceeding the coping capacity of the individual.

- Stages of response to disaster include, impact, heroism, acceptance, disillusionment, disorganization, and eventual recovery.

- Impact is often colored with shock and disbelief. In the heroic phase we face an acute stress response with intense alarm.

- In the acceptance phase, rescue operations create a brief feeling of calm that "it is over now."

- In the disillusionment phase the enormous effects of disaster are recognized and perceived. The illusion of safety and basic life assumptions about invulnerability are shattered.

- Individuals lose their sense of benevolence in life and belief in God's justice, convinced that there is no one to protect them in their hour of need.

- In the disorganization phase the sufferer begins to feel helpless, fearful, and vulnerable, and develops symptoms of PTSD, as coping mechanisms fail.

- The symptoms of PTSD are cyclical and can be triggered by anniversary dates or other reminders of trauma.

- PTSD is seen when one has experienced events that threaten serious injury or death for self or others, associated with intense fear, horror, or helplessness.

- People suffering from PTSD re-experience and relive the images of trauma, avoid whatever reminds them of trauma, do not retain parts of their memories, feel detached, and/or become irritable. They are hyper-vigilant and have an exaggerated startle response.

- Sometimes traumatic events are single episodes; at other times, they consist of sustained repeated events.

- The prevalence of PTSD in traumatized individuals varies between 15 to 30 percent. 70 to 80 percent of victims respond with growth and strength. (PTG).

- At times PTSD is combined with depression, anxiety, phobias, substance abuse, the undoing of character, or even breakdowns.

- Terrorism is the unlawful threat or use of violence against people, property, governments, societies, or religious groups for ideological reasons.

- Many terrorists have been abused or humiliated, and loathe being a victim; they become paranoid and focus their hatred on victimizing others. Some act on delusional or fanatical religious or political beliefs.

- Responses to terrorist attacks include PTSD symptoms, awareness of loss and possible future threats, feelings of anger or revenge, mobilization, and patriotism.

- At a later stage, there may be increasing disillusionment, loss of idealism, self-protectionism, doubts about leaders, and scapegoating.

- In order to recover from PTSD, one must regain one's sense of safety, relive and discuss the traumas over and over with trusted people, write and complete a comprehensive narrative story of the traumas, clarify fiction from reality, find adequate support from family, friends and support groups. Reliving and re-exposure to trauma images may initially provoke anxiety, but it gradually desensitizes the nervous system. One must find some meaning in the experiences and process feelings of guilt, anger, grief, betrayal, helplessness, revenge, and fear. This is best done in spiritual 12-step survivor groups, which help the individual to change attitudes, regain a belief system, integrate the traumas in life and identify triggers. One of the best adaptive approaches to PTSD is for the individual to practice the Step 12 program by listening, helping, and caring for other traumatized individuals in a survivors group.

- Other approaches to treatment include desensitization such as eye movement desensitization and reprocessing (EMDR) or adaptive rocking desensitization (ARD), group therapies, medications, anxiety management, cognitive therapy, and critical incident debriefing, as well as spiritual approaches aimed at finding meaning in trauma experiences and giving "PTSD" a new meaning: "Peace, Tranquility, Sanity and Dignity."

Rationale for writing this book

Psychological trauma and post-traumatic stress disorders trigger a human response that focuses more on banishing painful memories, rather than on sorting them through.

After all, certain violations of the human spirit seem too horrible to remember or to talk about.

Yet the memories lie hidden beneath the surface, intruding on our thoughts at will. We may try to deny or repress them, but atrocities and violence refuse to be buried. The ghost of the trauma can haunt the victims relentlessly until their stories are told.

Indeed, as we understand the past, story narratives help us to reclaim the present and future. Clearly, remembering the truth of suffering is the main prerequisite for healing. Survivors of trauma often report contradictory and fragmented stories, at times undermining their own credibility, but when the whole undistorted truth spills out, the recovery process begins. Only then can non-verbal and secret expressions of trauma fade away and the victim's anguish be transformed into spiritual awareness.

Writing a book about suffering, trauma and growth did not come easily for me. It evolved over many years. During the 1970s, I became heavily involved with the plight of sexual abuse victims, whose suffering proved intense and contagious. I treated hundreds of rape victims, from a two-year-old girl who had acquired syphilis to a brutally violated 60-year-old nun. Experiencing the agony and helplessness of these victims, I fought in many courts to make the symptoms of PTSD admissible as evidence in rape trials.

During the 1980s, my involvement with borderline patients and families of victims of incest and abuse increased my interest in the field of trauma and led me to take on the position of coordinator of a PTSD research and treatment program. Throughout these 30 years, I came to realize the healing power of speaking the unspeakable and lifting the barriers of denial from pain and repression.

This book is the culmination of three decades of clinical work with trauma victims. It presents spiritual solutions for human suffering and advances the concept that suffering can lead to strength and spiritual growth.

I have written this book for both sufferers and students of PTSD, the patients and the therapists. Each chapter highlights insights into the spectrum of human beings response to suffering and how that suffering can lead to greater spiritual growth. Before taking the reader on this journey, I will take the liberty of sharing a portion of my own story and explain how trauma affected my spirit.

Chapter One: My Story

Unless you assume a God, the question of life's purpose is meaningless.
        — Bertrand Russell

Blessed are those who trust in the Lord.
        — Jeremiah 17:7

Early childhood and family life

My drama began long ago. Perhaps chance or fate played a hand in my life. I was born and raised in a loving extended family in Iran. My father was an enlightened man with a deep sense of compassion and a vision of historical purpose. In his childhood and youth, he had been raised by an orthodox Jewish family. Due to his remarkable knowledge of the Hebrew Bible and the gift of a melodious voice, he had become a cantor in the local synagogue. He was well known in the city of Kashan as a wise man with fine musical talent and the ability to entertain. He used to travel frequently to the city of Hamadan for business.

It was in this city—which contains the tomb of Esther—that Cyrus the Great issued his decree for the rebuilding of Jerusalem. According to Jewish tradition, the book of Esther will have great importance in the Messianic Age. Shortly after the Bahá'í Faith was introduced to Hamadan, a mass conversion of Jews to the new religion began around 1877, when at least one-third of the city's Jewish families became Baha'is. My father had been in contact with some of the charismatic Bahá'í teachers, former rabbis in Hamadan, and he became convinced that Bahá'u'lláh[4] was the long-awaited Messiah.

---

4   A title meaning "The Glory of God," and the name of the Prophet-Founder of the Bahá'í Faith.

The social position of Jews in Iran during the late nineteenth century was unstable and precarious. Although at times they were accepted by the Muslim majority as "people of the Book," and treated relatively well, they were considered a minority that had to pay special taxes and were thought of as "untouchable" (najiis) in the Iranian community. For the most part, they were severely persecuted, segregated, forced to live in ghettos and wear a special sign showing their Jewish identity.

For Jews to become Bahá'ís, however, was to put themselves in mortal danger, since Baha'is were considered heretics deserving of death or annihilation. Killing them was considered a sacred duty for Muslims. Thus, I was forever in awe of my father's courage in taking such a risk. As is still the case in Iran today, heretics were asked to recant their faith or be killed.[5]

There is great similarity between the early history of the Bahá'í Faith and that of Christianity. For my father, it was absolutely clear that he had found the Messiah and that he was willing to give his life for the new faith. Like most other Bahai's, he never recanted his faith. His conversion had stirred great conflict in his Jewish family and among the Jews in Kashan, but he was spiritually on fire and unshakable.

Among his many qualities, my father was a true spiritual healer. He sought inner knowledge and had an intense commitment to his fellow human beings. This particular trait led him to set up tents in our backyard to house as many as 20 Jewish refugees during the later mass exodus of Jews to Israel.

My father never lost sight of his own emotional wounds while struggling to create meaning for others. Rather than expecting someone else to serve as his healer, he chose not to reveal his pain to others. He proudly preferred to minister to his own wounds from within. His intense devotion to the Bahá'í Faith had helped him to teach and bring at least 500 more family members and friends to the new Faith. This phenomenon of conversion spread very quickly among Jews and Zoroastrians—the two major religious minorities at the time—since the Messianic proofs from the Bible and in the Zoroastrian sacred writings were clear and unequivocal. There seemed to be a powerful spiritual transformation moving across the land and creating a new culture of progress and freedom.

---

5   Readers interested in greater detail about this early period of Bahá'í history in Iran may refer to the work of historian Habib Lavi et al. (1999) and Susan Maneck (1990–1991).

My mother was the eldest daughter of a Sephardic Jewish rabbi. She became a Bahá'í following a dream in her youth. As a result, she, like my Father, endured much suffering from the deep family prejudice until she married my father. She adored him and perceived him as her inspiration, telling us often that a man should inspire his family. She did not expect anything from my father but for him to face his own anguish as she did. To her, this was the root and sign of their strong devotion to one another.

My parents' mutual strength impressed me greatly. In my childish innocence, I marveled at their emotions, hopes, and dreams. With blissful fantasies of omnipotence, I thought at times that I, too, knew everything and was the master of my own fate. I survived several serious illnesses as a child and was therefore nicknamed "Lucky." From my earliest years, I felt attracted to the good and the positive. This I owed to my mother's contagious optimism.

The greatest gift my parents gave me was their encouragement to independently search for truth. My father's many wonderful stories and teaching tales provided a subtle path for my search. His fairy tales taught me how tears could change people's hearts. Our family suffered deep sorrow, but we all considered tears to be the foundation of love. A Sufi prayer I knew asked for one's heart to be shattered so that it could contain limitless love. My family cherished this belief, so I learned as a child that suffering could give birth to compassion. This principle later became one of the main themes of my existence.

Twenty-two members of my extended family, including my grandparents, uncles, aunts, and cousins, lived in several apartments in a large communal house built around a spacious yard with a swimming pool and many fruit trees. This house was located in one of the poorest neighborhoods in Teheran, very close to the Jewish ghetto of "Sare' Chal," but surrounded by the homes and businesses of many poor Muslims.

These people were generally hostile to Jews and especially to Baha'is, to whom they displayed a condescending and prejudiced attitude, considering them "najjis" or untouchable "infidels." Encircled by such hostile neighbors, we were each other's sole support. Boundaries between our family members were blurred—both a blessing and a considerable problem, as respect for privacy and separateness was not a birthright, and premature knowledge of sexuality was par for the course for all the children. But in periods of crisis or illness, family members assumed each other's responsibilities, giving all of us a sense of confidence and continuity. I cannot imagine how my life would have turned out without the comfort of this communal family experience. One touching example: my uncle Isaac had adopted one of my orphaned cousins; in order not to cause any sense of strangeness for this cousin, my uncle taught all his own children to also call him "uncle." This was a mystery to me until he explained his reasoning several years later.

At the age of two, my oldest sister had fallen on her head from the second floor and from then on suffered epilepsy. Her seizures were frightening to me, but my mother had taught all of us how to take care of her during a seizure. Her helpless condition might well have been one of the initial reasons for my interest in medical education, which began when I was six or seven years old.

Following the 1917 Revolution in Russia, the Bolsheviks had invaded northern Iran and, and with their Iranian communist sympathizers, looted my father's two stores, reducing us to poverty. It was only from my mother's stories that I heard about a time when my father had been prosperous. My uncle Isaac was the only family member who had a radio and most of us crowded into his apartment often to listen to music or shows. He probably enjoyed having that special privilege. Both my father and my uncle Elias were musicians, singers, and entertainers. So we had the blessing and pleasure of many private family mini-concerts and comedy sketches. These were soothing remedies in our otherwise traumatic lives.

Education, persecution, and terror

My elementary school was an Anglican Missionary project called "The School of Light and Truth," staffed by converted Persian Anglican nuns, called "Miss," since they believed they were the brides of Christ. We also had some Jewish, Muslim, and Zoroastrian teachers, as well as some Iranian Christians. Although loving and kind, the nuns were strict disciplinarians and rather harsh in the punishments they meted out to the students. We learned Hebrew in order to read the Bible in its original language and English to read books, such as Lorna Doone and Robin Hood. Joyous and lively Christmas festivities were filled with the wonderful tales about Christ. Sending me and my siblings to this school was my father's way of exposing us to European thinking along with its good education. Although the school had only six grades, it was enough to strengthen my belief in God and His messengers. Indeed, I can say that the combined input of my parents, my grandfather, and my schoolteachers made God a member of our family!

With my limited understanding, I perceived everyone in my school and neighborhood, even those who were cruel and savage, with the untainted eyes of a child, unable to separate the reality around me from my imagination. My father would often recite passages from the writings of Bahá'u'lláh, such as this passage from Hidden Words, which I particularly loved: "O Son of Spirit: Noble have I created thee, yet thou hast abased thyself." Thus, I perceived all these people as essentially noble and only corrupted by inadequate education. That way, it was easier to be forgiving of their hostile actions.

Accepting my father's enchanting tales as my own reality, they became the bedrock of my development. No matter what happened to me, I could reenter a state of innocence by remembering a story, shedding my cynicism, and looking at the world through the loving spirit of my father. Returning to such spiritual innocence did not require much of an effort. All I had to do was to stand still and the magic of the tales would take hold of me.

Relying on my parents' compassion, I felt emotionally strong, even though we faced severe persecution and harassment as followers of the Bahá'í Faith. The Muslim neighborhood around us was chaotic and crime-ridden. Immediately next door was an opium den which was often raided by the police. The addicts would usually run to the roof and try to get in to the neighboring houses to hide. We received them many times and led them out through the back door. Only a block away, there was a house of ill repute where a number of Muslim or Jewish prostitutes worked. They were also raided frequently by the police. Most of the other neighbors were Shiite Muslims and very hostile to Baha'is. They did their utmost to bully us, stone our house, or verbally and physically harass us.

As Baha'is, we believed that the Creator had made man in His own image and that God was a transcendent reality who ruled and maintained all existence. We also believed that God had formed a covenant with humankind to lead people into love, fellowship, and unity by sending divine messengers throughout history. Bahá'u'lláh, we believed, was the latest messenger of God for our time. Since the majority of the Muslims in Iran perceived the prophet Mohammad as the last messenger and what they called the "Seal of the Prophets," they heavily disputed this idea. Thus, from its earliest beginnings, they saw Bahá'ís as the hated heretics of the nation or the so called the misguided sect.. Baha'is in many parts of the country often lived in turmoil, suffering constant harassment, unbearable hostility, continuous death threats, and daily oppression. These traumatic experiences were more intense among the lower classes and those communities who had deeper prejudice against minorities. Those who were more educated were more tolerant of minorities. Yet persecution was always a threat during times of political or social upheaval in a country in need of scapegoats.

I have no claim on truth, but the personal experiences of multiple traumas during my own childhood and youth unveiled to me the significance of spirituality on trauma resolution and growth. To me, trauma and spirituality operated as two sides of one coin.

Years later and after completing my training in psychiatry, my interest in PTSD was triggered by my years of exposure to personal trauma. Moreover, these same experiences became the foundation of my own spiritual growth and sensitivity toward other traumatized individuals.

Growing up in a repressive culture as an identified heretic, particularly during middle and high school years, I was chronically abused by my classmates, neighbors, and the community at large. As with all the members of my family, I was often threatened with hostile brutality, which precipitated intense feelings of helplessness and fear. Many Bahá'í leaders, doctors, lawyers, and other successful individuals were tortured and murdered for their beliefs. Others were harassed, oppressed, dismissed from places of work, and dispossessed. Members of my immediate family were physically assaulted, humiliated, or threatened with death.

As a child, I became a repository for memories of martyrs and stories of tragedies that had occurred during a hundred years of genocide against Bahá'ís. Fear and nightmares were my daily companions. Terrifying images of aggression smothered my natural spiritual being, like a fire under ashes.

Many of my classmates from the various political groups bullied me mercilessly, beat me, smashed my teeth, stoned my house, urinated on me, and threatened to kill me as soon as their party took control of the country. As I mentioned earlier, these attacks were more common in the poverty stricken areas of Teheran where we used to live.

Although my father had enrolled me in what he thought was one of the best high schools in Tehran, called Dar-al-Fonoon (College of arts and sciences), it was anything but a center of knowledge. The principal was a child molester who was later arrested and sent into exile. The school itself was chaotic, ruled by brute force and attended by thugs and delinquents. These boys, some of them very strong physically, bullied others, attacked teachers with knives and other weapons, and generally terrorized everyone with regular fist fights and abuse. Even though the principal brought police and soldiers to keep a semblance of order, the thugs stole anything of value, from light bulbs to the PA system and lab equipment. The teachers labored in an atmosphere of fear and disrespect and a few of them were corrupted, asking for bribes to give a passing grade. My geometry teacher was hostile to Bahá'ís and flunked me one year for no reason, with the result that my father had to bribe him to change his mind.

Ghader, one of the Muslim bullies who used to torment me, knew well my feelings of frailty and fear at being in an enclosed space. He was physically strong and ruthless. His father was an influential police officer and he felt immune from punishment. Once after the school hours, he locked me in the school coal room, a dark and frightening place. For two hours he banged his thunderous hands on the door. He said he was going to leave me there to die. I could not see anything and was afraid that I would suffocate. No one knew where I was and I could not escape, no matter how hard I tried. His twisted laughter was terrifying and I screamed continuously for help. I was afraid he would kill me. Finally, a passing teacher heard my cries and rescued me. Complaining to the principal was useless, as it would only bring down the wrath of the bullies and expose me to more attacks. Our next principal was a heavy-set wrestler who often used a log to attack and hurt unruly kids. His approach to bullying was to call the culprit and his victim to his office, where he would ask them to demonstrate what had actually happened. As the abuse was going on, he would join in, attacking and beating both parties. He hated the Baha'is in school and once assaulted me with a pair of scissors because I carried a small Bahá'í prayer book in my pocket. I had no one to complain to.

One evening as I headed home, four bullies from my class spotted me in a dark alley. One of them was built like an adult, with broad shoulders, a beefy neck and massive legs, though he was only 13. He had already been suspended or kicked out of most school programs. But in my school, he was in the boxing club, and most kids were afraid of him. The bullies, all carrying switchblade knives, shouted that they were going to kill me. My heart pounding with terror, I ran as fast as I could, screaming for help. But no help was forthcoming. At the time, it did not dawn on me how cowardly I must have appeared to them. I could only run for my life, hearing their jeers and laughter behind me. My heart pounded and my legs pumped like a hot rod. After running for 10 to 15 minutes, I saw a house with an open door. I crept in and shut the door behind me. I knew no one in this house. I was afraid of being caught as an intruder or a thief. I descended to the basement and hid there for a while, bursting with fear for at least two hours before I dared to leave the house and return home. After that incident, I was thankful not to be hurt. As these painful events kept occurring throughout my childhood and adolescence, I began to see and compare my misery to the fate of other Baha'is being persecuted or even murdered all over the country and thought my portion of torture was relatively light. At times, I could not attend school for days, for fear of running into my school bullies again.

The Bahá'í community and my extended family served as my psychological refuge, offering a powerful sense of kinship and strengthening my confidence to move on. We felt like the early Christians, destined to sacrifice our lives for the spiritual rebirth of mankind. The Bahá'í sacred writings encouraged us to have spiritual distinction, to love mankind, to be faithful, steadfastness, and to respond lovingly to hatred and abuse. I tried hard to remain firm in these principles and continued to treat my tyrants with compassion. Many years later I encountered Ghader accidentally. He approached me with tears in his eyes and apologized profusely for his conduct and asked me to forgive him. He called me an angel and attributed some of his own change of heart to my kindness.

Stories of the heroic lives of the Bahá'í martyrs of the 19th century reinforced my sense of responsibility. Strong belief in the afterlife and the presentation of death as a messenger of joy were soothing influences as I struggled with traumatic events. Yet the never-ending cycle of trauma continuously challenged my belief in human values.

My own encounters with trauma as a young boy were at times less than heroic. My PTSD symptoms often made me feel lost in a world of absurd pain without any ultimate order. During my early childhood, the horrors of World War II had compounded my family's anguish. Before the invasion of Allies, we heard daily remarks by our Muslim neighbors that Hitler would soon arrive and destroy all Jews and Baha'is. The Allies invasion was an attempt to prevent the Nazis from attacking Russia from the south. A multitude of Jewish refugees from Eastern Europe were later brought to Teheran by the Allies and housed in crowded destitute tent cities. As a result, food was rationed and an epidemic of typhus fever caused tremendous suffering for everyone. American soldiers guarding these tent cities were the only kind people we encountered among the Allies.

This period was marked by the bombing of military installations in the capital city, the arrest and exile of the monarch, Reza Shah to South Africa, famine, street demonstrations, mob threats, and chaos. When my beloved uncle died of typhus fever and several members of my family became seriously ill, I thought I could bear no more. I asked God what I had done to deserve this torment.

The traumatic events from my high school days caused me repeated PTSD arousal symptoms. I startled easily and walked around in a state of deep anxiety. I had acquired a dreadful, inexplicable consciousness of imminent death. I experienced a range of emotional responses associated with PTSD, sometimes chronic and sometimes acute. During the years after Mohammad Reza Shah was brought to power, there were many times when Baha'is were used as scapegoats to divert national attention from other issues or crises. I heard radio reports predicting the impending genocide of our fellow believers. These broadcasts during my teenage years, along with the frightening news of killing, looting, arson, and even the destruction of homes and cemeteries, engendered a continuous sense of terror in me.

My father's purpose in life had been to keep the family together, so that his children could have the security to develop their natural spiritual capacities. But he realized that, much as he loved and provided for us, there were many social limits to raising well-adjusted children in such a prejudiced culture. He also knew the terrible cost to his own health of maintaining a sense of tranquility. Repressing his own fear and anger in order to appear strong resulted in high blood pressure, a chronic cough, and other physical symptoms. My mother's style of loving is something many people never acquire. She did not possess much in the way of material comforts, but gave generously. She had a tender way of combining love, discipline, and respect, often sacrificing her own needs for those of her children. I will never forget the many nights that, lantern in hand, she would search the alleys around our home to find us and bring us home safely.

I was 11 years old when my father's health began to fail. It was hard for me to deal with that reality, and whenever I shared my concern he insisted that he was fine. I went on deceiving myself, believing that he would indeed be fine. At night, he suffered from shortness of breath and often dozed off slouching forward against a wooden stick. In the daytime, when we went for a walk, he frequently had to stop to catch his breath. One night when I was 13, he called me into his room and talked to me seriously about his illness: emphysema and heart failure. He told me that no matter how much it would hurt to lose a father, I was to be strong and helpful to my mother. The conversation that night still causes me intense pain. He told me that his heart was failing, that he did not have much more time to live. My childhood ended that night. I was overtaken by a wave of emotion, and cried hard. I wondered why God was punishing my family this way.

My father was not afraid of death. He saw it as a "messenger of joy." His faith was strong, and he felt that, come what may, everything would be fine. We were children of his second marriage and all very young. He wanted to make sure we were taken care of after his death. Over the next several months, he talked with me many times. He tried to drill into me a sense of responsibility. He encouraged me to remain firm in my faith and out of trouble. "Always let God guide your life and no one else," he said. "God has spared your life many times, and you should never give up."

My maternal grandfather was a rabbi, and my deep love for him had brought me very close to the Jewish side of our family. As a child, I had been to his synagogue many times and had witnessed the Jewish rituals for remembrance of suffering. Their immense sense of community was a ray of hope, and the possibility of exodus made life more tolerable for them. Indeed, after years of preparation and hope, immediately after the establishment of Israel as a nation, a mass exodus of Jews from Iran began.

The Jews had numerous days of ritualized mourning and prayer, so they did not have to keep their suffering private. This was an immensely important aspect of resistance to trauma, as it created a transcendent meaning for all suffering. My reaction to the dreadful condition of the Baha'is was to intensify my family bonds. The family was all I had. We had become totally interdependent. I soon realized that it was easier for me to talk about "us" rather than "me." All things became "ours" rather than "mine," as I let go of the illusion of self.

We could all contain our nightmares, fears, paranoia, and agitation much more easily when our family members were together. Faith was our only refuge. Spiritual convictions helped us to process painful realities. They became the building blocks of our self-perpetuation and survival. Our assumptions, although helpful in providing an illusion of safety, further isolated us within the community at large. In such an environment of segregation and fear, we experienced our daily share of trauma with all five senses. We appraised them communally and adapted to them as best we could.

As a young child, I was taught to believe in the unity of mankind and in the need to mingle with people of all creeds. But these assumptions were incongruent with my environment, causing me great confusion and at times dissociative reactions. I had my first out-of-body experience at age 13. It was very frightening to see myself sleeping on a couch and yet walking around. I suffered from night terrors, anxiety attacks, palpitations, indigestion, and insomnia. Many of my family members also suffered from sudden panic attacks and depression.

For the sake of survival, and in order to distract myself from the oppressive environment, I focused heavily on learning and achievement. In school, I was often the first to arrive and the last to leave. I was hard on myself when I made mistakes and studied diligently to correct them. Constant study and strong self-discipline honed my skills and helped me stay at the top of my class. I became a bookworm. To protect myself against the bullies, I made a pact with a huskier classmate: he would act as my personal bodyguard and I would do his math assignments.

Gradually, I learned how to deal with intimidation. I strengthened my ties with the Bahá'í community and deepened in my spiritual practices. I behaved like a soldier in hand-to-hand combat, totally supportive of and enmeshed with my family members and friends. In 1955, when Iranian government officials destroyed the Bahá'í National Center in Teheran, there was also a court hearing, in which some Bahá'ís falsely accused of murder. When we learned of a plot to assassinate the lawyer who was defending the Bahá'ís, a group of devoted youth (including the author) put their lives in danger to protect him from certain death.

The collective experience of oppression caused the social boundaries among the Bahá'ís to become blurred, leading to a form of intense interdependence. This heightened sense of unity served as my only safe haven in a culture of anxiety. Aware that my Jewish family members were free to join the exodus to Israel, I also began to think about the future as my sole avenue of hope. As a child, I had learned about America and began to prepare myself to take refuge there, by any means, and as soon as possible. The future became a vehicle for me to prove my honor and courage. The only meaning that I could find in my suffering was to save my family and friends, some day in the distant future. I was aware that my experiences could never be reversed or erased, but my defiant soul had chosen to give them a completely new meaning. This was one more reason for my decision to become a doctor.

I realized as a youth that having a quest, a direction, a sense of meaning decreased my pain and despair. I knew that no one could change my basic attitudes. My father had strongly encouraged my search for meaning. It soon became my treasure chest of hope. His endless tales and stories helped tremendously. The poetry of the classic masters Rumi, Hafez, and Attar provided a set of lofty ideals completely aligned with my religious beliefs and those of my Jewish heritage. I read T. S. Eliot's "Wasteland," which impressed me deeply as a youth. I came across sections under "what the thunder said" and learned the thunder's message: to forgive, to look inside, to learn, to care for others. and to follow the righteous path. These were the gateways to meaning for me. I became aware of my uniqueness and started to pursue my educational goals. Marlon Brando's movie, "Teahouse of the August Moon" taught me that pursuit was far more important than achievement. My childhood traumas intensified my faith, as my concerns shifted to the positive aspects of life, to detachment from self, respect for others, and transcendence. There were so many ordinary people who looked the other way in fear when confronted by tyranny. My hope was not to do so.

The Bahá'í sacred writings had taught me to be "generous in prosperity and thankful in adversity, a treasure to the poor and an admonisher to the rich, an answerer to the cry of the needy, a haven for the distressed and an upholder and defender of the victims of oppression."[6]

My vivid dreams and the practice of meditation helped me recognize the evil demon of the "self" as I learned how to bear witness to it. When I postponed confrontation with that inner darkness and begun to rationalize or deny, I struggled as a youth to confront myself in order to become an instrument of transcendent hope and love. The life stories of such historical figures as Christ, the Buddha, and Bahá'u'lláh were instrumental in reviving a spirit of hope, service, devotion, and steadfastness.

Passing of my Father

For several weeks my father's physical condition worsened. His doctors could no longer do anything to reverse it. Emphysema had led to severe

---

6   Bahá'u'lláh, *Epistle*, p. 93.

heart failure, and he knew his end was near. On the night of his death, my father slipped in and out of coma and at last gasped, his mouth fell open, and his life was over. I was 14 years old. The family members turned to the poetry of Hafiz, following a Persian tradition that this great poet knew the unknown and thus could guide people spiritually. What appeared was a sad poem about leaving without saying goodbye.

The next few days after his funeral, were an eternity. Like a book suddenly closed, he had left me forever wondering what he wished me to do. I frantically cried, as my mother tried to calm me.

My father's death left the family feeling even more helpless in the face of tremendous difficulties. I felt deep despair for that entire year. Losing him meant separation from my core. It meant losing my ability to center myself. Self-deprecation and guilt came easily. I felt ugly and diffuse. I almost failed school that year. Like Peter Pan, I had become a boy who now refused to grow.

Compulsive repetition of trauma in revolution

A crisis of faith

For a while, I lost interest in school and almost flunked that year. Later, my history teacher, who respected Bahá'ís, took a fatherly interest in me. A complex but charismatic man with no children of his own, he wanted me to be everything I could be. He was obviously frustrated by my deep depression. He helped me to survive in school by introducing political issues. I soon found myself collaborating with the Iranian National Liberation Front, led by the late Prime Minister, Dr. Mohammad Mossadegh, and a revolutionary movement called the "Third Force."

At that time I knew little about PTSD symptoms and specially the concept of the "compulsive re-enactment" that happens to victims."[7] So I started

---

7   Compulsive re-enactment (also known as repetition compulsion, trauma addiction, or compulsive re-staging) was identified by both Janet (1899 and 1911) and Freud (Strachey, 1962). Some trauma victims themselves become victimizers or violent; others become self-victimizers and relive or re-enact their traumas through co-dependent relationships or masochism. This phenomenon is seen as a way of achieving mastery over the helplessness of trauma. It is similar to therapeutic approaches of exposure desensitization, in which the individual is repeatedly confronted with memories of traumatic events. Immediately after re-enactment, the brain releases endorphins which calm the victim. Some individuals become addicted and continue to re-enact traumas for the pleasure created by these substances.

my re-victimization behaviors along with thousands of other unhappy Iranians in a futile revolution. I joined demonstrations against the former government's police and military forces, since, like others, I had identified the regime as our national oppressor. We all felt that a corrupt dictatorship had poisoned the nation and that needed to be purged from our midst. I had several traumatic experiences during these political demonstrations, some of them almost fatal. I had been taught by the party how to avoid being a target and some of the tactics I had learned certainly prevented me from being killed.

But I had returned to my habit of splitting, classifying people as either angels or demons. During the events of that period, the government had used the police and military forces as well as the Constitution to remove Prime Minister Mossadegh from power, there were bloody uprisings, some of which left more than a thousand people dead in one day. The Secret Service (SAVAK) and the military would attack the demonstrators with bayonets, guns, grenades, and tanks. One young girl stood heroically in front of a tank but the driver ruthlessly drove over her, crushing both her legs. At one point, I was attacked with a few of my friends by a group of soldiers and we began to run. One soldier hit me hard in the mouth. Bayonet in hand, he looked ferocious. I could taste the blood in my mouth. He then hit me hard in my left elbow and I heard a cracking sound and felt intense pain. The crowd was running desperately and the soldiers were following us. I turned down a small alley and, fearing for my life, flattened myself against a wall. Some of the attackers came into the alley but ignored me and followed my escaping friends. I hid in some garbage and sat there, quaking, until the sound of screams and bullets faded away. Although many of my young comrades perished that day, I somehow miraculously survived. The bloody street rallies and the images of young people being crushed or killed by explosives or stabbed to death with bayonets revived my PTSD symptoms as I became more vigilant and possessed by fury. Although it eventually healed, my elbow remained permanently bent.

During this period of frantic political activity and protest, I had become confused and dangerously distracted from the spiritual, non-partisan Bahá'í teachings. One extraordinary day in the midst of a rally, witnessing the despair of my friends and feeling victimized and miserable, an amazing feeling washed over me. I cannot adequately describe it, as it defies logic. But it is engraved in my memory forever. A living silence visited me, reaching deep into my soul. My fears suddenly melted away. I was filled with a wonderful serenity. The illusion of being a revolutionary disappeared and I felt a deep love, as if my father were taking hold of me. For a moment I saw my father looking at me with deep sorrow in his eyes. I was bewildered and overjoyed, but somewhat ashamed of what I had become. It seemed to me that the pain of seeing what was happening to me was causing him great sadness. I immediately decided to quit politics and withdrew temporarily to a remote mountain village in order to meditate and lick my wounds.

Later, I attended some of the court trials of Dr. Mossadegh, who was accused of treason. There, I met the famous lawyer Mr. Shahgholi, who was assigned to defend the former Prime Minister. When I learned that he was a Bahá'í and that he was conducting seminars about religion and spirituality, I began to attend. Gradually I decided to return to my spiritual roots, participate actively in Bahá'í life and, at the same time, try for a scholarship for medical school.

I studied long and hard and was eventually accepted. At the university, I rejoined a loosely organized Bahá'í student club and met Mr. Faizi, the man who was to become my spiritual father. His loving guidance filled the vacuum of my life. As he listened compassionately to my story, he was the embodiment of love and acceptance. His presence among this group of disillusioned youth made it safe for me to explore my spiritual nature again and recapture the powers of my soul. Cradled in this man's unconditional love and devotion to our group, I was able, once again, to free myself from the prison of darkness and deceit that surrounded us. It was not long before the intensity of Mr. Faizi's love burned away my depression and confusion, and revived a sense of hope and steadfastness. I had begun my journey of post-traumatic growth.

Gradually, I allowed my spiritual energy to fill me with peace. I felt reborn and open to all the potential entrusted to my soul, and, in the words of the Bahá'í writings, able to rid myself of "attachment to all created things." I felt forgiven and transformed. One night in a soul-stirring dream, I realized that I was not, and never had been, alone. That universal animating power, my hero with a thousand faces, had always been present. I needed to open my inner eyes and gaze upon His beauty. When I awoke, I prayed hard with tears of joy. I decided to use all my powers to serve humanity. The door to the past memories was not closed, but they were integrated with my new being. A door had been unlocked as the mystery of spirituality worked its will.

Medical school

Medical school was exciting and often filled with fun-loving times. Out of several thousand annual applicants, only 250 could get a full government scholarship for the entire medical school course, and I was fortunate to receive one. Everyone in my family was thrilled by my success and from the second year of pre-med started to call me "Doc."

I was assigned to a subgroup of 40 students who studied together at the college or in its affiliated hospitals. Many of these fellow students had a keen sense of humor and we had many laughs with our professors. There were 20 Bahá'í students in my class and we dedicated ourselves to service and to assisting the poor. Since I was working part time for one of the pharmaceutical companies, I was earning a fairly good income. Together we rented a garden and cottage outside of Teheran to provide first aid, initial medical and literacy services for the indigenous villagers.

I already spoke English relatively well and managed to translate some medical books into Persian, and co-authored several volumes with the late Dr. Farrokhroo Parsa for high school students.[8] My academic and social activities during medical school gave me special status at the university and I was able to graduate in 1960.

Beginning the study of PTSD

After finishing medical school, I married and moved to the United States to pursue further education. When I completed my training in psychiatry and child psychiatry, I launched myself into a lengthy study of trauma and its wake.

Having come from a medical and scientific background, I had become used to viewing human beings as a vast reservoir of organs, tissues, cells, and molecules, organized in a dizzyingly complex physical system. As such, I believed that medication, cognitive and behavioral therapies and psychodynamic approaches were the best remedies for human existential and emotional problems. But in the course of my study of PTSD, I discovered a much deeper state of consciousness in all human beings, completely separated from mundane everyday life. I realized that as psychological healers,

---

8   Years later, Parsa became the first female Secretary of Education in Iran, and after the Islamic revolution was hanged for her pioneering work for women's rights.

we had sent our spiritual roots into exile by changing psychotherapy—which, after all, meant "care for the soul"—into a lifeless practice of illusions, images, arbitrary labels, and beliefs. We had assumed that the human brain and emotional problems are determined by chemical transactions, ignoring the effect of intense existential experiences of our lives on mental disorders. We had now acquired a broken brain and needed medications or shock therapy to correct its function!

I felt, in order to overcome the consequences of society's alienation from the soul, that psychiatry and psychology was in need of fundamental revision. To escape from the prison of our defense mechanisms, we needed to enter the garden of love and spirituality. To release our deceptive thought processes from what the great Sufi poet Rumi called the "four evil birds" of slavery to matter, we were challenged to let go of the soul-contaminating habits of greed, lust, power, vanity, and narcissism.

For years, men, women, and children have walked into my office with feelings of terror, anxiety, emptiness, loss of meaning, depression, disillusionment, hunger for spirituality, and yearning for fulfillment. Feeling shrunken and demoralized, they have had to deal with the skeletons of frightening secrets beneath overwhelming emotions. I became more and more sensitive to the suffering of these victimized people as I met with hundreds of traumatized patients. I recognized the profound relationship between trauma and spirituality. In group therapy sessions, I discovered that love for one's fellow sufferers can be a healing balm for those facing post-traumatic emotional challenges.

Because I find it difficult to write about such love in logical fashion, I shall use a metaphor to present my understanding of what I think love means. Legend has it that the loving radiance of the prophet Joseph, while in prison, awed his fellow prisoners. One of them questioned him about his hidden recipe for happiness in the face of so much adversity. In reply, Joseph compared himself to a grain of wheat, first buried in the ground in the cold of winter, intended to blossom into a stalk of wheat in the spring, and then be crushed into flour, made into dough and baked in a fire to evolve as bread. Once eaten, the bread would then take human form. Joseph explained that he knew that the anguish of any one stage would lay the foundation of his transformation in a later stage. Thus, he could love all those who had put him through the pain of adversity and wait for the glorious outcome.

Love determines not only how well or poorly we function, but colors how we experience life. Empirical fact-finding and rational thought can never explain the intuitive, tender, and romantic nature of love. Love focuses on faith, illusion, destiny, and the warmer interpretation of existence. It tolerates ambiguity and contradiction as various facets of human experience. The best way to focus on love is to tell love stories—stories that unite the apparent and the hidden, joy and pain, life and death. We are psycho-historical beings, capable of a love in keeping with our true worth. Love opens our inner vision to the highest potential of the human being for transcendence. Love does not err.

The union of our bodies and souls is an "I-Thou" affinity.[9] Any attempt to separate this amazing connection reduces us to mere objects or subjects of illusion. Love, the union of our inner core, is our human nature. Without it, we have no relationship with ourselves or with others. It removes the traces of prejudice, fear, hate, and inhumanity by opening our hearts to the blossoming of flowers, the sound of bells, and the color of compassion.

As a child psychiatrist during the 1970s, I became heavily involved in the treatment of sexually abused children. Young victims—unlike older family members who had been silenced by society for many generations—began to talk and reveal their horrifying secrets. Simultaneously, during those same years the women's movement brought new awareness of the intensity of violent crimes against women. I met hundreds of victims of all ages and began to speak out in their defense in the media and in the courts. My first paper, "Developmental Variations of Rape Trauma Syndrome" was published in 1984.[10] I was then appointed by the Governor of Missouri—a state known as the capital of incest—to a committee for the prevention of sexual abuse. I presented a series of television programs called "Incest: The Invisible Taboo."

By this time, I had realized that people exposed to psychological trauma suffer from predictable symptoms. I also recognized that in order to study these symptoms, one must simultaneously focus on human vulnerability and resilience. My theoretical emphasis in trauma recovery became essentially transformational and spiritual. I found that I could synthesize my insights much better using a spiritual approach and more effectively help the victims. Later experiences confirmed this point of view—the subject of this book.

---

9   Reference to the term coined in 1937 by Martin Buber (1974).
10   See Stuart and Greer (1984), pp. 36–73.

PART I: The Dilemma of PTSD in the Age of Anxiety

Chapter Two: Human Nature: Noble or Sinful

Happy the man who stands firm in times of tests. He has proved himself, and will win the prize of life, the crown that the Lord has promised to those who love Him.
James 1:12

A tempest, unprecedented in its violence, unpredictable in its course, catastrophic in its immediate effects, unimaginably glorious in its ultimate consequences, is at present sweeping the face of the earth.
Shoghi Effendi

Vignettes of calamity and suffering

Fred's story: Man or beast

In a moment of contemplation during a PTSD group session, a man I'll call Fred posed a simple question to the group and to me: "Doc," he said, "what do you think of me? Am I a man or a beast?"

As I scanned his face, the question caught me off guard for a moment. A 46-year-old Vietnam veteran, Fred stood six feet tall, squarely built, with broad shoulders, several scars on his round, sunburned face, a firm chin, upwardly curving lips and yellow teeth. His eyes bore the unmistakable calm and deadly gaze of a killer. His hair was sandy gray. Fred's serious demeanor made it impossible to take him lightly or joke with him about anything. The group members all knew this and respected his gravity. He often became annoyed by this, and generated an air of malice. One could read a danger-ous, calculated craftiness in his manner. Perhaps a malignantly self-centered man, he projected an air of confidence and talked smoothly.

He then said: "I'm confused about my nature, Doc. Sometimes I be-lieve I am like a sheep and at other times I consider myself to be a beast. What do you think? I am so seriously confused. Sometimes I am so naïve, it is ridiculous; and sometimes I am so cunning I feel like a monster. I let authorities control my mind. I conform softly and follow their commands, even when their demands are illegal. Military leaders, police, bank owners, doctors, priests, and anybody in power are attractive to me. I have a sort of blind faith in them, and you, too, Doc. I follow your directions as if I don't have any convictions of my own."

John, one of the group members, interrupted him, saying: "Is that what you call a sheep, Fred?"

"Well, maybe I am not a sheep," Fred replied. "Perhaps I am a cha-meleon. I figure that when somebody makes a decision for me, I am less responsible for the consequences. It was so easy to be in the military. I had no personal decisions to make and nothing to be responsible for. Yet some-times I ask, if I'm a sheep or even a chameleon, why my hands are so stained with blood?"

I asked if he was referring to his Vietnam experience. "No way, man. I'm talking in the present tense. Right at this moment, sitting here in this group, in front of you, I could waste you for the silliest possible reason. See this knife?" Pulling a large switchblade out of his pocket, he continued. "I never go anywhere without it. Since the end of the war, I have maimed, hurt and perhaps killed people. I can hardly remember the reasons, but I am sure they were all for stupid reasons."

Another group member, Richard, blurted out with apprehension, "I know this, Fred! It's so intimidating to be around you. I've felt this way for months, but I have dreaded talking about it. How does your family take all of this? To be honest with you, at this moment I feel pretty shaky being around you."

I asked him if he carried a knife as means of keeping his distance from others. I felt that on some level, he was robbing me of the opportunity to be his therapist. Perhaps the complexity of his soul was sending me a double message: a wish to be intimate and, at the same time, a fear of closeness.

Under such conditions, I had to walk on eggshells around him, trying to figure out his next move.

"Are you giving up on me, Doc? Is that it?"

"Not at all. We all share your confusion to some degree," I said. "You took the risk of passing through the building security and brought a weapon here. You know the regulations against the presence of weapons in this office. So what shall we do now?"

"It's not like that, Doc," said Fred. I'm not as mixed up as you may think. I have changed. Perhaps some of the group members have noticed that. I came here for help, not to harm anyone. I was in the "hole" for many years. I'd hate to go back to the penitentiary. True, I've used force to break other people's will or their bones, but now I feel bad about it. I want to get away from all of that. People talk trash about Hitler or Stalin, but I feel almost as bad as those guys.

"Did you ever see the movie 'The Seven Beauties'?" he continued. "I often ask myself, what would I do if, like the movie's main character, my survival depended on killing others? Would I kill my friends or family members? Strangely enough, I fear I might say yes. Now that's horrible. You know what I think? I think for every Hitler or Stalin in the world there are thousands of people like me, who accept orders to kill or torture, some even enjoying what they do. I did. I enjoyed killing those gooks. Even if they were civilians, it didn't matter to me. We didn't know who 'Cong' was and who wasn't. Sometimes I just went berserk. Has anyone in this group ever gone mad or berserk? Initially, I was ordered to kill, but then, as time passed, I started to enjoy the act of killing on my own. It was a sordid form of fun, man. Beastly, but exciting: atrocities, tortures, burning homes, you name it. I did them all. I felt powerful and ruthless. I didn't listen to those folks cry. To me, they were not real humans or children. As I look back nowadays, I realize I was not alone in doing that. I feel so many men are savage killers like me. I figure you wouldn't hesitate to kill me if you could save your own life."

When he stopped to catch his breath, Fred suddenly burst into tears.

"Fred, before you go any further," I pleaded, "let's see if you can bridge the gap with all of us by giving me that knife."

"Scared of me, Doc?"

His penetrating, fierce eyes lost their light for a moment as he moved away from me and took a deep breath. I felt anxious, but kept staring back at him. Then he bent over and handed me his sole symbol of control. His voice was hoarse and he mumbled now, revealing self-pity.

"I'm married now, Doc. I have two kids. I need help. When it comes to my own children, I'm so soft you can't believe it. I can't talk loud to them. I would kill anybody who tries to hurt them. In my life, there are many opportunities to lose control and hurt somebody, but for the sake of my kids, I let go.

"I knew someday I would be punished for my crimes, but I didn't know the extent of my penalty. You see, when God dishes out punishment for crimes, mine seem the lesser crime. I am broken now. I am a monster in sheep's skin. Sometimes I daydream about being a military leader or a king, using all sorts of lies to hide my own brutality. For the sake of national security, I would justify vengeance and humiliation or even murder."

He shook his head and went on, without waiting for a reaction.

"National security—it's the biggest lie our leaders use. It's something they use to help others relinquish their will power and follow orders. It's true that perhaps all of us have a Dr. Jekyll and Mr. Hyde in the closet. There were times when I thought we should nuke Vietnam. It didn't matter to me if 20 or 40 million people died, as long as I would be free to go back home. I hated those people. I hated the South Vietnamese more than the North Vietnamese, and yet I had gone there to fight for their freedom. Freedom! Whose freedom are we referring to?"

He started to shout. "What's the meaning of this crazy life?"

Prompted by a thought that had caused strange feelings, Fred sighed and continued, "I have never been happy with my church's position. Catholics claim that man was born in sin. It was only the mercy of God through his Son who died for us, that we are redeemed. I don't buy that. I believe man's violence is the consequence of what he endures. If you look at how I grew up, the abuse and torture my father put me through, you may understand my violence better.

I do not know what vanity could I have wounded as a newborn child and what emotional or physical illness caused my father's coldness to me. Was I a child whose very life was a reproach? I was treated with such hostility by my parents that even the neighbors pitied on me.

I didn't have a lot of choices. I was a simple, everyday victim. As a young kid, I think I did believe in justice and goodness. I thought that someday my father would be punished. I wanted to believe that God was a loving creator and everything would be all right at last. But that day never came. As I grew older, I learned the real truth. I see a whole nation morally bankrupt. We have lots of Hitlers and Stalins here in this home of freedom. We are the ones who destroyed Berlin, dropped the Hiroshima bomb and destroyed Vietnam."

His tone of voice softened noticeably, and when I glanced at him, he smiled reassuringly. He was silent for a few minutes, and then began again.

"I believe the conditions we grow up in, either exaggerate or decrease our physical aggression. I have not ever shared this before, but today I will tell you what happened to me. It's strange, but I can trust you guys."

Here was a man who had several times harbored suicidal thoughts, who had challenged the police to shoot him, and who had been saved only by the courage of his wife, a man who had kept his war experience under wraps for fear of retribution, suddenly deciding to blurt out his deepest secrets.

"In Vietnam, I killed three American soldiers. They were going to rape a little 12-year old Vietnamese girl. Seeing what they were up to reminded me too much of my own childhood. I pleaded with them. I threatened them. They gave me no choice. I shot them all. No one ever found out about my crime. I fragged[11] their bodies. God knows how long I have suffered thinking about this."

Tears welled up in his eyes, and with a heroic effort to contain them, he turned his face away. He seemed to feel small and ugly. He sank into the chair and continued in a mumble.

"The Vietnam War corrupted me. It was invented by the worst of our politicians, money mongers and drug dealers. The soldiers were pawns. We were sent there like Christians to the lions. We thought only of our own survival. In those days, life was cheap. It was hard to feel anything. Many times while I was in that place I wanted to die myself. I was hoping that a bullet would just explode my brain. Too many friends had died and life seemed worthless. But then part of me really didn't want to die. Killing gave

---

11   "Fragging" is a slang term used in the Vietnam War for assassination (using a fragmentation grenade) of one's unpopular military superior. Fragging was more commonly used as a term to describe friendly fire in Vietnam.

me such high energy. For a moment, when I killed those three guys, I felt high. I had warned them to let the little girl go. They wouldn't. They were undressing and preparing to rape her. I couldn't take it. I guess you could call me a war criminal. I am as corrupt as anybody else. Maybe I am a *gook*. I became a *gook* with the first man I killed. From that moment, I imagined myself as a killing machine. I think I changed drastically and became a stranger to myself."

Fred's meandering thoughts illustrate how our process of imagination-reflection-intuition leads us to an awareness of our dark side. The theater of our memory presents clusters of images linked by archetypal fantasy. Distorted, hideous representations can become essential aspects of these dark memories. We frequently depend on these twisted images to reinforce our own personal mythological themes. But recognition of our fantasies as they play out through our lives helps us to look directly into the unconscious to make sense of the daily struggle.

Dealing with Fred's life story, guilt, suicidal behaviors, as well as my own confusion in confronting a war criminal created one of the most difficult challenges not only for me in my professional work, but also for the group members. At times I was overwhelmed by my contradictory emotions in dealing with a killer-saint, wanting to surrender him to the authorities or let go of my relationship with him. At other times, realizing there was a national amnesty for Vietnam veterans, my hope was to help him return to a more normal and productive life. If he were spiritually transformed, he could be a great ally in helping other veterans deal with their dark secrets of war.

Mythology and spiritual metaphors, presented in the context of group therapy was my only refuge. I decided to talk about the myth of Achilles[12] and the Trojan War to the group and encourage them to discuss feelings of betrayal. The book *Achilles in Vietnam: Combat Trauma and the Undoing of Character* by Dr. Jonathan Shay (1994) was extremely helpful. Such symbolic stories eventually helped me, Fred, and the group members become more trusting of each other and understand the context of his terrible experienc-

---

12   According to Greek mythology, Achilles was the bravest hero of the Trojan war. When he was born, his mother, Thetis, tried to make him immortal by dipping him in the river Styx. As she immersed him, she held him by one heel and forgot to dip him a second time so the heel she held could get wet too. Therefore, the place where she held him remained untouched by the magic water of the Styx and remained mortal or vulnerable. In many cultures to this day, any weak point is called an "Achilles heel."

es. He was able to perceive his background of tyranny, aggression, violence, murder, guilt, and fear as vehicles for spiritual growth. Group and individual work with Fred continued for two harrowing years before he could integrate his split personality into integrity and wholeness. He has continued to be a volunteer helper with other war veterans and hopes someday to study law for greater defense of veterans.

Soul Loss

Soul loss—or "susto," a name given to PTSD in some Latino cultures—refers to an acute state of terrified helplessness or loss of meaning in life. It indicates the process through which alienation from one's spiritual nature leads to obsession, addiction, anxiety, violence, and depression. Psychological counsellors encountering trauma victims may try to remove or alleviate their symptoms without being mindful of the "soul loss" concept. But the spirit, the generator of intuition and imagery, does not focus on relieving symptoms or lessening pain. Rather, it tries to remove disillusionment, to create meaning and satisfy spiritual hunger.

The soul continuously strives to achieve a balance between pain and pleasure, failure and success. Thus, although the metaphoric and spiritual approach to the resolution of trauma may seem old-fashioned, it is actually radically new. It taps into ancient classical notions of the soul, while advancing new psychological concepts.

John Keats, the romantic English poet, referred to "soul making" as a way of finding connections between the soul and human life (Stillinger, 1982). To deal with the soul, we must first define it: it is a non-material entity, and, as such, it cannot be described with reference to time or space. The soul is that self-sustaining, imagining capacity of inner vision, and is present even when the ego, consciousness, and subjective awareness cease to function.

According to most sacred scriptures, the soul is independent of the physical body and the events of earthly life. Sometimes called the "faculty of inner vision," the soul is the basic component of psychic life and the creator of spontaneous and inventive patterns of imagery. The soul enables the human being to encompass a variety of viewpoints and allows for the widest spectrum of expression. The mansion of the human soul has many rooms, many bright colors, and many voices. It can explore allegorical meanings and produce stunning insights, images, dreams, and fantasies. At times, victims of trauma lose this fundamental capacity of the soul and feel lost.

What Jung and his followers saw as a "partial personality" is, in reality, an aspect of internal spiritual relationships or, figuratively speaking, a community of the soul. These images create reality, since the soul serves basically as an image-maker, seeing all things in a multi-faceted way. Ignorance of the soul makes our lives godless and profane, as we become possessed by the ego, our defense mechanisms, and our biased thinking.

The Swiss psychiatrist Carl Jung conceived of the soul as a "collective universal image."[13] Since the soul emanates from the Creator—in effect a mystery of God—we cannot claim the soul as our own. To think otherwise is to take a timeless, infinite phenomenon and confine it to within our finite minds and mundane experience. In other words, the human mind comes from the soul and not the soul from the mind.

The path of spiritual growth is liberally strewn with afflictions, tests, and difficulties. Wounds and breakdowns enable the soul to move toward deeper awareness of psychic realities, yet psychological trauma may throw the soul temporarily out of balance. It may create a crisis of conscience on the personal, social or therapeutic level, leaving us spiritually confused. In fact, traumatized people often carry an altered self-perception and a distorted picture of reality. They may "lose" their souls and become alienated from others and from their spiritual center. They may lose their sense of self as loving and moral beings, that is, until a spiritual metamorphosis takes place.

Throughout my years of practice, I came to see the transition from affliction to love as the only effective remedy for the resolution of the effects of trauma. I saw that trauma creates a paradoxical moment of reflection and puzzlement. The soul then intervenes to move from the manifest to the hidden, using metaphor as its vehicle. Sensitive to all aspects of living, the soul surges with creativity.

The complexity of the human soul makes it difficult for trauma survivors undergoing individual psychotherapy to gain spiritual balance. For whenever we try to reduce the soul to definitions or dogma, we ignore the soul's basic nature and miss the significance of such issues as mind-body, God-soul and nature-nurture interaction. Rather, spiritual balance comes

---

13 See Moore (1992), pp. 22–24 and Hillman (1997), p. 128.

more easily within a community of trauma survivors, who each practice the art of surrendering to God. In a group setting, it takes much less effort to identify the truly human issues of love, value, justice, change, the soul, and God. There, the group milieu provides the bedrock for spiritual awareness.

More than 30 years of international research has demonstrated the uniqueness of the healing process for each individual. Yet professionals in the fields of psychology and psychiatry now recognize that enhancing spirituality can be a powerful remedy in the resolution of trauma. Recovery finds expression more easily in spiritually directed groups than in individual psychotherapy.

Recovery from soul loss

Calamities and spirituality are like the two sides of one coin. Victims of severe trauma initially feel unprotected, vulnerable, and unable to trust others. They may feel betrayed, abandoned, abused or violated. However, sooner or later, we can each see PTSD symptoms as metaphors of meaning. The truth of the human soul comes to us in poetic and symbolic language, almost like a beam of light in darkness leading us to post-trauma growth.

For thousands of years, spirituality and an attitude of prayer, along with a strong and loving support system, have helped to insulate victims of trauma against soul loss. This approach is valuable primarily because human beings have an innate desire to make sense of their experiences. Most traumatic events are painful, unbearable, and confusing for the sufferer. In spite of that, tragic stories present solid evidence of the positive value of human life. Within a strong community of survivors and with a renewed sense of spirituality, traumatized individuals regain their hope and learn to carry God's benevolence to other sufferers. I have encountered many people who have learned to love again while traveling the path of spirituality with fellow sufferers in a group of survivors. Tapping the capacity for love serves as the cornerstone for recovery from aggression, vulnerability, and the whole complex of trauma-based emotions described in the stories that follow.

I shall present a detailed narrative about the state of the soul in psychology in Chapter 14 of this book.

Domestic violence: Love or hate?

Lisa's story

Lisa, a beautiful 28-year-old woman, told a horrendous tale of sexual abuse, including ritual abuse by her mother, father, and an aunt. She had worked through her emotional difficulties and managed to complete a degree in social work. With an instinctive tact that never quite deserted her and a desperate, enduring, and harrowing grief, Lisa often brooded about her past experiences. Her grief was not easily observable, but the tone of her voice revealed her pain. She often talked about the disturbing flashbacks of her childhood abuse.

Lisa wondered why men are so violent and brutal. She had vague recollections of sacrificial rituals during which she was warned to remain silent or risk being killed. She had never been able to understand her flashbacks of these events. Whenever she confronted her parents, she received nothing but denial. Nevertheless, her images of these traumas were recurrent and troublesome. During many years she had re-consolidated these memories with more intense emotions.

Throughout her professional life, Lisa had felt compelled to study violence and aggression. In this particular session of group therapy, she began to explain why.

"For some people violence seems to be a show. Football, wrestling, boxing, and the martial arts are understandable to me. I know intuitively that Hulk Hogan is never really hurt. Yet I detest violence. I'm not sure how many people know why they act violently. I consider violence in self-defense as somewhat acceptable, but violence to cover up some inner fear freaks me out. I know that most fears are not real. They're just illusions. Yet everybody participates in this kind of violence claiming that they are doing it in self-defense or to preserve personal, family, social, or national security.

"Survival is another big excuse. For the sake of survival, anyone could kill and destroy, without feeling responsible or guilty. I was pretty badly abused myself and had thoughts of revenge for years. On numerous occasions I thought about killing my mother, my father, and my aunt. I knew their brutality and wanted to get even. Without revenge, there seemed to be no justice. I thought many times about 'an eye for an eye.' But then I felt guilty being so angry. I've known many friends who experienced abuse, trauma, and abandonment, but they survived and remained strong and resilient. They had no thoughts of revenge. They could forget and forgive much more easily than I. They lived with others and could experience love. Their lives were in total contrast to mine. My mind seemed broken, fragile, and confused.

"When my revenge fantasies became strong, I often felt weird. I knew that my family had destroyed my life, but to feel so outraged about it made me very self-critical. My father is a sick man, a blazing alcoholic and very disturbed. My mother, I think, has sold her soul to Satan. I hate to go home to visit them. But when I do, on holidays, I sometimes lose my sanity and go straight back into the madhouse. Every time I'm there, my father manages to get dead drunk and find his way to my bed in the middle of the night. There are no locks. He wants to mess with me again. He wants to persuade me to return home. He talks about his desperate love for me. He claims that his life and death are in my hands. He apologizes and intimidates with no shame or inhibition. I kick him, slap him, and scream. I get sick to my stomach and want to throw up on him. My lunatic mom takes sides with him and says I am making a scene.

"Last year I called the police on him for attempted rape. They did nothing. They just embarrassed my mom, who refuses to leave the creep. I swear to God I will never go there again! My belief in the goodness of man has been shattered because of my father. I remember fleeting moments in my childhood when I did believe in love and justice, but I was robbed of those convictions. All the lies, cover-ups, and brutality in my family destroyed my peace of mind. I fear them. I know that they really do not love me."

A sense of victimization commonly accompanies prolonged traumatic experiences. When a victim of trauma can escape a tyrant, he or she may not have to endure trauma a second time. By contrast, war, captivity, detention in a concentration camp or years spent living under abusive family conditions all imply repeated traumas without the opportunity to escape. This pattern generates a long-term state of victimization, with the victim feeling always at the mercy of the perpetrator.

Domestic violence is perhaps the most common source of victimization. For abused children and women, the home is indeed a prison. There are no bars on the windows and no visible barriers, but the invisible psychological barriers are powerful and brutal. Dependency, economic and psychological subordination, as well as physical force, keep the victims trapped. A special type of relationship based on coercion develops, which forces the victim to submit to humiliation.

The perpetrator's ego thrives on exerting superiority. It draws strength from a rational but paranoid vision. Such an ego manipulates, victimizes, and destroys in order to establish brute power. This distortion of the powers of the soul can lead to grim cases of sadomasochism, in which the struggle for power actually destroys the life force of another human being while corrupting the perpetrator's spiritual nature. Genuine spiritual power, under these circumstances, degenerates into tyranny and victimization.

Exposure to repeated or protracted violence often leads to the loss of emotional control, difficulty processing information, and uncertainty in discriminating stimuli. Stories reported by hostages, concentration camp survivors, and prisoners of war reveal that their perpetrators used similar approaches to coerce, subjugate, and demoralize. Although domestic abusers have no specific training in torture, they tend to use the same methods to humiliate and victimize. They create terror and helplessness to establish control and destroy their victim's sense of autonomy.

For most victims, the mere threat of death or violence works as well as violence itself. Once the victimizers have achieved full control over the victim's mind and body, they become not only the main source of terror, but also a solace in the hope for food, comfort or a kind word. This granting of small favors further debilitates the victim's resistance. In prison camps, a combination of terror, isolation, intermittent reward and forced dependency may lead to absolute compliance and submission. Fear may be intensified by violent outbursts of rage, which destroy any possibility of resistance to the perpetrator's power. The victim's bonds of attachment to others may be severed by forced isolation, which, in turn, intensifies the emotional dependence on the tyrant. The victims may start to see reality from the point of view of their victimizers.

Examples abound. Battered women may be forced into sexual practices they once detested. Prisoners may be broken to the point where they become completely passive, sub-human creatures for the sake of survival. Victims of prolonged trauma or domination violence may be prone to hypervigilance, agitation, furious outbursts of temper, and arguments at the slightest provocation. They have no capacity for calm. They practice altered consciousness to bear the unbearable. They hold contradictory beliefs to play tricks on reality. At times they direct their rage inward, harboring thoughts of suicide. Abused children display self-destructive behaviors such as self-mutilation, excessive risk taking, or even suicide. Traumatized people can lose their natural life force, provoking others to abuse them in masochistic fashion, as if they were victimizers of the self.

The prevalence of abusive relationships and the breakdown of normal human relations rank quite high among traumatized individuals. At times, totally submissive victims can transform themselves into dominating victimizers. As Thomas Moore explained:

The sadomasochistic splitting of power has the characteristics of all symptomatic behaviors: It is literally destructive and involves a polarization in which one side of the split is apparent, while the other is hidden. People who turn to violence are visibly controlling; what is less obvious are their weakness and feelings of powerlessness (Moore, *Care of the Soul*, p. 97).

For some victims of battering, on the other hand, a compulsion for repeated exposure to trauma works as a convoluted route to recovery. This tendency, labeled "trauma addiction" by some researchers and "co-dependency" by others, can contribute to eventual emancipation and healing through gradual mastery.

Many victims of violence identify with and take on the characteristics of the aggressor by becoming hateful abusers, covering up for their vulnerability and reverting to victimizing behaviors. In order to replace the feelings of helplessness with an illusion of power, they victimize others. The case of Patty Hearst and the Symbionese Liberation Army as well as numerous victims of torture is good examples.

Male victims commonly become the aggressors, while female victims tend to respond more passively, sometimes falling in love with a violent, abusive individual. Often women who act as perpetual victims are not aware of their own indirect or co-dependent methods of control.

Yet another pattern of behavior is seen in some PTSD sufferers. When they or a loved one are traumatized, the intense hatred of helplessness becomes addictive in itself. The mind begins to compare an imagined secure, powerful self-ideal with the injured, inadequate, and vulnerable self. This comparison generates hatred toward the provisional self for failure to be strong and to prevent trauma. The coping capacity of these individuals is shattered and they feel incapable of influencing their destiny.

This was the fate of Lisa who had carried her intense hatred of both parents along with a pattern of self victimization. Several months of group therapy, made her aware of her addiction to trauma and need for self protection.

Paranoia about the recurrence of trauma in many victims is common and soon takes over. Minor triggers remind them of their helplessness, at times causing a change of identity. This shift takes place in the hope of gaining greater control over that very sense of dread. They may lose the capacity for intimacy, thus hurting others with much greater ease. Loss of hope, self-blame, the inability to judge and appraise events realistically, and to maintain boundaries gradually combine to create a feeling of alienation from the individual's own soul. Feeling like either a passive sheep or a beast, the sufferer finds it much easier now to devalue and dehumanize both the self and others.

Spiritual struggles and questions about God's benevolence or justice are common among victims of trauma. They find it difficult to recapture their childhood faith. In order to overcome rage directed at oneself or projected onto others, the sufferer must learn to see these behaviors as normal responses to abnormal conditions. Violence serves as an expression of the dark side of our souls. Disowning or rejecting the dark side blocks our recognition of the soul's power.

Turning the other cheek is a way for many trauma victims to deny their dark side. They become passive and submissive. They deny the power entrusted to their souls. Simply writing down the soul's experiences and passions creates a mighty sword of self-empowerment (Moore, 1992). The magnificent power of the soul must be captured in our imagination. We must feel and own our dark side, with all its passions and turmoil. If we desire a soul-filled life, then the fantasy of innocence must go and the two sides of the soul must integrate. This process leads us to overcome self-blame and regain happiness.

The main function of group therapy is to prevent paranoia and detachment from destroying the possibility of intimacy. Group members must assist each other by tuning into each other's dark side and by accepting and validating rage reactions.

Obsession with death and dying (necrophilia)

Kenny's story

Kenny, a 36-year-old African American, had been formerly hospitalized because of a homicide/suicide attempt involving his entire family. He candidly reported that the two young children from his eight-year marriage had suffered intense abuse and brutality at his hands. Kenny was a victim of physical abuse by his own father and rape at the age of 12 by one of his uncles. When I first saw Kenny, his long, unkempt beard and disheveled hair could not conceal the rage in his piercing eyes. He looked mean and his comments confirmed the impression. He expressed paranoid thoughts of betrayal and suspicion. Kenny said he felt tormented by wicked impulses and asked if I could help him.

"Cure me, Doc." He said. "Save my innocent kids. If you can't cure me, then help me die."

Handing Kenny pen and paper, I asked him if he could draw freely whatever came to his mind, without censoring his thoughts. His spontaneous drawings were saturated with images of suffocation, beheading, torture, and stabbing. He seemed tormented by bitter memories of abuse by his father. He had suffered a psychotic breakdown after being arrested by the police for reported child abuse.

Kenny's madness made him feel in love with the idea of death. He continuously thought of suicide and of going home to kill his wife. He obsessed about having sex with his wife's dead body, hoping to have the biggest orgasm of his life. "I will kill myself then in ecstasy. Nothing could top that!"

Kenny's cruel compulsion to abuse his wife and children had lasted for many years, in stark contrast to his own longing for help. His family members feared him to the point where they became paralyzed and unwilling to report his battering to the authorities. Immediately after his hospitalization, his wife and children secretly escaped to another state, and were not heard from again.

Kenny was fascinated by the thought of corpses, filth, and destruction. He was a fountain of uncontrolled rage. In a serious distortion of reality, he felt that for many years *he* had foolishly succumbed to the needs of his family. He had been *their* slave, but no longer!

Like many batterers, Kenny had shaped the psychology of his family victims out of his own fears and did not think there was anything wrong with him. Grandiose, secretive, and paranoid, he felt bitter that he had to lie and steal to pay the family's expenses. He often felt he was living someone else's dreams. To him, work, play, food, shelter, and love were all stereotypes of conformity. He hated them all. But death was enchanting, and he often thought of going to cemeteries to smell the scent of death. He felt utterly alone, and when his manipulations failed, he simply reverted to violence or to thoughts of suicide.

With his typical habit of bullying, Kenny would burst into my office without knocking and demand immediate attention. He talked loudly and used threatening language to intimidate me. He had little respect for other people, especially for those he considered "sissies." His business partner, who had tolerated several months of brutality and abuse, had secretly taken all the company's assets, furniture and accounts, escaping to safety. Kenny considered the man a true sissy.

Hospitalization seemed to improve his condition, so Kenny was transferred to a less-restrictive unit of the hospital, from which he suddenly disappeared. Police were notified of his escape but could not locate him. We learned several weeks later that he had moved in with one of his sisters. Intense arguments and hostility had broken out between him and his brother-in-law. At last, in rage, he had set that family's home as well as his own car on fire. He was arrested and incarcerated.

He had another psychotic breakdown in prison, necessitating a transfer to a closed state hospital unit. There, one of the female psychiatric technicians, who had a fascination with killers and aggressive men, became attracted to him. She tried to help him escape again, although he abused her shamelessly. A nursing supervisor, aware of this unholy alliance, knew of the technician's long history of exposure to abuse and intervened by moving her to another unit. At that point, Kenny went berserk. He was so violent that it took eight staff members to restrain him.

"She is mine," he screamed. "You cannot take her away!" The thought of losing something that belonged to him was unbearable, as domination of others was his only answer to his own fear of life. Kenny would often lie awake at night, as he could see better in the dark and felt more alive and energetic. Darkness and death, he said, were the only things he was quite sure about.

After discharge from the state hospital and a period of cooling down, he approached me again and asked for help. I assigned him to individual and group therapy. Within the group, he had done occasional inner-child imagery, and it was easier for him to attend group sessions and accept guidance from fellow members. In one particular group session, as he elaborated on his extreme selfishness, he declared his confusion with reality.

"I often live in a world of delusion" he said. "I behave like a baby. I am troubled with reality and often feel at the mercy of my immediate sensations. I can't understand what is going on. My reactions to the events in my life are mostly emotional and farfetched. I often think that people are conspiring against me. I have fooled some people—especially women—to believe in me, but sooner or later they find me out.

"A few years ago when I started my engineering company, I hired some men to work with me. For a while I had absolute power over them. I felt all-powerful. Nobody could put limits on me. Day by day, these people became alienated and left. I had thoughts of hurting or killing them. I was paranoid and thought people were in a conspiracy against me. Anybody who looked at me could see the shining eyes of a crazy man. Now things are changing. I feel depressed and lonely. Looking at my childhood and what has happened to me, I feel ashamed. I don't want to be aroused into rage anymore. I don't want to return to the world of the insane."

Although Kenny gradually invested some of his capacity for love into other group members, his real change of heart took place after three stormy years of challenging recovery work.

War and martial values

Throughout history, the military class has promoted a set of martial values which included courage, honor, loyalty, duty, perseverance, and dignity. In this value system, ranks and positions were assigned according to one's valor and heroism. The presence of such values was beneficial in preventing unusual atrocities and eventually led to modern international agreements, such as the Geneva Conventions.[14] As long as the influence of God (or

---

14   The Geneva Conventions, dating from 1863, consist of four treaties which set the standards of international law for humanitarian concerns, the treatment of non-combatants, and prisoners of war.

other deities such as Mars) could be invoked in a given war, moral values were given greater credence.

In legends handed down to us from pre-recorded history, it was alleged that wars were settled by the wrestling of two mythical heroes, without bloodshed. Human life was considered sacred. However, with the advent of the city-state and empires ruled by kings aided by a warrior class, the idea of conquest and violent conflict became a feature of life for thousands of years. Wars were waged in the name of one god or another, resulting in unbearable injustice and deviant behavior.

In modern times, as moral values have eroded, the prevalence of atrocities has increased, shattering all codes of martial values and benevolence. Such deviations and atrocities have been studied in the behavior of Korean and Vietnam War combatants, as well as the participants in the current wars in Iraq and Afghanistan.

The desire to kill, as a manifestation of man's dark side, can evade all moral scruple and generate unbelievable atrocities. Combatants and killers—when they are not lying to themselves—often report that their experiences of killing were arousing and addictive. At times such arousal was consummated in unnecessary or random killing. The so called "adrenaline rush" of combat has been reported in many recent studies of soldiers, gang members, police officers, or other individuals in the act of killing.

Fortunately, atrocities have always been compensated by the expressions of conscience and love. General Giap, the leader of the forces of North Vietnam, reported in a television interview that for every act of atrocity committed by American soldiers, there were ten acts of compassion.

The loss of moral and spiritual values in modern day societies has taken yet another form: civilian violence. A gradual decrease in the importance of old military values, compounded by control of military forces by civilians, has deprived society of the ritualistic martial arts, which earlier functioned as a systematic approach to the channeling of youthful aggression, particularly in situations of abuse/trauma and PTSD. Without sanctioned outlets, violent aggression has spilled over into our streets and neighborhoods, spreading the use of guns to millions of civilians. The repression of martial art values, honor and dignity, has led to social chaos, increased trauma, and the massive prevalence of PTSD. Violence and abuse are at the root of the everyday increases in mental illness, personality disorders, family breakdown, and child development deviations. The more disturbed the population becomes, the greater the preponderance of personality disorders, aggression, love of death, atrocities, and violence. The threat of nuclear war, on the other hand, has further eroded moral values around the globe. As we contemplate the mass demise of civilian populations in the fraction of a second, the old military values, regulations, and conditions, chivalry and honor, simply vanish.

According to the sociologist and psychoanalyst Erich Fromm in his book *Anatomy of Human Destructiveness* (1991), one of the major consequences of war is "necrophilic violence," attended by the significant enjoyment of killing or abuse. This phenomenon generates a feeling of power, a fascination with danger, and a deviant interest in atrocities, torture, and death.

As they increasingly identify with popular soap opera figures, a number of youth today report that they consider killing for a price to be legitimate. In order to close a deal, some state that they might consider killing another human being—if the price is right. Many boys also seem callous about rape, thinking that if they spent money on a girl, they have the right to forcible sex with her.

The prevalence today of wanton violence, drive-by shootings, murders, massacres, explosions, and terrorist bombings has intensified the universality of trauma reactions. This correlates with a deep loss of soul in our communities, which provokes helplessness and a need for power, and further promotes violence, addiction, and greed.

In chapter 14, we shall discuss the topic of human nature in greater depth, with a special focus on the "ego," the "self," and defense mechanisms.

Chapter Three: Understanding Trauma and Terror

My calamity is My providence, outwardly it is fire and vengeance, but inwardly it is light and mercy. Hasten thereunto, that thou mayest become an eternal light and an immortal spirit.
        – Bahá'u'lláh[15]

A fireman spoke through a newscaster to an invisible audience of television viewers, his gaze not quite meeting the camera lens. His clouded eyes vaguely searched for a place to connect, settling instead into what is often called the "thousand-year stare." The journalist asked questions about the man's tough-minded bravery, but his mind's eye had fled to another place, seeing instead atrocities he had been forced to see—not only the first time, but now in countless flashbacks.

He was remembering his lost comrades as he recounted his experience of the terrorist attacks on 11 September 2001, which reduced the 110-story towers of New York's World Trade Center to a six-story heap of rubble and ash. He described how the man-made volcano swallowed up the lives of more than 3,000 men and women, many of them firefighters.

When the newscaster asked him about his own grief, the firefighter responded, "It doesn't matter what I feel. I will get up, and go on, and do what I have to do. None of my grief is even worth mentioning; knowing what the others went through and what their families will continue to go through for a long, long time." He tried to sound reasonable and strong, but his face betrayed the never-ending hollowness he would continue to feel for many years to come.

---

15   Bahá'u'lláh, *Hidden Words*, Arabic No. 51.

After every disaster, war, or family catastrophe, the participants enter a new period, not only of grieving, but of coping. The coping mechanisms involve the body, mind, and spirit. Sometimes they take a toll that seems too great to bear. Often they leave the sufferer wondering, "What is happening to me? How can I get through this? Will life ever seems worth living again?"

Victims of the great Asian Tsunami, Hurricane Katrina and the Iraq War experience and report the same sense of confusion, despair, and loss of meaning. In the months after the massive underwater earthquake off the coast of Sumatra, survivors were wrestling with the mental health impact of the disaster which had caused 280,000 deaths, half a million injuries and had left five million people homeless. The World Health Organization[16] reported that between 30 to 50 percent of the victims were suffering from severe PTSD and other psychological disorders such as anxiety, depression, psychosis, substance abuse, psychosomatic illness, and the desire to commit suicide. To help the millions of victims in Darfur, China, India, Indonesia, Burma, Thailand, and other areas, thousands of psychiatrists, psychologists, and mental health workers responded in a massive worldwide rescue effort. Some of their stories, presented at the "Global Disasters Challenges" conference in Atlanta[17] were as heartbreaking and shocking as those of the 9/11 victims. People were found in a complete state of shock, unable to face the massive destruction, death, chaos, and devastation. These stories are common for victims of other earthquakes, hurricanes and natural disasters or war. However it is not always a catastrophic or national tragedy which can initiate these feelings of confusion, helplessness, or loss of meaning. A sudden brush with death or a childhood tainted with suffering can create a personal war within.

Whatever the cause, the struggle forces the sufferer to find a way through the maze. As I faced this challenge in my own youth, and later through the tragedies that befell my clients, the greatest strength came in embracing the phrase (from the passage quoted above), which can make the suffering not only bearable but worthwhile: "My calamity is My providence."

It is a supreme challenge to find meaning in trauma without trivializing the suffering of any of those involved, whether yourself or others. Perhaps you have crashed or maybe slowly careened into your own wall of pain. Per-

16   Bulletin of the World Health Organization 83(6): 401–480, 2005.
17   "Global Disasters: Psychiatric Medicine and Public Health Challenges," Special Session of the American Psychiatric Association, Atlanta, Georgia, 24 May 2005.

haps some series of events in your life has triggered the range of responses we now call PTSD. If so, you may find it helpful to step back and take a detached look at the symptoms, first to be assured that your response is quite normal. Before we can search for the "providence" in the "calamity," we must first consider the nature of trauma.

Definition of trauma

Human life is inherently stressful, particularly when actual or covert events threaten one's psychological or physical integrity. At times we face existential stressors, such as a dysfunctional marriage, divorce, aging, unemployment, disability, chronic illness, or the death of a loved one.

Disasters and calamities create severe disruption, often beyond the coping abilities of the individual or society. The four characteristic features of trauma experience include:

1. Exposure to catastrophic events;
2. Re-experience of the traumatic event;
3. Avoidance of triggers that might revive the memory of trauma;
4. Increased arousal symptoms such as flashbacks.

A comprehensive listing of disasters and traumas is impossible within the scope of this book, but the following are the most prevalent sources of PTSD:

Natural traumas

Natural traumas include famine, drought, hurricanes, tornadoes, floods, volcanic eruptions, earthquakes, fire, lightning strikes, epidemics, serious fatal illnesses, mental illness, and severe injury or death of a loved one. Given the incessant and comprehensive attention given by the media to such events, it is hard to find anyone who has not been affected directly or indirectly by one or another of these disasters. In the searing images of the survivors of death, destruction, and misery in the aftermath of a tsunami, hurricane, famine and earthquakes, we clearly see the signs and symptoms of PTSD, as well as the heroism of millions of individuals or communities. Natural disasters typically call forth emergency humanitarian responses from whole communities, nations, or the world.

While, heroism is often the first response to the initial impact of these events, it sooner or later gives way to disillusionment and confusion. But in time, humans learn to reorganize, recover, and return to something resembling their pre-disaster condition.

Man-made traumas

By far the most dramatic forms of PTSD are related to man-made traumas. These include war, terrorism, arrest and unjust imprisonment, abuse of human rights, torture, massacre, concentration camp experiences, riots, the killing of loved ones, arson, battery, assault, life threats to self or loved ones, genocide, rape, sexual abuse, incest, physical abuse, atrocities, explosions, prisoner-of-war or refugee experiences, ritual abuse, police brutality, betrayal, acts of violence, and domestic violence.

In his book *A Terrible Love of War* (2004), James Hillman counts some 15,000 wars waged and recorded over the past six thousand years. The history books are littered with wars which were seen to have had a determining influence on our history, with their "heroic" leaders virtually deified in statues, magnificent plazas, parks, streets, national holidays, and memorials. Others merely resulted in vast human waste and destruction. As of this writing, many wars still rage across the planet, most of them bringing nothing but daily trauma and devastation not only for the combatants, but for the civilians victimized or displaced by them.

The primary example of man-made trauma is, of course, war. The relationship between combat experience and PTSD has long been established, with suicide, proneness to accident, mental and medical disorders among the prime symptoms. The Veterans Administration reports the incidence of PTSD among combatants in the current Iraq war to be on a scale not seen since Vietnam.

Roger, a veteran of Operation Iraqi Freedom, was in the ER of a local hospital when other patients alerted the staff about his intense agitation. Multiple attempts by staff and security guards were unsuccessful in calming him down. He began to run around the ER yelling "Incoming! We have to get them before they get us! He hid under a desk as if taking fire. He was obviously sleep deprived and hyperactive, scanning the environment with a terrified mood and loss of contact with reality. He seemed to be re-experiencing combat memories one of the cardinal symptoms of PTSD. Since antiquity warriors have returned from battle with physical and psychological wounds and healers have tried to relieve the pain of injured bodies and tormented minds.

Situations like mentioned above are quite frequent in veterans of war, demonstrating the toll of combat, the high cost of war and the intense problems of dealing with trauma emotions.

Technological traumas

Technological traumas include plane or train crashes, accidents, electrocutions, gas or chemical spills or explosions, nuclear reactor accidents and other accidental tragedies resulting from the malfunction or breakdown of man-made objects or human error.

Terrorism: Re-enacting early trauma in violence and war

Terrorism—the unlawful use of violence against individuals, groups, governments, or nations—is usually motivated by political or religious ideologies. As the life stories of some famous terrorists such as Adolph Hitler, Saddam Hussein, Timothy McVeigh and others reveal, many were abused, humiliated, or traumatized in childhood and suffered disrupted attachment patterns as a result. They lost their trust in human beings, loathed being a victim, identified with their aggressors and became victimizers themselves, obsessed by hatred, malignant narcissism, and the thirst for revenge or power. Some are even young people displaying rage against classmates with semi-automatic weapons.

It is not overstating the case to say that the 20th and 21st centuries represent an age of terror and violence. It is estimated today that approximately one-third of any given population will be exposed to a severe traumatic experience. In diverse segments of the world, violence and psychological trauma are so rampant that we can now identify entire cultures where trauma and PTSD are seen in epidemic proportions.

The lives of some of history's most notorious "terrorists" help to illustrate the root causes of their use of violent methods for ideological or political reasons. In many cases, as mentioned earlier their terror reflected the various forms of trauma they had experienced in their own lives. Hitler's brutal father almost killed him twice. He was full of rage as a young man and very close to a psychotic breakdown, when he developed a paranoid delusion towards the Jews as "poisoning" what he termed the "Aryan" people, that is, white European non-Jews. Although this delusion saved him from overt psychosis, it became the motivating force behind the Holocaust and

WW II. Hitler's success depended on the group and national fantasies of millions of other people, who shared histories of childhood abuse or violence. When nations suffer from thoughts or fantasies of "poisoned blood," war itself and the acts of terror perpetrated in its name become purifying acts, believed to magically regenerate the nation. Thus, war may be seen as a sacrificial ritual designed to block the resurgence of trauma memories by re-enacting feelings of victimization upon scapegoats or what psycho-historian Lloyd deMause called "poison containers" (1982, 2002) According to deMause, war can be a form of mental disorder.[18]

Both victims and victimizers need to find scapegoats in order to project their unacceptable emotions and find relief. Scapegoating brings a sense of comfort, security, hope—even rebirth—even when it results in war and the suffering of others. Thus, in times of national or social crisis, political leaders will sacrifice the scapegoats or "poison-containers" under the banner of patriotism and saving the nation.

In his book *Reagan's America* (1984), deMause documents a history of child abuse by the former President's alcoholic father, which led to his political ambitions in later life and his focus on the Soviet Union as a "poison container" (an "evil empire"), and the grand military build up for Star Wars. In his own biography, *Where is the Rest of Me?* (1965), Reagan refers to some of these events in his childhood.

One prominent figure in the Islamic jihad movement, born into a prominent upper class family, was attracted to writers who advocated a return to traditional Islamic values in order to free Islam from the influence of Western "infidels." After the 9/11 attacks, two of his daughters were killed in a bombing incident. He and his followers were implicated in the assassination of Egyptian president Anwar Sadat, whereupon he was arrested with hundreds of others, imprisoned, and tortured. His hatred of the West intensified and led to more terrorist actions, killings, and bombings. After much world travel, he helped to build a strong anti-West movement and became a lieutenant of al-Qaeda. His brand of terrorism is based on ideo-

---

18   According to deMause (1982, 2002), some of the unconscious motivations influencing terrorism include i) unusual economic success, along with feelings of guilt for having greater social advancement than one's parents; ii) pleasure from sinful behavior; iii) deviation from moral values learned in childhood; iv) traumatic experiences and poverty. Other causes include mental and emotional problems (particularly PTSD), the degree to which a nation promotes freedom and democracy, and extremes of idealism, pseudo-religious ideologies, and nationalism in which human life is devalued, etc.

logical/religious motifs, colored by personal and family traumas. There are limited reliable data regarding the psychological makeup of many modern terrorists. We only know that there are great differences between suicide bombers and other terrorists.

Timothy McVeigh, born in 1968 to a 15-year-old manic depressive mother, was not a natural-born killer. He was raised in a dysfunctional family in the poor suburbs of Buffalo, joined the army as a refuge and became an excellent soldier. He saw many atrocities in the Gulf war, but received a Commendation Medal from the army. He was emotionally torn about his war experience, as he did not think Iraq was a direct threat to the United States. He returned home with severe PTSD and went to war with America itself. He despised government agencies, such as the FBI and the ATF, that were responsible for assaults against people's rights and freedoms. Following the incidents in Waco, Texas against Branch Davidians and the assault against the Weaver Family in Ruby Ridge, McVeigh decided to take revenge against the FBI agent who had killed Randy Weaver's wife. His brand of terrorism was linked with multiple, life-long traumas and victimization.

The third wife of Mao Zedong, and the main leader of the bloody Cultural Revolution in China(1966–1976), re-enacted her own personal history of trauma over a ten-year period of terror, torture, killing, and assassinations, until she was arrested, imprisoned and later committed suicide. She had been heavily abused by her alcoholic father and ran away from home at age 13, only to find herself among teen-age prostitutes in Shanghai, where she led a miserable life. She eventually joined the communist party, met Mao, and become his third wife. When Mao Zedong betrayed her with his fourth wife, this still young and beautiful woman transformed her rage into acts of terrorism which continued until her final arrest.

Terrorism and the concept of "jihad"

After the 9/11 terrorist attacks in New York, the concept of *jihad* in Islam has come to the fore in the public consciousness, and been endlessly studied and debated.[19] Many Muslims understand the *Lesser Jihad* to represent the individual struggle to purify one's soul, as distinguished from the *Greater Jihad*, which calls for the defense of Islam under attack. Sufi mystics, such

---

19   *Jihad* as been studied and described by many researchers such as Omar Nasiri (2006), Daniel Byman (2008), and Brynjar Lia (2008).

as the poet Rumi in his famous story of the "Merchant and the Parrot," described *jihad* as the death of the ego or self in love, leading to personal resurrection. (In Rumi's view this dying in love and resurrection was the *Greater* Jihad and the defense of Islam in war the *Lesser* Jihad).Current proponents of *jihad* direct their violence against the West, particularly the United States, viewing specific countries as "enemies of Islam."

Needless to say, widely varying interpretations of these concepts have led to a multitude of conflicting arguments, confusion, vast destruction, and indescribable human suffering.

Suicide bombing

The number of suicide attacks in recent years has increased dramatically from the handful in 1980 to more than 500 in 2005. It is impossible to determine the exact numbers as we do not have clear and verifiable reports. They are occurring on foot, in cars, in boats, planes, on donkeys, bicycles, buses, and even in submarines. Contrary to public belief, most suicide bombings result neither from despair, poverty, nor abuse. Rather, the perpetrators tend to be motivated by pseudo-religious or nationalistic ideologies, and are targeted at presumed "enemies." The groups advocating suicide bombing feel they are disadvantaged by an imbalance of power against these enemies and consider suicide attacks a convenient tactic to take revenge on or demoralize the other side. Supporters of these tactics may consider those who carry them out as martyrs or heroes, defending a particular national, religious, or other cause.

Thus, suicide bombers are seen as courageous individuals who sacrifice their own lives to achieve their goals. They consider these goals to be more important than human lives. They serve as models for many young or old individuals, who are taught to consider martyrdom as the greatest honor. They come from many different socio-economic backgrounds, education levels, and, at times, from apparently normal family backgrounds. Extremist beliefs are significant when combined with mental programming, special training and group support.

In some Muslim communities, such martyrs are celebrated and admired, even by their own mothers. These communities often react with moral outrage at perceived attacks against Islam and sacred values. The fact that many suicide bombers were friends or classmates and have strong personal attachments to one another tends to encourage their actions. The goal is the same, however: to kill as many people as possible in order to frighten their adversaries.[20]

Violence

"Violent Times, Borrowed Space"

> In those moments when
> I'm trying to forget
> the uncertain path
> of my inadequacies
> I allow my soul
> to take refuge
> among the mysteries
> of the world
> of solitude and silence.
> Not to blur what surrounds me
> nor to curse what my mind
> can not touch nor bend,
> rather, to admire with reverence
> the immensity and beauty
> of this, our Universe.
> Then,
> I emerge from the depth
> of my self imposed exile
> asking always the same question . . .
> "why must creatures of this world
> engender such violence
> when they are but leasing
> their teluric space
> for only just a while?
>
> — Carlos Pappalardo

20   In his book *My Life is a Weapon: A Modern History of Suicide Bombing* (2004), Christoph Reuter tells of one particular suicide assassin who left a "Spiritual Instruction Manual" in his briefcase, in which he had written, "You will notice that the plane will stop, then will start to fly again and that is the hour to meet your God." Readers may refer to some of the following sources for further information about suicide bombing: Rosen (2005); Barlow (2008); Pape (2005); and Griset and Mahan (2003).

Let us now look briefly at the American statistics on violence from various available sources. Over the past several years, there have been from 25,000 to 30,000 murders each year. Sixty-five percent of the victims have been between the ages of 15 and 24. Three million cases of battering are reported by women each year. Combined woman and child abuse make up at least 70 percent of these cases. Seven million children witness the battering of their parents annually. Two million elderly are abused each year. There are 1.8 million cases of violence against children, and an estimated 2.7 million children suffer verbal, physical, or sexual abuse each year. Some 15 to 49 percent of the population is at risk of having PTSD as a consequence of rape, assault, serious injury, disaster, terrorism, or war.[21]

In the war against international terrorism and in the two wars currently being waged in Afghanistan and Iraq, the number of casualties from all the countries involved is staggering. The impact of media portrayals of suicide bombings and atrocities, have created an unprecedented state of public anxiety and psychological trauma. Official Army statistics between January and August of 2005 indicate that 19 to 21 percent of returning veterans suffer severe PTSD and other emotional problems, the most severe symptoms occurring in soldiers deployed for more than 12 months. This is particularly true for those involved in actual killing, combat, or the handling of dead bodies. Post Deployment Health Reassessment (PDHRA) reports considered the rate of medical and mental disorders in the returnees to be above 35 percent. The VA, PTSD cases increased from 120265 veterans in 1999 to 215871 soldiers in 2004. The cost of care rose from 1.7 billion in 1999 to 4.3 billion dollars in 2004. Suicide rates amongst returning veterans from Iraq, have reached alarming levels, all a direct consequence of PTSD. Many veterans do not seek help for fear of being stigmatized.

One might well ask what generates such appalling violence in the world. Sociologists and legal authorities offer the following as among the important factors:

- The collapse of traditional values in the Western democracies, to the extent that only 11 percent of all families are now what one would call "traditional" or "nuclear;"

---

21   Statistics based on reports of the Criminal Justice Statistical Analysis Center (2000 to 2005) and the US Department of Health and Human Services Administration on Children, Youth and Families (2006), available at: http://www..acf.dhhs.Gov.Program/cb

- In the United States, adequate child-care is lacking for at least half the child population;
- The number of young, unwed mothers, or those without partners has risen dramatically;
- Seventy-seven percent of children in modern-day families grow up without the influence of a father.

Included are the many conditions which aggravate the spread of violence, such as disorientation and insecurity during a life transition, resentment of a pregnant young wife, helplessness in custody battles, the pressure of rampant consumerism, inadequate health care, prenatal or neonatal brain damage in children, job insecurity and disregard for employee needs during corporate takeovers, racism, covert segregation, emotional numbing to death and murder diminishing the value of life, inadequate support systems for victims of violence, epidemic PTSD, exposure to media violence and worship of violent heroes by youth, the spread of weapons—some 240 million guns in American homes—the practice of blaming the victim, low tolerance of frustration, inadequate parole systems, crowded courts and prisons, insufficient numbers of police officers, and the collapse of ethics among leaders.

To illustrate: a young gang member asked another subway passenger, a teenage girl, to give him her earrings. When she refused, he shot her, pulling the earrings by force from her ears. During his trial, he blamed *her* for not cooperating, saying, and "If she had given me her jewelry, I wouldn't have had to shoot her!"

My interviews with youth gang members incarcerated in various juvenile institutions revealed their frequent exposure to violence in early childhood, including shooting, stabbing, torture, abuse, and exposure to death. Almost half of gang members show symptoms of PTSD, such as hypervigilance and flashbacks.

Oscar's story

Oscar was a six-year-old child who was referred to me for aggressive, violent, and angry behavior, temper tantrums, and hatred of his mother. For some reason, his mother had never bonded with him. His parents denied any history of verbal, sexual, or physical abuse. They believed he suffered from attention-deficit/hyperactivity disorder (ADHD) and were asking me to give him medication to calm him down.

I gave Oscar a piece of paper and crayons asking him to draw anything he wished. He drew a frozen mountain covered with snow and ice. At the bottom of the mountain, was a tree between two igloos, with a large empty hole in it. I quickly deduced from his drawing that Oscar was depicting his emotionally frozen home, his desire for, and fear of, autonomy, and the possibility that he had suffered a major trauma at around the age of three. I asked his mother to be more truthful about their family history—insisting that something traumatic had happened to him which had frozen his emotions. Weeping profusely, she reported that when Oscar had been three years old, his father's favorite brother had been killed in the collapse of the World Trade Center towers in New York. He was devastated and furious, began drinking heavily and became very suspicious of everyone around him. She said, "He began abusing me physically and berating me for no reason. I could not take it anymore and asked for a divorce. He became more outraged and abused me even more. On several occasions, little Oscar came to my defense, trying to push his father away. But he was treated brutally. I wanted to report the abuse or run away, but my husband threatened to kill all of us. Then, after a few months, he calmed down, apologized, and asked me to forgive him. For Oscar's sake, I agreed to stay, but our home is not happy any more. I am traumatized badly and can't forgive him. So I guess Oscar is right. Our home is like a frozen igloo. My husband also insisted that we forget the events of post 9/11 and never talk about it. I thought perhaps Oscar had forgotten about those days. But I see that he is not stupid. Maybe my submission to his father has angered him. So now he is angry at me and in a way has started to behave like his father during those dark days."

Domestic violence, child abuse, and violence against women

According to a recent report by NPR broadcast (7/17/08), a victim of domestic violence dies or is severely injured every ten hours in the United States. For countries such as Russia, the incidence is 10 times higher, almost one casualty per hour.

Domestic violence is a pattern of behavior used among family members or within the home by one person to oppress, dominate, and control another person or persons. Such abuse occurs among people from every socioeconomic, racial, educational, cultural, and religious background. It may occur between partners in a relationship, married or not, living together, separated, or dating. It may also occur between siblings, between parents and children, between adult children and elderly parents, or between other relatives.

Domestic violence occurs in predictable cycles, characterized first by tension-building behavior, such as criticism, yelling, angry gestures, swearing, coercion, and/or "looks" which then leads to violence. This may take the form of sexual or economic abuse, destroying or damaging property, neglect, abandonment, desertion, emotional and verbal abuse, corrupting, stalking, coercion and threats to intimidate or terrorize, and blaming the abused party for causing the abuse or of being responsible for the behavior, personality, or character of the abuser.

Child rearing practices around the world vary from indulgent, North American and European cultures to those of authoritarian societies in Asia, the Middle East, and Africa. Although prejudice against and abuse or neglect of children are still prevalent in Western cultures, the statistics on abuse, abandonment, and neglect of children are far greater in the developing nations, especially in Islamic countries. It is estimated that there are at least seven million cases of child abuse annually in the United States, but the incidence in developing countries may be far greater and more severe. Children are not only exploited for labor, war, prostitution, and sexual slavery, but are often the targets of mass indoctrination in the hatreds and prejudices of their elders. Incest and sexual abuse/rape of girls and boys are endemic and physical abuse reaches inhuman levels. Political leaders, anthropologists, sociologists and governments—when they do not outright deny the issue—avoid addressing the consequences of child abuse.[22]

In societies the world over sexism, discrimination, and violence against women create a ripe environment for massive traumatic experiences. Women who are victims of oppression have little self-esteem. Their profound experience of injustice and violence leads to a sense of helplessness and a desire for revenge. In most societies women are still praised as feminine and dutiful if they sacrifice their personal needs to submit to their husbands' "conjugal rights."

---

22   Douki et al., 2003; Watts and Zimmerman, 2002; de Mause, 1998 and 2002, Chapter 5,

Centuries of misogyny create an atmosphere in which, in many cultures, the birth of a girl is not celebrated. From an early age, she is tolerated as a burden, to be married off as soon as possible. In many cultures, girls and women are not only deprived of education, but even of proper nutrition and health care. Seventy-five percent of the world's illiterate people are women.[23] In most cultures of the world, reflecting the fact that women have been traditionally regarded as the property of men, marriage laws heavily favor the rights of men.

Rape—whether in marriage or outside of it—is still not viewed as a crime in many countries, and rapists or customers of prostitutes are rarely prosecuted. Rape of women and children is commonly sanctioned as a weapon of war. Sexual desire and sexuality are taboo, and at least 130 million women in the world have been subjected, either as children or teenagers, to female genital mutilation.[24]

Victimized mothers frequently educate their sons to be aggressive and vengeful. Massive sexual abuse of both women and children, including boys, leads to a feeling of humiliation, later exploited by charismatic leaders to create terrorist martyrs, combining self- and other-victimization.

Bobby's story

As an eight-year-old, Bobby was referred to me when physical abuse was discovered by the Division of Family Services. His father was a fundamentalist preacher, who had victimized his wife for many years in Bobby's presence. But this had been kept secret to avoid a major break-up.

When Bobby was six years old, his mother had died as a result of severe injuries which were never investigated. Her violent death had caused Bobby deep grief and loss. He had lost his only source of love and felt miserable. He had stolen and hidden a number of his mother's bras and underwear, and when he missed his mother most keenly, he would put them on secretly in order to feel loved again. After discovering this practice, his father had decided the boy was possessed. His only way to save Bobby from the devil was literally "to beat the devil out of him." One of Bobby's teachers had discovered and reported the abuse. He was temporarily separated from his

---

23   Hepburn and Simon, 2006.
24   Female genital mutilation (FGM) is the surgical removal of the clitoris, usually performed on very young girls.

father and placed in a foster home, pending further evaluation and therapy.

Bobby's father rejected my explanation that his son's behavior was a form of intense grief and PTSD, saying that he did not believe in any other authority but the Bible. He sincerely believed he was doing the right thing and that no one should interfere in his family affairs. Since I could not influence the man, and, with the intention of finding an ally in a more sensible person in his congregation, I asked him to invite me to his church, in order to learn more about his belief system and practices. He took my interest seriously and invited me to a church service one Sunday morning. Among the some 400 people present in the Full Gospel Church, I was hoping to connect with someone emotionally and ask for help. The speaker that morning was a man who, before he was born again through the influence of the church, had spent some 30 years of his life in and out of prison. He had displayed a number of his prison photographs on the stage, and, after his fiery speech, announced that if Jesus could reach and transform a wretch like himself, He could save anyone. I told Bobby's father how impressed I was by the sermon, and asked if I could go forward and ask help from the preacher, who seemed to be a man of God. He agreed. I then approached the preacher, introduced myself as a physician, said that I was treating the child of one of the brethren, and that I needed his help in order to avoid any mistakes. He responded kindly and asked the entire congregation to rise and pray for me. He then proceeded to speak in tongues, and in an emotional ritual—during which some women fainted and others sang in praise—he conferred the power of God to my hands.

This event brought me closer to Bobby's father and I managed to persuade him to see his son as emotionally distraught, and in need of love, rather than beatings. After several months of therapy, Bobby felt better and eventually returned to his father. I lost contact with this family for several years. But when Bobby was 18, I received a call from the police requesting Bobby's psychiatric files. I learned that, after a few years, his father had remarried and that his wife had given birth to a little girl. When Bobby had displayed jealousy toward his sister, the father once again believed him to be possessed by the devil. The beatings and physical abuse began again, reviving Bobby's painful childhood memories. In a fit of rage and hypervigilance, he had attacked and severely wounded his sister. He was arrested, tried as an adult, and sent to prison.

Reactions to the victims of trauma and violence

Traumatized individuals—particularly victims of violence—often behave as if they were immigrants in a foreign land or aliens in exile. Their unbearable experiences are foreign or irrelevant to the average citizen and they often feel abandoned, misunderstood, isolated, and forlorn. Like the "ugly duckling" in the children's story, they are considered misfits, often knocking on the wrong doors for recognition or support.

Victims of violence—especially war veterans—are so dismayed by this lack of recognition that they often prefer prison, homelessness, or isolation to living with their families. Isolation decreases their bitter imagery of trauma and helps them avoid confrontation with painful triggers. Some of them continue the cycle of trauma and violence either by self-victimization or harming others in revenge.

For centuries, people have endured suffering in circumstances beyond their control. Because of their unusual behavior, these victims are often rejected by society, and labeled "borderline" or "hysteric." Like a black bean in a bushel of green peas, they are the odd one out, rejected even by their own kind. Those who are naturally more sensitive or temperamentally intense, suffer unbearable heartbreak. Their wounds deepen as they face the additional cruelty of rejection by society.

Psychiatrists sometimes try to diminish the pain of traumatized patients and remake them by encouraging a form of denial or "psychic surgery," pressuring them to simply "get over it." Even though the symptoms of PTSD are virtually universal, the victim's intensity of feeling and persistent reliving of experiences are thought by many practitioners to be abnormal, and are therefore dismissed.

The symptoms of PTSD are even widespread in folklore and literature, along with descriptions of the brutality which brought it about. In the writings of Balzac, Hugo, Shakespeare, and Somerset Maugham, we read gruesome tales about those who have achieved spiritual transformation, but whose peace of mind is interrupted by painful baring of the soul, despair, and a pervasive sense of impending doom.

In two of his major tragedies, the 13th century poet Nezami used the phrase "event stricken," or "calamity stricken" to encompass a full clinical description of PTSD. In *Henry the IV, Part One*, William Shakespeare gives us a vivid, true picture of PTSD in the character of Hotspur, as expressed in the words of his wife, Lady Percy:

> *Tell me, sweet Lord, what is't that takes from thee*
> *Thy stomach, pleasure and thy golden sleep?*
> *Why dost thou bend thine eyes upon the earth,*
> *And start so often when thou sit'st alone?*
> *Why hast thou lost the fresh blood in thy cheeks*
> *And given my treasures and my rights of thee*
> *To thick-ey'd musing and cursed melancholy?*
> *In thy faint slumbers I by thee have watch'd,*
> *And heard thee murmur tales of iron wars,*
> *Speak terms of manage to thy bounding steed,*
> *Cry "Courage! To the field!" And thou hast talk'd*
> *Of sallies and retires, of trenches, tents,*
> *Of palisadoes, frontiers, parapets,*
> *Of basilisks, of cannon, culverin,*
> *Of prisoners' ransom, and of soldiers slain,*
> *And all the currents of a heady fight.*
> *Thy spirit within thee hath been so at war,*
> *And thus hath so bestirr'd thee in thy sleep,*
> *That beads of sweat have stood upon thy brow*
> *Like bubbles in a late-disturbed stream,*
> *And in thy face strange motions have appear'd,*
> *Such as we see when men restrain their breath*
> *On some great sudden haste.*
> *O' what portents are these?*[25]

Although many psychiatrists and psychologists have fluctuated in their attention to trauma, at times even denying its existence, the Vietnam War, and the disasters of 9/11 and Katrina have changed their views significantly.

---

25   Shakespeare, *Henry the IV, Part One*, Act II, Scene III.

Brief history of professional approaches to the post-trauma syndrome

Medical and psychological practitioners have vacillated over time in the degree of their awareness of the effects of horrifying events on the patients they treat. But this awareness is rarely retained for long. Denial and dissociation are evident in the health care establishment, as well as in individuals or communities. Psychiatrists have had periods of active interest in trauma in the past, as well as periods when the subject is ignored completely, for the very subject of trauma arouses intense controversial reactions which challenge anyone's core beliefs and vulnerabilities. It is much easier to talk about and bear witness to acts of God, beyond human control. But when terrifying events are man-made, we tend easily to take sides with victims or perpetrators. This poses a serious moral dilemma, as we cannot remain neutral. The community often forgets victims of war or violence. It is easy to distort the facts of their trauma in an attempt to draw the veil of oblivion over unpleasant or horrible events.

For many centuries the psychological nature of trauma symptoms were denied and linked to "body damage." Such terms as "irritable heart," "cardiac neurosis," "shell shock," and "hysteria" have served as a kind of denial of emotional suffering. But, in reality, these represent attempts to discredit the victims and render them invisible. Three times in the past century we have witnessed a surge of investigations into trauma, to be followed immediately by a loss of interest. Pierre Briquet (1859) was perhaps the first clinician to link hysteria and physical symptoms to a history of psychological trauma. Hysteria was an archetypal psychological illness in women which was picked up by the anti-religious political movements of 19th century France. After Briquet, James Putnam, in a brilliant paper (1898), reviewed mechanisms of regression in post-traumatic conditions, where emotions were displayed in simple reflex body symptoms. Jean-Martin Charcot (1887), the patriarch of hysteria studies and his student Pierre Janet (1889) clarified the relationship between trauma, hysteria, sexual abuse, and children's impostor syndromes. According to Janet, emotions following intense trauma lead to regression and lack of integration, where traumatic memories are dissociated and repressed. The victims lose their capacity for conscious narrative formation, developing what he termed a "memory phobia." Dissociation, however, does not soothe the heartbreak of trauma. The victims, deprived of the natural connection to their spiritual nature, become obsessed and compensate for thoughts of the trauma with anxiety, intrusive thoughts, somatic problems, and disturbed sleep.

Although Janet vividly elucidated the link between psychological trauma and emotional illness, his hold on the field of psychology did not last long. Soon there was talk of simulation, suggestibility, and moral weakness. What followed were such notions as "cowardice," "diseases of the will," "neurological concussion," "loosening of the synapses in the brain," "secondary emotional gains of trauma response," and the "predisposition to vulnerability."

All these fanciful terms—and what came to be known later as "compensation neurosis"—were simply powerful means of blaming the victims for their fate. Abuse and harassment of former soldiers and the wholesale denial of the traumatic impact of sexual abuse on women or children slowly took hold. Janet and his ideas were put on the back burner and psychoanalysis took psychiatry by storm. The study of hysteria, which had so captured the public imagination, was repudiated.

The fruits of Charcot and Janet's studies were the independent formulations in the mid-1890s of Sigmund Freud (1962), Bruer (1955) and others, describing hysteria as caused by emotional trauma. Although Freud initially claimed to have recognized the source of hysteria in concepts such as childhood abuse and war trauma, these insights were soon replaced by a focus on unconscious childhood sexuality and "intra-psychic conflict." Although Freud was at first aware of dissociation with regard to painful past physical or emotional experiences, this awareness was drastically reversed when he emphasized hysteria as a defense against unacceptable Oedipal (sexual) or aggressive strivings of the child, thus postponing any attention to trauma for several decades.

The study of shell shock or combat neurosis began in the United States and England after WW 1 and reached its peak in the Vietnam conflict. Eight million men died during the years 1914–1918, shattering European cultures and the moral values of the day. Exposed to the unremitting horrors of war, men broke down, became helpless and hysterical, and lost the illusion of manly honor and battle glory. Some became mute. Military leaders tried to suppress such casualties of war, but the numbers were so great that military psychiatrists had no alternative but to fight back by coining the terms "shell shock" and "war neurosis" to deal with the problem. The collapse of war culture and the rise of anti-war associations encouraged their research. Eventually, the last frontier of trauma awareness was overcome by the feminist movement, which focused attention on the victims of violence and sexual abuse.

One gifted man, Abraham Kardiner, in his now famous book, *The Traumatic Neuroses of War* (1941), researched the psychological, epidemiological, biological, social, and cultural aspects of trauma and outlined the classic manifestations of PTSD: the trauma orientation, virtual irreversibility of symptoms, absurd labor of victims to overcome a Sisyphus-style curse,[26] and personality changes. Kardiner, a former student and patient of Freud, worked in the Bronx, New York clinic of the Veterans' Administration, hoping to make a contribution to psychoanalysis. He worked with veterans suffering from "war neurosis," but, writing of the veteran's recollections, intrusive memories, and misery, he was overwhelmed by his inability to cure his patients. For a brief period, he switched to the field of anthropology to avoid his own traumatic childhood memories. Following in the footsteps of Janet, he also linked war neuroses with hysteria, although he disliked the bias implicit in that term.

Today, thanks to the work of such researcher-therapists as Shoshana Zonderman (1975), Aphrodite Matsakis (1994), McFarlane et al. (1996) and numerous others, we have become fully cognizant of the "therapist's trauma syndrome" from which Kardiner suffered so keenly.

---

26   In Greek mythology, Sisyphus was a king punished by having to roll a huge boulder up a hill, only to watch it roll down again, and to repeat this throughout eternity. See Hamilton (1942).

Chapter Four: Post-Traumatic Stress Disorder—Symptoms and Cycles

The mind and spirit of man advance when he is tried by suffering. Man is so to speak, unripe: the heat of the fire of suffering will mature him. The greatest men have suffered most.
— 'Abdu'l-Bahá[27]

PTSD symptoms

The human response to traumatic events may be either: positive—leading to future emotional growth—or negative—leading to depression and isolation. Four criteria are usually considered necessary for correct diagnosis.

5. Exposure to severe trauma, along with horror and helplessness;

6. Repeated re-experiencing of the trauma;

7. Avoidance symptoms of PTSD;

8. Arousal symptoms of PTSD.

PTSD can result from a single traumatic event or repeated exposure, and can be intensified by other stressors such as loss of support, unemployment, and poverty.

Individuals exposed to major traumas often respond with horror, helplessness, and a numbing of the senses, as if they cannot react at all. They

---

27   See van der Kolk et al., 1996.

feel dazed, unaware of their surroundings and unable to understand the new reality of their condition. Some experience amnesia for at least a portion of their experience, and others act detached, as if watching a movie of disasters happening to someone else. Later on, as a way of gaining mastery over their emotions .they may revisit the traumatic event frequently through flashbacks, nightmares, intrusive thoughts, or images.

The initial reaction to trauma is called Acute Stress Disorder. This stage lasts from several days to several weeks, and, in 70 percent of victims, usually subsides within that period.

Victims then enter a chronic phase, which we call PTSD. During the acute stage emotional regulation is impaired and individuals are easily overwhelmed by the imbalance of cortisol levels in the blood in the adrenergic and hypothalamic-pituitary-adrenal (HPA) systems of the body. This issue is discussed with more detail Chapter 10.

This post-trauma period usually involves a two-phase process. Certain symptoms of PTSD create a sense of chaos and a shattering of the individual's sense of self-cohesion, while the numbing responses promote order and reorganization. These fluctuations of symptoms help restore the victim's sense of control over trauma memories. Thus, we can consider PTSD as the transitional coexistence of two opposing states of mind.

Acute phase

After traumatic events, the psychological defense systems remain in a state of permanent alert. In this condition, the traumatized individual startles easily, sleeps poorly, and overreacts to any small provocation. He has flashbacks and suffers from intrusive thoughts, anxiety, fear, panic, phobias, multiple worries, restlessness, rage, violent emotions, guilt, shame, grief, helplessness, and a dread of the return of the traumatic event. This state of physiological neurosis may produce fear that retelling the tale of trauma will overwhelm others. The sufferer may endure nightmares, manic behaviors, hallucinations and even psychotic symptoms, and even engage in self-mutilation, Or, he may lose the ability to control emotions or even to discriminate between threatening and non-threatening stimuli.

These painful symptoms often make afflicted individuals feel like emotional hemophiliacs. They feel vigilant about danger. They demonstrate a fragmented fight-or-flight response to any stimulus that triggers the autonomic nervous system. In the acute stage, if we play tapes of combat sounds to PTSD veterans, their heart rates accelerate, their blood pressure increases, and they become very agitated. Their bodies remain on the alert, as they cannot tune out annoying stimuli. This explains why, in this acute stage, it is far more important to create a sense of safety and security than to engage in debriefing, therapy, or re-exposure to traumatic memories.

Thus, during the first few days after a terrorist attack, we usually observe in the victims varying states of shock, disbelief, denial, fear, anxiety, insomnia, and depression, sometimes accompanied by numbness. In subsequent weeks, behavior may be characterized by an awareness of loss, anger, revenge fantasies, and increasing solidarity. These emotions later change to disillusionment, self-serving behaviors, surrender, or mistrust of leaders. Eventually, attempts at adaptation and reorganization appear and lead to acceptance and rebuilding.

Chronic phase[28]

In this phase, we are confronted with four categories of symptoms:

1. Reliving and experiencing intrusive images of trauma, including flashbacks, nightmares, intrusive memories, and a general state of activation;

2. Avoidance, the effortful numbing of emotions to create a sense of safety, and avoidance of triggers which revive memories;

3. Arousal of the autonomic nervous system, characterized by the fight-flight-freeze syndrome, hypervigilance, exaggerated startle reactions, insomnia, irritability, and anxiety/panic reactions;

4. Associated features, such as depression, substance abuse, character changes, or psychosis appear in roughly 50 to 70 percent of individuals suffering from chronic PTSD.

5. No clear relationship between these symptoms has been observed, as they vary according to each individual.

---

28   Some 30 percent of all traumatized people develop chronic PTSD. The majority of victims recover from the acute phase by processing and integrating traumatic memories and return to normal functioning and post-traumatic growth.

Flashbacks

These are defined as the sensory re-experience of past trauma, activated by a variety of triggers. Long after the traumatic event has passed, victims relive the experience as if it were happening in the present. Time seems to be arrested at the moment of the trauma. The memory intrudes into consciousness repeatedly in the form of nightmares or revisualization, known as flashbacks. Insignificant reminders may cause the same degree of arousal as the real threat, as the individual cannot discriminate trivial from important information. Even a very safe milieu of therapy may seem dangerous, as the survivor cannot be sure when a reminder may appear.

As Kardiner (1941) suggested, trauma sufferers may fixate on a vivid sensation or an image, often dwelling on a horrible visual image that recalls their painful experience. Words are inadequate or unavailable to the survivors to express their horror. During the traumatic event, the body's high release of adrenaline may shuts down the encoding of memory separating images from words or metaphors..

As with the alert state hyper-vigilance can generate reactions of mistrust of others, paranoia, hyper-emotionalism and hyper-awareness.

Reliving and other intrusive symptoms

After traumatic experiences, the psychological defense shields are paralyzed and the individual remains in a state of permanent alert. He may sleep poorly, be plagued by nightmares about the trauma or other symbolic triggers; he may overreact to minute provocations, and have continually intrusive thoughts causing anxiety and panic attacks; or he may develop phobias, and experience grief or rage, feel violent, guilty, shameful, or helpless. The victim may be fearful of the return of trauma events and avoid communication in order not to overwhelm others.

Self-victimization

Another symptom of the chronic state is the victim's tendency to recreate the trauma or re-enact a painful situation as a form of self-victimization. Freud named this behavior "repetition compulsion," as his patients seemed addicted to the trauma without being consciously awareness of their behavior. Recent research shows the value of this compulsive behavior as a pathway toward the eventual reintegration of the personality, a step toward turning trauma into spiritual growth.

Guilt

Some victims of abuse come to believe that what happened to them was deserved because they were or might have been bad as children. Overwhelmed by guilt, they try to become as good as possible in order to reduce their feelings of rage about the injustice suffered. They then self-denigrate or self-victimize in order to make others happy and to avoid further abandonment or rejection. These individuals develop a fear of, or guilt about, pleasure, growth, or prosperity, feeling that they do not deserve happiness.

Victimization of others

In contrast to self-victimization, some 20 percent of PTSD sufferers and victims come to believe that there was nothing wrong with *them*, but perceive their environment as hostile and abusive. Because they feel victimized by parents, caretakers, perpetrators or educators, they try to avenge their suffering and pain by identifying with the perpetrators and, as was described earlier, become victimizers themselves. This group of victims also displays a pattern of re-enacting their traumas in aggression and violence, whenever further trauma, abandonment, or reminder dates trigger renewed threats. Such victim-cum-victimizers can appear either in one individual, or in minority groups or whole cultures.

Avoidance and numbing

These reactions are used to create feelings of safety. They are related to dissociation of memories and emotions and the attempt to shut down the arousal state. Generally, they postpone recovery and act like tranquilizing medicines, at times necessary for survival, yet making PTSD more chronic. When trauma victims feel completely powerless, their consciousness alters and their defense systems shut down. They may freeze emotionally and feel paralyzed. At times, the victims display a false sense of calm, which actually disguises their pain and terror. This state of numbness constricts awareness and lets the individual disconnect from the reality of the traumatic event. Perceptions become distorted and the victim experiences time in slow motion. The victim may feel that the event is happening to someone else, or that it may be a dream. Her face may reflect the distant thousand-yard stare, as she has nearly lost her soul.

On the positive side, this trance-like state of numbness can be a normal coping device to reduce pain and terror. However, it can create symptoms such as avoidance or withdrawal from others, mental blocks, amnesia, decline of awareness, breaks with reality, depression (to conserve mental energy), apathy, fatigue, oversleeping, and physical symptoms that distract from the traumatic memories. The victim can also experience genuine memory loss, problems with new learning, loss of motivation, loss of meaning, sudden dependence on others, emotional detachment, relationship problems, an inappropriate lack of feeling, a paralysis of will, surrender, loss or denial of reality, out-of-body experiences, loss of identity, and a dimming of all emotional reactions. Victims often suspend their judgment and feel anesthetized but safe.

This response, coupled with an intense increase in the release of endorphins (the body's natural pain killers), helps the body reduce its level of chaotic arousal after an incident that creates terror. Substance abuse is another mode of psychic numbing for trauma victims. Many victims who cannot release adequate amounts of endorphins rely on alcohol or drugs to achieve the same anesthesia. Up to 70 percent of Vietnam veterans with PTSD later used alcohol or narcotics for self-numbing, to avoid thinking about the meaning of their painful memories.

Associated features

As mentioned earlier these features include depression, substance abuse, anxiety and physical illness. But victims may exhibit a gamut of other secondary symptoms including impulsive behaviors, the unraveling of character, and loss of sanity, delusional thinking, love of death, and survivor guilt.

The symptoms described so far may surface in cyclical fashion. At times, an individual might adapt briefly to her PTSD, showing normal coping skills and a sense of humor. She may go on socializing, working, and sharing with others, even processing memories, and exercising stress management. She may have a degree of control over her emotions and be quite able to distinguish important from trivial matters.

However, when a traumatized individual feels haunted by recurring memories and new triggers, she may suddenly become defensive or withdrawn. She may try to avoid personal relationships and become paranoid or detached. Her numbing responses can lead to memory problems or hallucinations. If this defensive numbing does not return her to an original adaptive state, she might enter an arousal stage and become prone to rage, violence, panic, loss of control, acting out, aggression, and loss of discrimination.

It is well known that fetal and childhood memories of trauma before age five are registered in the amygdala in the form of emotional memories. These memories remain dissociated from the context of trauma; thus, although victims are unable to remember the exact nature of traumatic events, their feelings of helplessness, abandonment, depression, terror, vigilance, and mistrust may remain to haunt them for many years. In these circumstances any future triggers of trauma memories may generate intense emotions and a relapse of PTSD.

PTSD cycles

1. During periods of remission the individual regains normal coping mechanisms and a sense of humor, is able to socialize, share stories, work, and manage stress; he may be emotionally calm and capable of discriminating trivial from significant issues.

2. During anniversaries, major holidays, or whenever individual faces triggers for trauma or new real or symbolic traumas, they may initially go into a defensive state of avoidance and withdrawal, in order to prevent further arousal. But hypervigilance, paranoia, detachment, numbing, physical symptoms, memory problems, and insomnia soon reappear.

3. If the period of defensive operations fails, another stage of arousal follows which is characterized by rage, violence and acting out, panic, loss of control, loss of discrimination, flashbacks, nightmares, reliving experiences and hyper-emotionalism.

4. After this period of arousal a deep depression with feelings of shame, guilt, hopelessness, despair, worthlessness and suicidal ideation may take over until another cycle of remission helps the individual adapt again.

As described in earlier chapters, PTSD often compels the victim to re-enact traumas. Thus, the compulsive repetition of victimization may chronically alternate with periods of intrusive or numbing symptoms.

Cognitive processing problems

Trauma and PTSD may cause regression and a retreat from normal memory processing and use of language or symbols to purely emotional memory processing. This may result in other problems including: decreased rational thinking, amnesia for certain issues, solidification or de-solidification of certain memories, poor emotional tolerance, splitting and white/black perception, boundary problems, fear of bonding or intimacy, re-enacting or repeating traumas, obsessive reliving of events, addiction to drugs or sensations, co-dependency, and all-or-nothing thought processes.

The sense of emotional abandonment can also engender similar symptoms, as well as submission-surrender, loss of capabilities, loss of pleasure, and blocking of thoughts or amnesia. Severe PTSD can lead to the undoing of character, personality problems, dissociation, and identity confusion.

Normal responses to abnormal conditions

It should be emphasized that all these symptoms and behaviors are normal human reactions to abnormal and extraordinary conditions beyond human tolerance.

Research shows that when animals or humans experience "inescapable shock" (IS)—that is, when escape from a traumatic situation is impossible or futile, as in combat or forcible rape—they demonstrate troubled flight responses to danger, learned helplessness, reduced action of neurotransmitters, paralysis of will, a marked release of endorphins, a reduced sensation of pain, and amnesia.[29] As has already been mentioned, trauma conditions initially trigger the release of chemicals such as adrenaline/nor-adrenaline, which cause arousal states and fight-flight-freeze reactions or reliving experiences. Depletion of these chemicals in the body then leads to a condition known as "down-regulation." Defensive numbing, avoidance, and depression may accompany this process.

Repeated and chronic states of abandonment and trauma in childhood create deviations in attachment patterns with caretakers. Such children may have anxious, hostile, dependent, or depressive attachment patterns which can influence their entire life.

We shall discuss some of the significant manifestations of PTSD in greater detail in subsequent chapters.

How common is PTSD?

Within the general American population, PTSD has been estimated to occur in 10 percent of women and 6 percent of men. The incidence is much higher in war veterans, estimated at 27 percent for women and 31 percent for men.

Rape and torture result in the worse statistics of PTSD. One month after rape or torture, PTSD is prevalent in 65 to 70 percent of all victims; many years later, the rates decrease to 13 to 20 percent. Children who are chronically abused display PTSD in 20 percent of cases, according to long-term follow up research. The risk factors for the appearance of PTSD include childhood emotional problems, panic disorder, poor education, a family history of mental illness, and earlier traumas. Women are more likely to experience trauma and to develop PTSD. Whereas men tend to become aggressive in traumatic situations, women suppress anger and tend to become more depressed, with the result that they are more likely to develop chronic PTSD. Women are also more frequently abandoned, intensifying the likelihood of PTSD in situations of rape or other traumatic experience.

---

29   Victims such as those resulting from terrorists acts or natural disasters often lose their faith and individual illusions of safety, become aware of their vulnerability, of God's inability to prevent disasters, and feel helpless. This may in turn lead to fear, loss of confidence, guilt, insomnia, bodily symptoms, isolation, and anger.

Assessment and evaluation

Clinical and informal evaluations miss PTSD in at least 50 percent of cases. To lessen this high rate of missed diagnosis, clinicians should focus on behaviorally structured assessments, with attention to:

- The capacity of victims for toleration of adversity as well as the strength of support systems available to them;
- The comprehensive review of all the past traumas and their impact on psychological growth;
- The frequency of symptoms and their intensity;
- Risk factors, threats to emotional or physical integrity;
- Temperament, vulnerability, and resiliency.

Psychological tests are generally inadequate for identifying chronic liars or those individuals, such as malingerers, who exaggerate their problems for purposes of secondary gain and are difficult to identify with psychological tests. Of all the available trauma-specific scales, the Trauma Symptom Inventory (TSI), and the Detailed Assessment of Post-traumatic Stress (DAPS), both developed by psychologist John Briere, have been found to be the most effective.[30]

---

30   Both these tests may be purchased through Psychological Assessment Resources in Odessa, Florida.

Chapter Five: Alienation, Abandonment, and the Search for Meaning

The philosophy, which is so important in each of us is not a technical matter; it is our more or less dumb sense of what life honestly and deeply means.
— William James

Alienation

Shirley's Story

Shirley was 31 years old when she and her daughter Lisa first came to my office. Shirley wore a dazzling green shirt, which made her harassed face look pale in comparison. The fire in her black eyes, sparkling yet gloomy, accentuated the expressiveness in her face. Her large mouth contracted and quivered whenever she cried or smiled. Her forehead, wrinkling at any mention of pain or fear, reflected sometimes the fatal and sometimes the serene. Shirley's face communicated her emotions so well that even the coldest of people could not resist being moved by her. Nevertheless, there was something missing from her eyes. It seemed as if her soul had departed, leaving her in a state of total loss.

Lisa, a fragile, emaciated 12-year-old, sat quietly during the first interview, like one of those people born to suffer. She moved and talked slowly, sucking attention from others. She had a large nose and a high forehead and seemed to have lost her youthful vigor. The helpless resignation in her soft voice contrasted with her mother's commanding presence. My initial impression of her filled me with intense pity.

Lisa and her mother reported that they had been raped together at home. Shirley was divorced. She did not generally trust people. As a loner, she was always cautious and vigilant. When their assailant broke into their home, he caught them completely by surprise. He was a tall, muscular, masked man with a harsh and frightening voice. Shirley remembered that when he assaulted her at knifepoint, a sense of paralysis had immediately overtaken her. Dissociating and pretending she was observing someone else's rape, she had not been able to scream or move. She had only prayed to God to protect her daughter, Lisa.

Lisa's voice, as well, had been silenced by fear as she watched the rape of her mother in horror. The rapist had forced himself on Shirley as if he were trying to humiliate an animal, and then, in front of Lisa, had hit her on the head with a pan. The blow momentarily knocked her unconscious, and she fell to the floor.

Assuming that Shirley was unconscious, the rapist proceeded to assault Lisa. But Shirley regained consciousness when she heard her daughter shriek. She felt a sudden heroic power and, with the speed of a ferocious cat, attacked the assailant with a butcher knife. Screaming at the top of her lungs, she punctured his chest. Bleeding and gasping for air, the rapist barely escaped death. The police apprehended him an hour later.

The rapist's capture and imprisonment could have brought closure for Shirley, yet the experience of her own brutality; vulnerability, and humiliation left her feeling ashamed and helpless. I'll never forget the depth and range of emotions expressed by Shirley and her daughter. Mortal terror and paralyzing fear of his freedom and return, rage, guilt, shame, loss, and betrayal overwhelmed them both. Being victimized had shattered their sense of resilience and security. Nothing was fair anymore. No one merited his or her trust.

Neither mother nor daughter had acted with promiscuity or disregard for safety, but their own paralysis of will, left them feeling defeated and shattered. Shirley told me she did not know how to be a woman anymore. She could not redefine her humiliated self. When they came for help, however, it was because of Lisa's anguish. She said many times that she had lost her soul.

I asked Shirley and Lisa to join my group of traumatized victims, and they began participating in the weekly sessions. For several months, they expressed their fear of having a nervous breakdown. They felt rage toward each other, toward the rapist, toward other family members, and even toward the neighbors, who could not have helped nor understood their suffering.

"I often ask myself if my experience of trauma was legitimate enough to cause so much pain, or if I am just faking pain for sympathy," said Shirley. "I have deep doubts about myself and feel alienated from all of you. I have been coming here for months and still, somehow, you seem like strangers to me. I don't know how to go about regaining my sense of trust. When I was in the hospital I couldn't stop crying, but sometimes I simultaneously laughed, and people started saying, 'She's gone crazy.' I was just responding to flashes of memory. When I was out of control, in the first week after the rape, every few minutes I relived the image of my daughter's rape and my helplessness, as I lay unconscious on the floor. I could not make sense of this much pain."

I asked one of the group members to read the story of the Lover's Journey (See Chapter 13) which explains in universal symbolism the struggle of human alienation from the soul. The story illustrates how adversity forces us to surmount barriers in order to recapture our spirits. Shirley was deeply moved and comforted by the tale. She suddenly saw a ray of hope that her assailant might have compelled her to improve her relationship with Lisa.

Shirley's dark cloud of guilt stemmed from the feeling that she had abandoned her daughter. In the months after the rape, she had become extremely protective, even smothering, toward Lisa. Chronically self-critical, she felt ashamed of being a rape victim and the mother of a rape victim. The sight of any tall, muscular man startled her and led to flashbacks. She felt fragile and thought about suicide.

Pain and trauma leading to spiritual alienation are central to the experience of the human soul. Pathology, fragility, and sickness are necessary components of spiritual growth. Most insights into the dynamics of psychology have been derived from the sick, the suffering, and the broken. The human soul frequently has to encounter illusions, depressions, anxieties, and compulsions. These psychological symptoms are signs of natural alienation. In recent years, we have recognized the inadequacy of medical models to help us understand spiritual alienation or what some call "falling apart." We have learned that the complaints and ailments of the soul may not be a form of sickness in the medical sense but, rather, a stepping-stone on the path of growth. They are indeed signs of frustrated spiritual fulfillment.

The spiritual models of human experience show us the possibility that illness, suffering, and disorders create new alternatives and perspectives. They are the foundation for transcendence after hitting rock bottom. The medical model enjoys labeling behavior in various categories such as catatonic, compulsive, autistic etc., and these terms have become our main means of communication about the human experience. Such arbitrary naming of the phenomena related to the soul and the human will remains as troubling as ever. There is no direct relationship between these words and the experiences they represent. Indeed the labels become insults when applied to anyone inappropriately. We must abandon them when dealing with spirituality and recognize that true therapy does not need names or etiologies and that the soul does not exist without its dark side.

Nature itself displays idiosyncrasies. For instance, abnormalities in the formation of a plant, if repeated by grafting or replanting starter roots, may lead to improvements or to a whole new type of plant, over time. This is why there are so many roses named after the individuals who first tried to reproduce an aberration and thereby helped the new flowers evolve.

This same evolution can take place in grafting the identity of a human soul. Thus, even nightmares, anxieties, and compulsions become essential to our lifestyle, work, relationships, and growth. These afflictions and abnormalities open a series of symbolic paths toward insight and meaning. This was what eventually happened to this mother and daughter.

Abandonment or separation sickness

O SON of LOVE!

> *Thou art but one step away from the glorious heights above and from the celestial tree of love. Take thou one pace and with the next advance into the immortal realm and enter the pavilion of eternity. Give ear then to that which has been revealed by the Pen of Glory.*
> — Bahá'u'lláh[31]

Shirley's vulnerability was a product of spiritual abandonment or loss, which seems to me the core of all human emotional ills involving powerless-

---

31   Bahá'u'lláh, *Hidden Words*, Persian, No. 7.

ness. Modern research has shed light on many aspects of attachment, loss, and abandonment. The separation cry of a young child, initially a cry of fear, rage, and protest, often trails off into a whimper of withdrawal, despair, and surrender. These reactions are necessary for energy conservation. They numb the emotional feelings of pain in order to soothe the infant. Yet they can evolve as the main sources of amnesia, loss of pleasure, and physical illness.

Besides influencing the basic mothering process and normal childhood stages of autonomy, abandonment also modifies our relationship to family members and neighbors. It affects our group and church affiliations, social activities, response to authorities and government, and even to God.

"I often felt that as a victim of violent rape, God had forsaken me," said Shirley, "and also my friends, my country, my relatives, and my neighbors. They had all abandoned my delicate daughter and me. I had been humiliated with violence, and no one cared. I faced my death and that of my child so closely that my soul felt crushed until the end of time. I utterly collapsed. Now, for months I have been lost in a world of illusions. All I can do is to protect my girl as best as I can. I know she hates me for overprotecting her, but I have no other choice."

Once Shirley wept intensely while sharing her anguish and asked if any group members could comfort her. Several members offered reassurance and affirmation to her. Some moved closer and embraced her. Shirley cried for a long time. She wanted to regain her sense of order and goodness.

A menacing but very common question plagued her. She wondered whether her reaction to trauma would overwhelm others, causing further abandonment. What if the group or the therapist betrayed her again? She longed for an almost cosmic mother, someone more powerful and more available than the group members at the weekly meetings. Nevertheless, this request for a comforting, mothering environment marked the beginning of her trusting alliance and the recapture of her spiritual integrity.

Vulnerability

Ronnie Janoff-Bulman (1992) wrote about the core assumptions that provide internal spiritual security during childhood, including a sense of:

- The benevolence of the created world, or the Pollyanna principle;
- The meaningfulness of life;
- Self-worth.

When consistency, security and a confident expectation of these values do exist, an optimistic view of life prevails. Such optimism can create a denial of death and childhood fantasies of omnipotence or indestructibility. In Western cultures, the overestimation of human control over random phenomena sometimes enhances this illusion of invulnerability. Such exaggerated perceptions of self or others are not reality-based and often create problems with adaptation.

The inner map of resilience depends on self-esteem, independence, self-discipline, recognition of personal talents, open-mindedness and the capacity to dream. However, even with a healthy sense of self, we do need human support, respect, recognition, empathy, affirmation, and acceptance to consistently succeed. A nurturing environment, together with personal resilience, helps us maintain our assumptions of a benevolent universe throughout our lives. But when reality does not confirm this inner map of security, we may choose to deny reality.

Exposure to life-threatening major traumas drastically influences our basic assumptions of invulnerability. Thus, a change in our thinking may render us incapable of assimilating trauma into our former schema of expectations and life experience. A sense of abandonment and terror always accompanies this intense vulnerability. One's environment appears as hostile and dangerous and forces the individual to face his own mortality. For many years the traumatized individual may dread the collapse of his world and his own instantaneous physical death. Thus, in order to feel safer, he has to create a fictional new world of power and illusion.

The mythical Norse hero, Balder, illustrates the illusion of invulnerability.[32] His mother had made a deal with all the gods to make him invulnerable. But in her rush to visit various Gods, she forgot the god of mistletoe.

---

32   See Frazer (1922) "The Myth of Balder," Chapter 62.

In the court of Zeus, Balder became a source of great amusement. Poison, spears, swords, and arrows were all ineffective against him, as he was protected by all the gods. His jealous arch-enemy, however, learned about the little god of mistletoe. One day, he made a poisonous spear from a mistletoe plant that ultimately ended Balder's invulnerability.

Eastern mystical psychology focuses mainly on the concepts of spiritual perfection. Mystical writers refer to a path of perfection that takes each individual through stages of search for knowledge, love and attachment to God, detachment from and renunciation of materialism, patience, trust, contentment, and freedom from self (ego). What they refer to as the faculty of "inner vision" is a separate mental entity, a shared frontier between the conscious and the unconscious mind. Imagination is part of this common faculty, which endows the human being with the capacity to combine illusion and inspiration—necessary for the exercise of free will.

Human illusions of safety or invulnerability may be inborn, experiential or associative. The inborn illusions of safety begin in infancy with primitive functions and reflexes such as grasping and sucking. For instance, an infant may suck his own thumb to feel secure. The experiential components of safety relate to good or bad mothering and memories during the formative years. The associative illusion of safety lead us to expect that the future will reinforce the impressions we formed in the past. These creative illusions may help or hinder our adaptation to trauma. They may be tools that simply help us cope or they may be pathological.

Spiritual attachment and security

Life energy is a unifying force that connects the natural world with the transcendent world. The highest level of mystical transcendence relates to the heart or the soul. All other components of human existence, including intelligence, serve as stepping-stones to spiritual transcendence and the knowledge of the soul. This inner knowledge is so secure that it cannot be stolen or robbed by trauma.

The human reliance on cognitive faculties and neglect of one's basic spiritual nature leads to a form of separation sickness far more disturbing than ordinary separation anxiety. Yet the development of our inner vision can connect the perceptions of the conscious, cognitive, rational brain with the inspirational insights of the unconscious, creative, spiritually transcendent mind. Our destiny is to unite with this spiritual energy. Only then can a person feel perpetually secure. This kind of security withstands trauma. In fact, it redefines trauma as a component of growth.

The great Sufi writer Mohammad Ghazzali, author of The Alchemy of Happiness, describes this experience with a parable:

> I was traveling one day in a caravan to another town. I had loaded all my manuscripts, research documents, notes, and books on a mule, to use them for future reference. Bandits unexpectedly attacked our caravan, and stole everything. They took my mule and all my books and manuscripts. I was shattered and miserable.
>
> What could I do without all of my original writings? I approached the leader of the thieves and introduced myself. I asked him if he could read or write. He noticed how disturbed I was and, puzzled by my distress, said he could neither read nor write.
>
> I offered him all I had and begged him to return my notes and manuscripts, since they were my main source of knowledge. The young thief thought for a moment and asked a question: 'You claim to be a scholar and a scientist, do you not?' Yes, I said, to which he replied, 'What kind of knowledge do you possess that an illiterate bandit can steal from you?'

Ghazzali then reports that the incident dissolved his beliefs about worldly knowledge and reawakened his spiritual and inward quest, saying, "It was only after years of inward journey that I learned the alchemy of true happiness. He who knows the soul knows God."

There is nothing closer to us than our soul. We are all aware of human free will. In other ways, we are not different from the animal kingdom. It is our soul that reveals our true identity, source, destiny, meaning, and the role we play in this world. Yet, too often, we focus only on our physical or material attachments and live in separation. We seem to be riding the steed of our soul, but in denial of its existence, going around and asking people: Have you seen my horse?

As Ghazzali and many other mystics of the East have persistently reminded us, we cannot see or feel our souls with the five senses. Spiritual reality is external to the time and space dimensions. The only way of experiencing the soul is through an inward journey. This journey is the unshakable essence of humanity's common spiritual experience.

Human beings cannot be robbed of their souls. It guides our mind toward a path of knowledge beyond the boundaries of physical science. The soul is but a river, which brings us to the ocean of reality, the universal consciousness. So as we begin to reclaim whatever abandoned us, we must remember to reclaim and re-attach to our soul.

The search for meaning

I am your creator. You were in my care even before you were born.
   — Isaiah 44:2

Although running away from pain can contribute to the process of awakening, it often leads to a divided self and estrangement from the soul. Yet we cannot run away from our true higher and transcendent self for long, much less forever. For many years as I struggled to integrate psychotherapy with spirituality, I lamented the artificial separation of mind and soul in my field and among individual patients. I longed for the leaders of research in psychology to courageously confront the issue and return to the roots of true inner reality. I knew that people could—and did—pretend to live and love by depending only on the "self," without any awareness of the soul. But I also knew that, sooner or later, illusions, expectations, and greed would all die and force them to delve deeper into their own spiritual reality.

For a long time, the Jungian school of psychology seemed the only discipline to emphasize the importance of the soul for modern man. In *Modern Man in Search of a Soul*, Carl Jung emphasized that none of his patients was ever healed without developing a spiritual orientation. Following Jung's precepts, I centered my attention mostly on what he termed the "unifying seam" of the soul. I hoped to enhance the spiritual growth of my patients as well as my own, by considering my work as a form of worship.

The contemporary pilgrims of psychotherapy have often separated themselves from the life-infusing myths of antiquity. These myths served as the primary emotional support system for primitive man, but not for people in our time. Modern day pilgrims feel isolated and pitiable, observing the wake of a dead God. When people belonged to living religions, psychology served as a minor branch in the realm of storytelling. Today, with the gradual death of organized religion, each person must work hard to tell his or her own story and to reclaim a spiritual identity.

Therapeutic narratives

Patients in psychotherapy for trauma tell frightening stories. Along the course of therapy, patients offer these narratives for another person, not necessarily a guru or a person of great stature, but only a compassionate listener.

As part of my path as a therapist, I chose not only to listen to my patients' stories, but also to tell them my own. I thought that if we explored together, we would come to know each other. The art of psychotherapy taught me how to be more honest and to remain in therapy for the rest of my life. I have found it helpful to continually retell my own story as I continue my pilgrimage towards meaning.

Viewing man's higher spiritual self as the "supreme Talisman" of God,[33] I have a deep longing for greater meaning in my own life as well as those of my patients. I wondered if getting a deeper understanding of spiritual pain could give my life more direction. I often engaged in lengthy discussions with my colleagues about emotional pain in order to discover the reasons for various outcomes.

One late autumn evening in California, I remembered the symbolism in the great mythological epic Mahabharata[34] which portrayed the loss of meaning. In one famous tale, a man runs away from a wild camel in a hot, empty desert and cannot find a safe place to hide. He is dying of thirst but finds only mirages. He climbs into a well for protection and hangs onto a small bush for dear life, finding a foothold on the slippery walls. When his eyes adjust to the dark, he is horrified to see that his foothold is nothing but the heads of four venomous snakes. He also notices a pair of black and white mice chewing the roots of the bush from which he hangs. At the bottom of the well, a fiery dragon is waiting to swallow him. Despite his state of panic, he notices a beehive dripping with honey close by. Reaching for the honey and tasting its sweetness, he forgets his predicament and falls to his death.

---

33   Bahá'u'lláh, *Tablets*, p. 161.
34   The Mahabharata forms one of the two major epics of Hindu scripture, the Bhagavad Gita.

Our own spiritual dilemma is strikingly similar: lost in the "desert" of a spiritual void, we thirst for meaning but rarely find it. We stumble on mirages or illusions of the "self," and sooner or later, the beasts of aging and illness haunt us. We climb into the safe "well" of friendships and family support, but they do not provide protection. Dependence on others is a slippery wall. The "mice" of the passing days gnaw our fragile bush of life, and our foothold proves shaky or dangerous. The dragon of death is ever present and the sweet honey of pleasure remains a continuing illusion.

In his search for meaning, the American writer, Sheldon Kopp, himself a victim of abuse and abandonment—and perhaps aware of the above mythical tale—offered the following list:

- This is it!
- There are no hidden meanings;
- You can't get there from here, and besides, there is no place else to go;
- We are all already dying, and we will be dead for a long time;
- Nothing lasts;
- There is no way of getting all you want;
- You cannot have anything unless you let go of it;
- You only get to keep what you give away;
- There is no particular reason why you lost out on some things;
- The world is not necessarily just;
- Being good often does not pay off and there is no compensation for misfortune!

Kopp's list is a sad litany of negation. Although in the context of PTSD such hopeless and gloomy perceptions of life are quite prevalent, for the majority of individuals who suffer adversity and trauma the opposite is true. A case in point was Kopp himself, who thrived in his personal, professional, and literary life after childhood trauma.

If we are taken in by this scenario and our own illusions, as we face the multitude mirages of life, we might well ask: Is there a soul and an afterlife? Is spiritual immortality possible? What is the real meaning of life? For many people, these questions have been answered in the affirmative. For example, Baha'is recite everyday as part of their prayers: "I bear witness, O my God, that Thou hast created me to know Thee and to worship Thee."[35]

But Kopp and others presume that "this is it!" and would have us believe that death brings everything to an end. Their philosophy is buttressed by some ancient legends, such as the epic of Gilgamesh,[36] the story of the king who did not want to die, a provocative metaphor for the ever-present dragon of death and the denial of immortality. Four thousand years ago, Gilgamesh ruled the city of Uruk in Mesopotamia. The people of Uruk had grown weary and appalled by his perfectionism and countless demands. When his oppression became unbearable, people complained to the goddess Aruru, asking her to destroy Gilgamesh. She refused to kill him, but, as a challenge to the king, agreed to create an enemy every bit as intelligent, cunning, and powerful, but a completely selfish brute, Enkidu, who existed solely to destroy Gilgamesh's pride. Covered with hair and raised in the wild, Enkidu challenged the king's rule, and for many years mighty Gilgamesh could not defeat him. At last the two decided to make peace, learn from each other, and work together. They went on many expeditions and adventures until the goddess Ishtar, who was in love with Gilgamesh, killed Enkidu in a fit of jealousy. Suddenly terrified by his own mortality, Gilgamesh decided to gain immortality by meeting the great master, Utmatishtim.

"The life that thou seekest," said the master, "thou wilt not find, for when the gods created mankind, they allotted death to him." In a heroic struggle, Gilgamesh eventually came to the plant of immortality at the bottom of the sea, but before he could partake of the plant, a serpent deprived him of renewed life by eating the plant.

This legend suggests that even with the support of gods, we cannot prevent the demise of our bodies. We are physically mortal and there is nothing for our bodies after death.

---

35   Bahá'í Prayers, 1988, p. 4.

36   One of the Akkadian epics; see also Campbell (1976).

Revising my practice of psychiatry

Moved by such legends and unable to accept the finality of death, I searched for another meaning to mortality. I conceptualized death as a possible new birth, a release, a freedom, and a resurrection. I did not seek a deterministic, soulless world prone to fast or superficial processes. I detached myself from illusions of pleasure and relinquished my search for a single source that provides security forever. Instead, I tried to experience the miracles we all seek throughout our lives, never losing sight of my own spirit.

I recognized that the human experience does not generate an ultimate wisdom that distinguishes illusion from truth. To resolve the endless confusion of meanings, I could have turned to arbitrary guides and to those considered authorities, or I could choose to personally search for truth. Inspired by the writings of the great Sufi poets, such as Attar (1984), I chose to seek for truth and meaning individually. I was invariably confronted by the multi-faceted nature of truth.

In the last few years of his life, a Sufi master had chosen silence and seclusion. On his deathbed, in response to the insistent question of a student, he uttered these words:

> *I have encouraged people to avoid hypocrisy and search for truth. I learned one day that truth is elusive, as anyone's truth may be someone else's deception. I also realized that encouraging others to search for the elusive is absolute hypocrisy. Thus I remained silent!*[37]

I, too, sought the nature of truth and, after long contemplation, arrived at the conclusion—right or wrong—that the only solution for me was to attempt a spiritual revision of my own professional work, in order to give my life greater meaning. The human soul has been exiled by the scientists of biology, statistics, behavior, and anthropology who dominated contemporary psychiatry. The time had arrived, I thought, to fundamentally change my own approach.

Venturing into spiritual depths was frightening. Learning to become sensitive to the "mysterious" and relying on the "inner vision" was, nevertheless, a way back to my roots, a homecoming of sorts.

It was thrilling to read the works of Hillman (1997), and Elkins (et

---

37   Shah (1967), p. 70.

al., 1988), who had so passionately contemplated spirituality in both their personal and professional lives. I thought about the messenger bird in fairy tales who appears and whispers in the hero's ears, revealing the wisdom of ages. Sheldon Kopp's book *Raise Your Right Hand Against Fear: Extend the Other in Compassion* (1988) had convinced me that imagination plays a dominant role in each person's experience of truth. The main dilemma, then, was how to separate spiritual truth from vain imaginations of the "self."

If our illusions of reality remain unexamined, we come to believe that our personal world-view reflects the only viable reality. We then consider those who disagree with us to be fools or liars. As a follower of the Bahá'í Faith, I have always cherished the pluralistic views and multiple realities symbolized by the image of humanity as flowers of one garden. This symbol had freed me from the needless suffering we experience when we apply one rigid personal vision to all situations. I felt free to respect and be nurtured by the enriching input of other people's realities. Thus, I yearned to help psychology integrate with its spiritual roots. My hope was not to commit the grave errors of Karen Horney (1970), who had searched for solutions through the ego.[38]

---

38   The reader may refer to Chapter 15 for further detail.

Chapter Six: Guilt

O MY FRIEND!

Thou art the daystar of the heavens of My holiness, let not the defilement of the world eclipse thy splendor. Rend asunder the veil of heedlessness, that from behind the clouds thou mayest emerge resplendent and array all things with the apparel of life.

    — Bahá'u'lláh, *Hidden Words*, Persian, No. 73

Rose's story

Rose's mother, a rather naive girl when she first married, was physically separated from her husband during her first pregnancy. He served abroad in the army while she went through the happy process of buying baby clothes and preparing for the event. When her pregnancy was complicated by rubella, she was suddenly forced to have an abortion. She suffered through the intense emotional loss of this experience without the support of her absent husband, especially difficult after she had spent so much time buying all the necessities for the baby.

This young mother felt suddenly vulnerable and fragile. When she accidentally learned about her husband's affairs with several other women, she was crushed. The ensuing bitter divorce made her cynical of all men, and it forever damaged her ability to trust. Many years later, when she met Rose's father, she was so frightened of men that he had to exercise considerable patience and compassion before she would consent to marry him.

Nevertheless, theirs was a dysfunctional marriage. Having tasted betrayal, she was watchful as a hawk of her husband's every move, incapable of trusting him. She constantly searched his face for interest in other women. She had learned to perceive events in fractions of a second, like a camera taking repeated pictures, so as to process them later, frame by frame. She could perceive the most unnoticeable aspects of an experience. She could read fleeting moments of betrayal in the depth of anyone's soul, even if such reflections were ill-defined. Paranoia and hypervigilance led her to drink heavily, as if numbing her senses might help her avoid the constant pain of betrayal.

Her husband's agenda was different. He loved children, albeit in a perverted way. He had waited patiently for his daughter, Rose, to grow older and to be the recipient of his sordid love. Although he was afraid of his wife's paranoia regarding other women and forever shut himself off from extramarital affairs, he knew that in his own home, some young girls were growing up to become love objects. He also knew that his wife was too naive to suspect such diabolical intentions in his love of children.

Rose, the oldest of four girls, was her father's first sexual victim, and was abused from age nine to thirteen. She was simply told that if she divulged a word about her father's "games," he would kill the entire family. Rose's mother, who had relied on alcohol to relieve the pain of betrayal, often resented her daughter. While she consciously wished no harm to Rose, she thought of her as being seductive and did not believe any of her hints that this quality came from another source within the home. Rose did not personally dislike her mother or her younger sisters, but at times, enraged with helplessness and confusion, she wished them all dead.

One after another, Rose's sisters each fell into the same trap. Although their mother eventually understood the nature of her husband's "love" for children—providing further proof to her of what she saw as men's absolute irresponsibility—the girls all felt unprotected by her during their tender years. Legal action, divorce, and the father's imprisonment did not change Rose's view of her mother. But by far the most disturbing issue for her was guilt. On several occasions, her father's sexual advances had aroused her to orgasm, and she felt ashamed of herself. She thought she had actually participated in a love affair with her father, concluding that he should not be the only one to go to prison. She had never shared her story, allowing her guilt to bring her to the brink of suicide before entering therapy.

Rose also felt deeply responsible for her sisters' victimization by her father. Her mother had told her on many occasions to watch her sisters and make sure nothing bad happened to them. On the other hand, she felt a sense of relief when her father switched his sordid interest to her sisters. They were all threatened with the same intense secrecy and dread of annihilation of the family. For many years, Rose had been filled with illusions of wisdom. Like her mother, she naively thought she knew everything she needed to know.

Our therapy sessions revealed Rose's fragility, profound depression, fear of criticism, desire to please others, and expectations of punishment. As I gently guided her to accept her emotions as adversities in the path of growth, I was able to "re-frame" her depression as a form of withdrawal to conserve energy. It was her way of facing death.

Although Rose had attended sexual abuse survivor group sessions prior to entering individual therapy, reassurances by group members had not insulated her from pain. One of her fellow group members had told her that even placing a chipmunk between a young girl's legs could lead to sexual arousal, but she continued to feel plagued by the guilt of her own participation. Her almost suicidal behaviors had frightened the group members, who insisted she seek individual psychiatric help.

Rose's obsession with traumatic memories prevented her from allowing any new information into her immobilized psyche. She suffered from a condition common to children of Holocaust survivors or to victims of war crimes, a condition of emotional confusion called alexithymia.[39]

Her complex emotions often showed in her face. Her morose, glassy eyes seemed blind to the world. They projected sadness and hopelessness. She felt ugly, especially when the slight tremors in the muscles around her eyes frustrated her. Her lips looked feverish and often took on a distasteful shape, as if she felt perpetually nauseous. Rose suffered from maddening self-blame. She seemed to anticipate being branded with melted steel or choked by a sadist, and the effort to endure often left her weak and fragile.

She had tried for years to suppress or alter her memories of abuse, but her coping mechanisms were of little use. Her flashbacks included masses of painful memories. She could never integrate these disgusting images into a meaningful or rational account of her story. She remembered actions without words and often let her body keep score of her trauma by physical symptoms. Dazed and distant, as if drugged, she often expressed the desire to die.

---

39   Alexithymia is the inability of a PTSD sufferer to put feelings into words, leading to over-reaction or inhibited behaviors. See Krystal, 1968.

Later, in an attempt to create a narrative of her mother's life, she began to recall her hostile-dependent memories of childhood. Initially in bits and pieces, and gradually with the help of a desensitization process, she retrieved many painful memories. She recalled her mother's paranoid accusations. She remembered her mother calling her a slut, shaming and criticizing her, without any recognition of her sacrifice or her attempts to protect her sisters. At times she had competed with her mother out of rage, feeling sorry for her father. But her main goal in life was to prevent the breakdown of her family.

Rose remembered her mother's alcohol-related hospitalizations and how she was left to act as the mother-caretaker of the family. In addition to her anger at her father's betrayal of her childhood innocence, she also felt enraged about her mother's cruel response when, at age 16, she had started to date in the hope of moving away from the family's hotbed of perversion. Her mother had threatened to arrest her 20-year-old boyfriend as a child molester. She recalled the many moments when she had planned to stab her mother and run away from home. Her amnesia, fantasies, and physical ailments all served as coping devices for her feelings of guilt over a combination of moral and spiritual betrayal, and complete abandonment.

Despite the numerous differences between them, Rose feared that she had become the reincarnation of her mother. Her guilt was compounded by her positive sexual response and arousal by her father, her desire to kill her mother, and her sense of responsibility when her mother actually died. She felt that she should also die and join her mother. Confirmation of Rose's horrifying abuse came later from her sisters. This led to a gradual evolution of her trauma narrative, in which she began to forgive herself enough to strive for spiritual peace. I encouraged her to return to her survivor group after the suicide danger had subsided, in order to continue her spiritual journey.

Self-blame is universal for traumatized individuals, regardless of the validity of the feelings in each case. Reports of European Jews who survived the Holocaust reveal this same baseless guilt over not having done more to save themselves and others. Some individuals use guilt as a defense mechanism against depression and the deadening of feelings. It seems that guilt magically brings the dead back to life. Self-condemnation has also been a common reaction to rape, battering, and even to death of a loved one. Some veterans who actually committed war atrocities have an even greater level of self-blame and guilt.

At times, self-blame is an adaptive behavior, but in most situations, it leads to depression and despondency. Some victims focus on specific behaviors committed or overlooked during the traumatic event. By doing so, they try to modify or correct such behaviors in order to prevent future traumatic events. Those victims who had a tendency to self-blame prior to the traumatic event endure more intense reactions, often non-adaptive and in which character becomes undone. They perceive trauma as further evidence of their unworthiness.

The characteristics of survivor guilt are common among the victims of the World War II atomic explosions, concentration camps, and those who suffer rape, betrayal, armed conflict, or natural disasters. Soldiers who have simultaneously experienced the roles of victim, victimizer and executioner have to face not only the fears and denials of the death images, but also the suffering of conflicting values. Self-condemnation, guilt, incompetence, and obliteration of meaning thus affect their lives forever.

Survivor guilt

Individuals traumatized in combat, violence, or disasters might question why they survived while others, whom they deem more worthy, did not. Victims of violence may also suffer self-reproach for having contributed to the cause of a disaster, an adversity or a violent event, or even for not having prevented it. They assume emotional responsibility for damages done to others. Many of my patients use irrational fantasies of self-punishment to appease their guilt. They demonstrate self-defeating behaviors, invite rejection from loved ones and seek new traumatic events, as if they are obsessed with punishment.

People traumatized by violence, combat, terrorism, civilian disasters, abuse, or rape, exhibit a high rate of suicide and self-destructive conduct. They sometimes report near-death experiences. Certain victims converse with guardian angels, imploring rescue from imminent death.

Many war veterans feel that they actually died in combat, and when they return, behave as if they were dead. Their intense grief and shame can lead to further suicidal attempts and eventual death. An estimated 100,000 or more Vietnam veterans committed suicide after returning to America, unable to tolerate their feelings of intense guilt. One Iraq war veteran said to me, "Doc, I know if I had done my job, if I was there for my buddies, none of them would have died. I know in the case of Bill's death, I was late. I didn't do my job. It was my fault that he never came home. When the time comes, Doc, I think I should join him. I didn't take care of him when he needed me. I should have taken those rounds myself."

The universal concepts of humanity, love, benevolence, trust, and morality are often distorted for individuals who have experienced trauma. As they face their moral responsibilities and experience images of trauma, a new form of victimization may develop. Their refusal to die or to kill forces the victimized individuals to suffer intense confusion and depression.

Survivor guilt is one of the most common features of PTSD. At least 20 percent of combat veterans and victims of the 9/11 attacks or the great 2005 tsunami who were interviewed by media reporters or aid workers admitted to depression, suicidal thoughts and guilt at not having been able to save their loved ones.

They suffer intense, unresolved guilt about their experiences and the very threat of death that defined their traumatic moments seems to pursue them like a demonic force. Guilt, along with the heavy psychological weight of their trauma, generates a long-term depression often characterized by insomnia, nightmares, and lack of initiative. The debased self-image of the survivor fuels guilty ruminations and further depression.

Angela's story

This 11-year-old girl was referred to me with a chronic history of running away from home, and later, from foster homes. Her earlier childhood experience was littered with exposure to domestic violence, parental divorce, and a highly emotional mother, who suffered from bipolar disease. This was compounded by the accidental death of her younger sister when she was six years old. At the time we first met, she was once again in her mother's home, displaying many signs of depression, anxiety, and PTSD. In an effort to establish a trusting therapeutic relationship, I had asked her to call me next time she was contemplating running away, so that I could "run" with her. She actually did call one day to report that she had decided to run away. I cancelled all my appointments and drove to her home and joined her for this adventure, having earlier received her mother's permission. We walked together for about four miles and arrived at a funeral home. Angela was breathing fast and appeared very apprehensive. She asked if we could go in. I agreed and we entered. She asked if I could get permission for both of us to view the coffins. After explaining the situation to the mortuary manager, he allowed us to go downstairs and view the coffins. In only a few minutes, Angela had regained her composure and, smiling broadly, said, "Everything is fine now! Can we go home again?" On the way back, our long discussion revealed a deep sense of survivor guilt, combined with childhood magical thinking. After the separation of her parents, Angela had assumed guilt for the divorce and had selected her younger sister to be a recipient of her guilt projection, and a poison-container for her rage, memories of violence and abuse, and PTSD. In a sibling clash with her sister she had once screamed, "I hope to God you die." When her sister was actually killed in a car accident a few of weeks later, her guilt over her curse, loss, and her own survival intensified. Now, any time she had a quarrel with her mother, she would fear her accidental death and would run to the funeral home—where her sister's body had been sent—to make sure her mother was still alive.

Survivor guilt in literature

Scientific interest in the survivor syndrome has rippled through literature, poetry, movies, graphic arts, and television. Experience has now taught us how to make more sense of these stories.As victims' wounds slowly turn into scars and tragedies become history, we try to uncover the buried wounds.

Despite the widespread interest in the clinical aspects and outcomes of PTSD which has emerged, overshadowing other psychiatric disciplines, we still seem reluctant to evaluate the impact of global events, such as the Holocaust, the devastation of the atomic bombs, war, and genocide. It seems that we are still averse to turning such highly emotional topics into detached scientific scrutiny.

The fears, guilt, and hope for redemption which characterize survivor guilt are much more clearly portrayed in folk tales, which generate a sense of courage to deal with these disturbing situations. One example appears in the literary account of a Hindu king's confrontation with a ghost, who symbolizes the hidden aspects of guilt, secrecy, and the thoughts which may haunt the sufferer throughout life. As recorded by Heinrich Zimmer in his book *The King and the Corpse*,(1948), the king engages in a struggle with darkness and manages to cover up for his guilt and anxiety with imperial complacency. The story unfolds as follows:

> Every day for several months a holy man in the garb of a beggar appears in the king's court, offering a piece of fruit as a gift. The king accepts the gift each day without paying much attention to it, passing it on to his treasurer, who throws the fruit into the attic treasure house. The beggar never asks anything for himself.

> One day, after several months of this mysterious charade, a pet monkey from the king's harem escapes and appears in the courtyard. The king offers the fruit to his monkey. As the monkey plays with the fruit and eventually bites into it, a beautiful piece of jewelry falls from the center of the fruit. The king, surprised, runs to the treasure house and finds the hundreds of decaying fruit with priceless jewels among them.

> The next day, when the holy man arrives again, the king questions him about the mystery of the fruit and the jewels. The beggar replies that by now the king has learned two important lessons: to look within, rather than superficially at objects and people, and to know that he can learn from anyone, even a monkey. The king begins to realize that the beggar is, in reality, a sorcerer and ascetic. The beggar offers the king a chance to become a hero by performing an act of exorcism. The king agrees to meet the beggar one night at the crematorium.

> When the king arrives at the burial ground, he realizes, to his horror, that the ground is covered with the remains of cremated corpses and hot burning coal. In the darkness, he can barely make out the charred skulls and skeletons and dimly hears the howling of ghouls and demons. The beggar instructs him to go to one side of the burial ground, cut down a corpse hanging from a tree, and carry it on his back toward the beggar. Trembling with fear, the king crosses the burial ground, The king is faced with a dilemma: if he utters a single word, the corpse on his back will jump back and hang onto the tree. The corpse poses difficult riddles for the king and announces that if the king does not answer the riddles accurately, his head will be blown to pieces.

> The king is caught in an agonizing paradox. He gives the correct answers to the riddles every time, but because he had to speak in order to answer, the corpse jumps back to its original position on the tree. Exhausted and confused by the time he answers the 24th riddle, the king is no longer able to come up with answers.

In anguish and humility, he declares that he will accept death without protest. At the very moment that he expresses his helplessness and humility, the spirit leaves the corpse, bows to the king and announces that the king had now become a hero. He has earned this title first by learning to look inside himself, second by showing willingness to learn from anyone, even a monkey; third by facing death; and fourth, by accepting humility. Thus, specter helps the king to free himself from the curse of the beggar and he becomes a hero.

Guilt and anguish may persevere over long periods of time. Like the corpse on the back of the king, guilt might generate riddles for the individual victim, and the resolution of each riddle can generate greater pain and anguish. The process may lead to depression, loss of joy, loss of productivity, and utter powerlessness. One might identify with the non-surviving loved ones and wish he could die. He may dread the return of the traumas or the sense of punishment and betrayal. And the agony of separation, abandonment and suffering may continue for many years. The fear of harming oneself or others is one of the seemingly eternal aspects of this disturbing human emotion.

Survival is a central theme of our lives. From early childhood, we struggle with fears of annihilation, murder, injury, or confrontation with danger. Our natural instincts alert us to the possibility of death. A survivor of life-threatening traumas or real exposure to death carries a number of characteristics through life that distinguish him from the average person. He has a dreadful knowledge. He has an intense sensory image of what it feels like to face death, especially if the traumatic event was persistent, horrifying, or sudden. These images are called imprints and represent our human vulnerability to disintegration or death.

The death image continually reverberates, raising questions about beginnings and endings, and leading to feelings of insecurity or melancholy. The mind rejects our first attempts at psychic numbing. It refuses to forget these grotesque images. Somehow, as we try to alter our sense of helplessness, we enter a stage of denial of our own mortality. We begin to believe we can escape painful realities, and this process of numbing then functions as a balm. Yet in the end, the illusion of flight from loss and pain is an evasion of all that life contains, and a very costly price to pay to erase our painful death images. Comfort becomes complacency when it demands that we reject our transient human condition and deny our mortality.

Frequently, a survivor shuns close relationships and thus feels worthless. At times he may "live in death" and project an image of danger to others through his acts of violence. Although violence can make survivors immune to the shadow of death, and although it is more tolerable than fear or guilt, it becomes an inner defense against dying that permanently curtails one's ability to love. Deviations of the capacity for love, nurturance, intimacy, and trust lead to a deep resentment of neediness. This then generates a perception that help is fake or unreal. False promises and betrayal of covenants make the idea of protection rather frightening.

Reliving guilt in group settings

Along with the explosion of information in the field of trauma, has come a dizzying number of support groups for trauma survivors. Group encounters help victims of trauma overcome their fears about relationships. In an emotionally supportive setting, survivors can re-examine death, mortality, and the limitations of human willpower. Survivor groups can often help each member understand the myriad tactics they may have used to provoke rejection and punishment. They can identify and explore self-defeating behaviors one by one and link them to the original circumstances of the trauma and the guilt. When a traumatized individual insists that seeking companionship in the outside world is not worth the pain of loss, group members can confront his desperate loneliness. Participants can begin to realize that life is filled with events beyond one's control. They can begin to see avoidance of intimacy as a denial of the limitations of human power. In reality, one has no control over the life and death of those people who are near and dear. Support groups remain available and steadfast until the new member can accept these truths.

The victim of trauma might ask, "Why has this happened to me? What did I do to deserve this?" It is impossible to answer such questions unless the victim evaluates his own individual images, symbols, and transformations. Survivor groups can help each participant find meaning in traumatic experience. They can help evaluate responses to the perpetrators of trauma, to natural disasters, or to combat.

Fear and denial of death is a central theme in group discussion, and spiritual approaches often assist the group in generating new meanings for this feeling. When individuals use guilt as a form of achievement, to appear as martyr or hero, the group openly discusses the meaning of such behaviors. They also discuss the relationship of the survivors to humanity. By helping each other to consider the universality of the human experience, they gain an understanding of the sense of unity which can promote peace and transcendence. When someone uses guilt to remain distant from others, the group can help him accept intimacy as a new adaptive response. They can encourage the struggling member to participate in social encounters and community life to recreate feelings of happiness and meaning in life.

Peer recognition allows survivors to recognize that they are not freaks and do not have to go through it alone. This usually leads to better communication of experiences in narrative. When we have a healing community of traumatized individuals, the victims can once again find that they can speak without acting out. Initially, the group discussions serve as part of a process of mutual affirmation and recognition. Recovery comes later when personal and individual narratives are developed and each individual shares his or her particular circumstances with the community. No person's suffering can be measured against any other person's anguish.

One of the most difficult steps in relinquishing guilt is letting go of pride. Learning to step forward in the path of love is the only way to relinquish self-pride. We can overcome loss and inadequacy by recognizing our spiritual nature and the spiritual nature of other PTSD sufferers. We can begin to see that all the treasures necessary for progress are already contained within our souls, that no one is free from adversity. Trauma may destroy coping mechanisms, but it invariably creates new possibilities for growth.

Victims of trauma often doubt that they are worthy of treatment because of their guilt. As they develop narratives, symptoms of guilt such as involuntary flashbacks decrease, and their reaction to old memories changes. Loving intervention from the community, especially through survivor groups, helps the participants learn to deal with denial, disillusionment, rage, and loss of meaning. With each other's help, members of survivor groups gradually develop human virtues. They become trustworthy and patient. They develop greater love and mercy. They avoid lying to themselves or others and become more spiritual.

Individual recovery

O MY SERVANT!

Thou art even as a finely tempered sword concealed in the darkness of its sheath and its value hidden from the artificer's knowledge. Wherefore come forth from the sheath of self that thy worth may be made resplendent and manifest unto all the world.

> — Bahá'u'lláh[40]

Emancipation from the bondage of death and guilt entails several stages of trauma recovery and spiritual growth. To reorder our lives, we must abandon loyalty to past memories and vicious cycles of victimization. Perhaps such memories will never disappear entirely, but our reactions to these memories can change and become more resolute. Renewal also requires modification of our sense of blame and guilt. Only then can we stop scapegoating and making poison-containers and gradually re-integrate positive childhood images.

When we learn that most PTSD symptoms are adaptive and necessary for the acknowledgment of the healthier sides of ourselves, we can begin to regain trust in others and ourselves. The tools for recovery are already available in our own souls. We need only to recognize our spiritual powers in relation to the cosmic reality. Learning to trust the divine intelligence imprinted on our souls in order to regain the sense of the miraculous is an essential step in recovery.

It seems to me that there is no way to recover from survivor guilt except in harmony with others. To do so, we each need to define ourselves as a spiritual being, to relinquish blind love and non-adaptive behaviors, and perhaps to practice a twelve-step program, carrying the message of hope to others.

This subject will be discussed in greater detail in Chapter 15 which deals with ego, thought processes, and human identity.

---

40   Bahá'u'lláh, *Hidden Words*, Persian, No. 72.

Chapter Seven: Trauma and the Body

Watch over your heart with all diligence, for from it flow the springs of life.
— Proverbs 4:23

Somatization: The physical expression of emotion

The human body—the inspiration for vast outpourings of exquisite poetry in virtually every culture of the world—keeps a complete record of both the traumatic and the joyous events of life. It registers millions of bits of information about every conceivable emotion.

The display of various emotional memories, registered in the amygdaloid complex of the brain as physical or somatic symptoms is called *somatization*. Simple forms of this process are nausea or diarrhea as expressions of fear, headaches or stomach aches, as reflections of anger, etc. Like our dreams and daydreams, in which the mind expresses emotional information in symbolic forms, physical symptoms are the non-verbal voice of our souls, which also communicate symbolically. We express joy or suffering through gestures and movements, but also through disrupted behavior, disease and altered perception. An explosion of new information about the mind-body relationship has shown the many ways in which psychological suffering and joy can affect the body.

Western medicine in the 20th century focused on cure and paid little attention to artistic-symbolic aspects of the mind-body interaction. Doctors often aimed at the eradication of symptoms before understanding their true meaning. In her pioneering work on the relationship of the mind and body,

Magda Arnold (1960) demonstrated how the limbic system of the brain[41] functions as a central information processing system, translating physiological and psychological information back and forth. Franz Alexander (1950) wrote extensively on the relationship between personality, emotional conflicts, and the endocrine system. He observed the link between environmental stresses and positive thinking, and discovered that trauma or threats to security in childhood seem common among people with neurosis or psychosomatic symptoms. He showed that organs such as the heart are not simply mechanical pumps but the symbolic center of love and courage, how colitis relates to repressed anger, and how pain could be absolutely symbolic. The chronic abdominal pain of sexually abused women serves as one well-accepted example.

Today's researchers now validate their psycho-physiological findings by synthesizing diverse sources of information. Trauma and post-traumatic stress disorders have become increasingly valuable as sources of study in evaluating the symbolic interaction of the soul and the body.

The mind-body relationships have been studied in detail down to the level of cellular functioning, revealing the following major pathways:[42]

- Through the adrenergic (sympathetic and parasympathetic) nervous systems, the brain connects directly to the eyes, salivary glands, heart and arteries, bronchi and lungs, stomach, pancreas, intestines, bladder, adrenal glands, etc. At the cellular level, these systems affect multiple functions related to energy, hormones, and the secretion of enzymes.

- Through the endocrine glands (the hypothalamus, pituitary, pineal, thyroid, hypothyroid, adrenal glands, ovaries and testicles), the emotional centers of the brain influence the regulation of basic metabolism, cell growth, sexual functions, kidney functions, electrolyte balance, and the flow of blood throughout the body.

---

41   Limbic system and its structures govern many of our emotions and motivations, particularly those that are related to survival, such as fear, anger, and emotions related to sexual behavior. Two large limbic system structures, the amygdala and hippocampus play important roles in memory. The amygdala is responsible for which memories are stored and where, possibly determining how much of an emotional response a particular event invokes.

42   See Chapter 10 for greater detail concerning scientific and biological research.

- Through the intricate connections of the central nervous system, the brain regulates emotional sensitivity, cognitive functions, gastrointestinal activity, the liver, the spleen, pancreas, the adrenals, the immune system, the release of endorphins, and a great number of neurotransmitter proteins, etc.

- The immune system including the thymus gland, bone marrow, lymph system, spleen, skin, neuro-endocrine hormones, receptor immune cells, antibodies, and immuno-transmitters are all under the direct influence of the emotional centers of the brain and respond to stress, anxiety, depression, etc.

Carl's story

Carl's wife brought him to my office in a wheelchair. A large-boned but fragile 40-year-old, he complained bitterly about his lack of balance and inability to walk. I had studied his medical files and knew about his recent brain surgery to correct a possible case of communicating hydrocephalus. He reported that surgery had not improved his gait or balance. He then described the full gamut of his physical symptoms, which seemed quite confusing. He had been unemployed for at least two years and had suffered from intense headaches, numbness in half of his body, muscle weakness, spasmodic muscle movements, nightmares, insomnia, panic attacks, and visual problems.

During a brief neurological examination, I noticed a lack of correlation between his symptoms and the normal distribution of nerves within the body. I also recognized his indifferent facial expression, traditionally called "la belle indifference," typical of hysterical reactions. I asked his wife to help me with the examination of his gait and movements out of the wheelchair. Immediately he squatted into an unusual position and proceeded to move in a well coordinated fashion by moving one knee forward with both hands then switching to his other leg.

Curious about this bizarre action, I took a few minutes to go alone to another room, where I imitated his movements to check my own balance. I found these squatting movements extremely difficult to imitate. They required unusual strength and coordination. I knew about a hysterical condition called *astasia-abasia*, in which the body translates severe emotional stress into the inability to walk and maintain normal balance. Carl's behavior seemed to match the description of this illness. His emotional indifference and even his occasional smiles as he struggled to move around tended to confirm my diagnosis of hysteria. Assuming there were intense psychological influences at work, I asked him to share his life story with me.

Carl began by talking about his truck driver father who was almost never home during his childhood.

"He drank heavily, often beating me and my mother when he was drunk," he said. "I hated him, and I was terribly afraid of him. Whenever he came home, I used to hide under the bed for safety. I could never look into his eyes, and that infuriated him. He thought of me as a sissy.

"I was barely five years old when my mother took off, leaving me with my father, without any mercy or protection. She said it was better for me to stay with my dad and learn how to be a man! I never saw my mother again. I was left with different relatives when my father traveled and moved from town to town. I never experienced a place I could call home. Like Frankenstein, I inherited different pieces of my mind from various people, never feeling like a real human. At times my father was gone for six months or more. At least I was free from his wrath during those days. Yet due to his many moves, I changed schools a total of twelve or thirteen times. I went to three junior highs and four high schools before I was 17. I had lived in nine different states, many different cities, and never felt settled. I had terrible nightmares about my father's abusive behavior, and for years they continued to haunt me.

"Once at the age of nine, I was about a half hour late getting home from school. He was furious. He picked me up and threw me against the wall. My head was gashed and bleeding. I was knocked out. When I regained consciousness, I was in a neighbor's home and my dad was gone. I was told I had 24 stitches in my scalp. No one did anything to protect me or to place me somewhere else at the time. I started to have severe headaches, and my fear of my father grew stronger by the day.

"When I was 14, my father remarried and I inherited a couple of stepbrothers and a nice stepmother. She was kind to me, but like all good things, her presence was short-lived. Immediately after my half sister was born, she also took off. I assume she couldn't take the abuse anymore, and I never saw her again.

"At 17, I fell in love with a classmate, left school, got a job and eventually married her. I worked as a mechanic and picked up the tricks of the trade fast. I was trying to settle down when I was drafted into the military. They sent me to training camp right after my baby girl was born. They made me a Seabee and, with minimal training, a helicopter mechanic. I was first sent to Cam Ranh Bay in Vietnam. I remember that my plane could not land for two hours, as the base was under attack. Soon I was sent to Long Binh as a door gunner. For eight months my orders were to shoot anything that moved. Killing people initially made me sick to my stomach, but I got used to it.

"Being in the air, surrounded by enemy fire, gave me a deep feeling of insecurity and panic. I often felt suspended up there, with no support. The sight of the GIs bleeding to death, their moaning and their cries, has never left me. My flashbacks never end.

"I don't know how it began, but soon I found myself deep into the heroin habit. The problem got worse and within a few months, I was caught and sent back home for rehab. The three months at rehab in Oklahoma were quite unsettling. I needed my fix to avoid my nightmares and panic attacks. Yet they couldn't debrief me due to repeated relapses.

"For some reason, they gave me a general discharge and kicked me out of the service. I had no place to go. I found my wife's address and tried to go back to her. Unfortunately, my wife had annulled the marriage and her brother put a restraining order on me. I never saw my daughter again.

"I was miserable and lost. I had no support and, against my instincts, I decided to visit my father. I was terribly shaky and still couldn't look into his eyes. In fact, I couldn't even talk. I just burst into tears. I needed him to hold me and let me cry. Instead, he slapped me hard and called me a sissy again. He kicked me out of his house and I've never gone back.

"In 1972, toward the end of the Vietnam War, my symptoms got real bad. I was miserable and returned to my only friend, heroin. Several rehab admissions and relapses later, I tried my hand at hard work to numb my feelings. Being a workaholic beats narcotics, but it doesn't leave you any time for intimate relationships. I remained utterly alone for many years. As a mechanic, I worked 14 to 18 hours a day. In order to avoid insomnia, I needed to be exhausted before going to sleep. I also moved around a lot, since I got fired from many jobs as soon as they recognized the instability of my mind.

"I went to New Jersey and met a Puerto Rican girl and married her. She decided to return to Puerto Rico, so I went there too, but my paranoia caused a lot of fights and eventually led to our divorce. Then I decided to go into the jungles in Puerto Rico, where I felt at peace. My symptoms subsided for a while. But then I was arrested in a case of mistaken identity. They thought I was an escaped prisoner. I lived in the prison for a while, until my case was clarified. I decided to go to Central and South America and then returned to New York. Finally, I came to California, where I continued to work 18 hours a day to numb my mind.

"Five years later, I married my current wife. The marriage has been very disturbed and difficult. We've had a lot of fights, but she's not even safe from me when I'm asleep. Once I threw her out of the window, and several times I tried to choke her in my sleep. Now she sleeps in a separate room and locks her door.

"A few years ago, I had a severe earache. I must have had meningitis. After that, I started to have these severe headaches, dizziness, blurred vision, and problems with my balance. The neurologists examined me and said my cerebrospinal fluid was not draining. MRI's and X-rays had shown a stretching and shrinking of parts of my brain. They decided to operate and put a shunt in my head. Well, they were the experts. What could I say?

"I was okay for a few days after surgery, but then the symptoms all came back. My headaches, blurred vision, numbness, nightmares, paranoia, violence, and anxiety all returned. I have been in and out of hospitals and received all forms of medications and treatments, but nothing has changed, nothing."

After a complete evaluation, I assigned Carl to a PTSD support group, where he took some time to establish a strong bond with several of the other members. Eventually he shared a complete narrative of his traumas with all of us. During these months of group therapy, he continued to relive helicopter attacks, B-52 bombings, the smell of explosives, and burning flesh. He still felt helplessness, paranoia, easy frustration, isolation, abandonment, restlessness, irritability, disgust, and a range of symbolic bodily symptoms, including abdominal pain, dizziness, sexual impotence, spasmodic muscle movements (an exaggerated form of startle response), headaches, difficulty swallowing, astasia-abasia, and "la belle indifference."

Several new neurological evaluations revealed no signs of acute hydrocephalus. His lab work was normal. The revision of his brain shunt did not show anything. His brain wave studies and MRIs were normal. It became clear that Carl's suffering stemmed from multiple childhood and adulthood traumas.

In group therapy, Carl realized that the Los Angeles earthquake and the destruction of his house had intensified his body symptoms. Months later, he gradually let go of all his medications and focused his energies on helping other trauma victims find a new life style. The development of his capacity to love again brought him closer to his wife. For the first time he was able to talk about her, using her first name rather than a derogatory nickname. When he received encouragement and validation from peers and tried to understand his own spiritual journey, Carl became more stable and eventually overcame his balance and gait difficulties.

Carl's story is reminiscent of the commonly heard tales of miracle cures or placebo response, situations in which a patient recovers due to a positive expectation of recovery, a delusion or a cultural belief. In some similar situations, a person may become ill due to a delusion or negative mindset. Emotional conflicts, traumas and faulty thought patterns can result in physical symptoms or what we think of as psychosomatic illness. A good example of this comes from another patient who complained for many years of intense shoulder pain. No medical interventions had ever helped him. Eventually, when he realized that his pain was in exactly the same site where his buddy's exploded head had hit him during combat, he was able to begin to work through his psychological grief and, consequently, his physical pain.

Some 60 to 65 percent of all PTSD sufferers experience physical as well as emotional symptoms. Of course, particular symptoms may have resulted from direct medical causes, but when physicians are unable to provide relief through diagnosis or treatments, the symptoms may, in fact, relate to trauma. Uncovering and treating the emotional pain behind a physical symptom can be challenging. A therapist who specializes in PTSD may be a great source of help in exploring these mysteries.

Chapter Eight: Generations of Suffering

Two are better than one, because they have a good return for their work. If one falls down, his friend can help him up. But pity the man who falls and has no one to help him up! . . . A cord of three strands is not quickly broken.
    — Ecclesiastes 4:9

The powerful effects of family alliance can set in motion both constructive and destructive forces. The restorative power of love that exerts its influence in the human soul must overpower many forces and dodge many "avenging hounds."[43] This chapter will explore the first of these forces, the family.

If group therapy offers opportunities for healing and growth, we can imagine the power of the biological family to influence healing. Yet the problems of many PTSD sufferers have their origin in their own families. In fact, many PTSD patients are vulnerable in ways they could not have prevented, since, as we shall see, psychological trauma often pass from one generation to the next. The cycle of psychological suffering, may catch everyone in its net, and, due to emotional contagion, trauma-generated symptoms are transmitted from parents to children and on to future generations. No society escapes some preoccupation with trauma and its trans-generational impact. The abuse of children, women, the elderly, and especially the disabled or mentally ill commonly occurs not only in folklore and literature, but in daily life, creating a perplexing paradox between the taboo against abuse in virtually all cultures and its universality.

---

43   The phrase used by the poet Aeschylus, who said, "To me these living horrors are not imaginary. I know them, avenging hounds incensed by a mother's blood."

The breakdown of personal identity, primitive handling of difficult situations, inadequate coping mechanisms used to face shattering events, and the cycles of victimization all surface as part of what can be a devastating family phenomenon. The ongoing deterioration of our social order, brought on by violence and trauma and enhanced by mistrust, paranoia, boredom, fear, boundary problems, and loss of meaningful attachment bonds all make PTSD a cunning disorder, very hard to overcome for some families, once afflicted.

Insights into the suffering of multiple generations come from studies in sociology, anthropology, as well as psychoanalysis. Reporting of trauma events has improved, and we now have better statistics, yet the stigma about revealing family trauma has not entirely vanished. At times, the living horrors of trauma cycles within families are so harsh that some who hear or read about them doubt they really happened.

Yet for those of us in the field of psychology, stories such as the accounts reported here are the norm for families with members who suffer from one or another psychosis or borderline personality disorder. I once had an office in the second floor of a large medical building. Windows overlooking an indoor courtyard with fountains and lights gave the office an aura consistent with the name of my program, The Hope Program. To penetrate the despair of some of my traumatized patients, I needed all the allusions and metaphors of hope available to me.

Early one September evening, as I conducted one of my weekly group therapy sessions for trauma survivors, the atmosphere felt anything but hopeful. A long silence revealed everyone's anxiety as the new member, Pat, introduced herself. To the members of this group—all victims of sexual or physical abuse, intense betrayal—such introductions often meant more horror stories and more collective pain. During Pat's eight-minute introduction, I could hear the sighs of the other nine members, followed by a loud, hostile exchanges, accusations, and tears.

But at the end, Pat and Mary, another woman in the group, made a sudden alliance and the atmosphere suddenly changed. For some unspoken reason, the two women appealed to each other and bonded instantaneously. They had each yearned for a significant alliance and now they had found each other.

It is not unusual for traumatized people to develop this kind of instant, intense kinship. At times, this takes the form of impulsive marriages between group members, who seem capable of reading each other's deep secrets or mutual feelings of pain. For Pat, this woman represented a reincarnation of her own daughter, a similarity which she expressed within the first few minutes of their meeting. The interaction and mutual empathy of the two women perplexed me, but I welcomed it. They saw in each other portraits of someone very important—perhaps a refuge and perhaps a glimmer of hope in a world of despair.

"Tell us about you, Pat" said Mary. "Do you have any big, dark secrets? Do you ever dump your guilt on someone else?" The earnestness of Mary's questions had a powerful effect on Pat, who burst into tears and launched into her tale, talking so fast, that it seemed she was afraid time would run out. As she spoke, breathing fast and holding her chest as if to prevent an explosion, the deep creases on her forehead showed her pain, and the occasional tear ran down her cheeks.

Pat's story

"My son-in-law, Tyson, has lived the life of a champion, so everybody calls him 'Champ'. I must say he is an enabler with a capital "E". He has this insatiable drive to please others and to accomplish a lot. He is a tall, handsome, muscular black man, always neatly dressed, rushing to do this or that every minute of his life. He is hyper and full of dash. He has gentle eyes but often seems sad and distant. To me, his most impressive feature is his bulging lower chin and his mustache".

"Tyson had warned us of his bad temper, but I had never seen him incensed. His parents were always sweet and caring. They said he had a happy childhood and was a straight-A student. And obviously he had learned good manners. He had a master's degree in engineering and worked for a fiber-optic communications company. At the time of his college graduation, I'm sure he never thought that someday he would go to jail for manslaughter".

"He told me once of his adolescent dream to build a ranch for runaway teenagers. For some reason, the freedom and know-it-all naiveté of teenagers appealed to him. For him, they were like living mythology, so he volunteered in psychiatric hospitals for teenagers just to be around them. He wanted to bring some hope into the lives of homeless and abandoned street kids".

"My daughter Mandy had been hospitalized in a special program for adolescent substance abusers by Dr. Amanat after we discovered her involvement with a gang of Satan worshippers, where she met Tyson as a volunteer. Mandy was a victim of incest and had odd behaviors, at times perceived as a character defect. Although she was well aware of her father's hatred of black people, she had used all her charm as a vulnerable victim, to seduce Tyson. I guess this was another one of her antics to get even and take revenge against her Dad".

"During one of the AA meetings, when Tyson was present, Mandy had volunteered to talk about herself. The following story is roughly what Tyson reported to me of that meeting:

> 'My name is Mandy, and I am an alcoholic. I was kind of forced into this program by my shrink. I think my parents should both be here. They pretend to be very religious people, but I have known their hypocrisy for years. Just to defy their bigotry I've been interested in the "people of the lie," as they are called nowadays. I felt drawn to Satan-worship as a form of defiance. My interest in these cults began when I was a young child. One of my aunts was supposed to be a witch, and I had heard strange stories about her. Then, a year ago, I was at a party when Tiny and his wife Diane joined us. Ladies and Gentlemen, the story I am telling you may seem stupid or unbelievable, but it is the honest truth and the main reason I am here tonight.

> 'Tiny was a fat, bald, ugly guy of 20 or so. He wore a long, khaki cotton robe and carried his pagan symbol on a long neck chain. His so-called wife, Diane, was simply gorgeous, but shy and passive. In his loud voice, Tiny argued about new paganism and promoted his group worship rituals, his natural lifestyle, and the ceremonies that went with it. He approached a really good-looking guy at the party and asked him if he would consider getting Diane pregnant. He said since he was ugly himself, he didn't want his child to look like him. Instead, he wanted the child to be attractive and wondered if some one else would consider the honor.

> 'The craziness and immorality of this all caught my attention. I had been a sucker for situations that would aggravate my parents for any reason. This was my way of rebelling against their hypocrisy. I decided to join Tiny's group as a teen-ager.

> 'My first encounter was chilling but tantalizing. There were 16 boys and girls in the dark basement of Tiny's home, imitating his crazy prayers, gyrations and dances. After a long hour of so-called

prayers to Satan, drugs were dispersed—mostly hash and crystal. I was ready to try anything. This was my way of making a fool of my parents, their being so God-fearing in front of everybody and having a Satan-worshiper for a daughter!

'Soon my mind was racing like a fast train. The energy rush made me feel powerful. I felt I could do anything. I was taken over by those intense rays of pure pleasure. Any fears or misgivings I had melted into rapture. I could not differentiate reality from the voices I heard inside. Then Tiny issued an order for all of us to undress, and we did. We had a free-for-all, with Tiny's wife as the queen of ceremonies. It was her duty. This ritual had apparently been repeated many times, and it happened many more after I joined the group, until Diane was finally hospitalized for a nervous breakdown.

'Soon afterward, I was selected as the cult queen. When I refused to participate in the ritual gang activities, they held me down and burned my skin with cigarettes. There are no words to describe the crazy feelings I experienced in these rituals. I could immediately understand why Diane had a breakdown. Being hooked on crystal is bad. But after I got high, all my emotions ran wild. I craved attention, and they gave it to me. I was numb, fearful, excited, hateful, and aroused. I was pretty much out of my body, waiting for the ordeal to be over. I would experience intense paranoia and start to hear mumbled voices in my head. I would tremble at the thought of losing my mind and scream as loud as I could. My screams were considered a necessary part of the ritual and generally ignored.

'I know this much about myself: that I seek trouble. I set myself up. Maybe I'm crazy, or perhaps I'm addicted to pain. But at the time, I was going there for free drugs and for all the attention I was getting. Anyhow, my parents noticed the cigarette burns, found out about the cult and called the police. Tiny is in jail now and I am here. I'm realizing that perhaps I'm an addict and have to do something about it.'

"Tyson was mesmerized and deeply moved by her story. He had already decided to help this beautiful, vulnerable, confused young woman. Perhaps he was a fool. Perhaps it was his destiny to walk right into the biggest trap of his life. Many heroes do foolish things in the guise of courage or compassion. When Mandy was sure of her conquest, she called me and manipulated her way out of the hospital against her doctor's wishes. Mandy knew our family's need for a sick scapegoat. We always had mixed feelings about her recovery. Without her illness, perhaps we had to face ourselves, and that would have been very hard to do.

"Tyson had asked Mandy to introduce him to my husband, Milton, but she had portrayed him as a lunatic who drinks too much and abuses the family. My husband hated blacks because he had been mugged a couple of times by African Americans. Two of my sons were football players and they were always around black guys. He hated that and gave them so much grief, they both left home

"Around the time that Mandy came out of the hospital, I began finding holes in my underwear or expensive dresses, and immediately assumed it was Mandy who was doing this to drive me crazy. But when the same holes appeared in my clothes when Mandy was in the hospital, I had no choice but to blame my husband, who swore he was innocent. A few times, I had found a knife stabbing a piece of furniture with a note attached to it. It read something like: 'This could have been you!'

"Mandy's father had many choice words for Tyson, when he learned about the relationship, but I was prepared. I was sick of my husband's power games. It didn't matter if I sent him to jail again. My daughter was a product of abuse, addicted to abuse and a monster of abuse. But compared to her father, she was an angel. Many years ago, when she confided in me about incest, I had her father arrested. He spent two years in prison, and letting him back into our lives was my biggest mistake. But now, I was fed up. I didn't care if he left us again. I was prepared to fight, and he knew it.

"My husband said, 'No daughter of mine is going to ruin her life with a black guy. If she pushes me, I will have to kill her together with her gigolo and go to jail for good.'

'You shameless bastard', I told him. 'Who was responsible for raising a rebel? You want to teach her morality now? Suddenly a child molester has become a conservative moral gentleman? Let me tell you something. I have been frightened of you for two years and kept my mouth shut, because I was the one who let you back here. No more!'

"He said, 'I've listened to you bad mouthing me a thousand times for those crimes. We went to therapy for three whole years. Are you going to push this nonsense on me for the rest of my life?'

"'You think I'm stupid, don't you?' I said. 'I've been afraid to tell you this for a long time, but I do know about your mother and your sister and your whole life story. At this moment, I don't care what you do to me or to anyone else. All I want to do is to scream!"

"When he realized that I had discovered his deep dark secret, Milton's face turned white as chalk. He mumbled that for 20 years, he thought his past was behind him, that he never imagined his wife would find out anything. He kept his private journal hidden in a very safe place, but now I knew everything. He sat down, hyperventilating and started to cry hard. Flashbacks of the horrible scenes of his youth tormented him. Finally, he had been discovered for who he was. At this very disturbing moment in his life, he was completely disarmed. The energy drained from his body; he felt paralyzed and robbed of his fight. Years of imprisonment, his own survivor guilt, the images of abuse, incest, his attempt to kill his own mother and the never-ending saga of his family life had exhausted him. He said later that he thought for a fleeting moment of killing me, his children and himself, but that it didn't seem like the right solution anymore. He cried helplessly".

"I do not know where to begin with my own story. I come from a home that was almost a prison. For many years before I married Milton, I thought of running away. I didn't have the guts to do it. I wanted to move away from the crazy part-time whore, who was my mother. There were rumors that she had killed her own 18-month-old son. She had strangled him with a chord and reported the murder as an accident. She had so many nervous breakdowns, going in and out of the state hospital, that nobody did anything to investigate or punish her.

"As a child, I was abused in every form or fashion you can imagine. When I was 15, my own mother tried to sell me for 500 bucks to one of her sex customers. I hated her for it. Then I met Milton, a handsome, intelligent man who looked to me like the rock of Gibraltar. I needed an island of security, and he was it. I was 19 and naïve. He was successful and rich. When he proposed to me, I didn't for a second think of our 20-year age difference. I had never known my father, and Milton seemed to be quite a loving man. I could relate to him as both a husband and a father. I married him without any investigation of his past.

"Milton said he had left his family when he was 17 to join the military and never returned home. He had war traumas and didn't want to talk about them. I didn't care to ask either. The first two years of marriage were blissful. I had everything I wanted. It seemed almost like a fantasy. But they say all good things come to an end. They did after our two sons and Mandy were born. My husband started to drink openly and, little by little, pressures built up. He had financial and union problems, and we got the brunt of it.

"Mandy was a difficult child to raise, and I felt left alone to take care of everything by myself. I had a feeling Milton was hiding something very dreadful from me, but I couldn't put my finger on it. Once when Mandy was three years old, on a day I call Black Friday, I found the keys to my husband's safety deposit box. I forged his signature and looked inside. To my horror, I found his book of confessions. It made me sick. Two hundred pages of horrible confessions he had kept to himself. Such a fool I had been to believe his stories. I threw up reading those pages and suddenly became frightened for my life and for the lives of my children. His miserable story was more tragic than any novel. But there it was, fully open to my aching heart.

"So as we sat and talked about Mandy and Tyson that day, so many years later, I told him for the first time that I knew about his childhood, his alcoholic father, his physical abuse and his act of trying to shoot his own mother. I had learned about his years of prison, his breakdown and all the other trash in his past. Milton cried for a long time, and eventually said: 'Pat! I swear to God and I told you a thousand times, I am not doing those awful things. I never wrote any notes to threaten you. I never put any holes in your clothes. I am broken. My soul is dead now. I am lost. Whatever you want, I'll go along with you. I am not the man of my youth anymore. In those days, I was really crazy. I tried to kill my mother because I saw her as responsible for my misery. I know, I have caused too much trouble for you and the kids but I am trying to bring some sense to our house. I want to be the loving father I never was before.'

."From the time Mandy was a little girl she hated me but was devoted to her father. At times she would pretend to be the woman of the house. Out of sheer stupidity, I would think it was cute. I must have thought to myself that they were good for each other. Perhaps I knew, on some level, that my husband could still return to his old molesting behaviors. But I hid it from myself and tried to do other things just to forget it all. I felt trapped and confused. I dreaded death, and thought perhaps that he knew I had found out about his past. His temper toward the boys and me grew worse by the day, but we couldn't talk about anything, since my heart was so filled with revulsion for him. I often felt like a concentration camp victim who had a sadist guard for a husband. I hated to have sex, as I had lost all admiration and respect for him. I think he sensed my fear and disgust, but he was afraid to bring it up.

"Killing him would have been my greatest joy. But I was a coward at heart and frightened for the children. Often I had thoughts of using his magnum to end my misery, but I had no guts. When Mandy was nine years old, her behavior began to change, slowly but drastically. She started breaking our belongings and sometimes tearing my clothes. I would give her more beatings. At times she sent me obvious signals about incest, but I was blinded by stupidity. She wore high heels at home and heavy makeup, yet I thought she was simply competing with me. For three years my husband had betrayed her innocence. She was 12 when she finally confided in me.

"I called the police. Milton was tried and went to prison again. He spent two years in jail, and by court order, we all went into family therapy. The court psychologist, a fanatical Christian, wanted us to work toward eventual forgiveness and resolution. Pity! She did not know how sick we all were.

"I can't comprehend how I accepted Milton back into my life. I found out that Mandy had another unholy alliance with him: she was a closet alcoholic. During those three years, he had introduced her to alcohol and used it to manipulate her. She had been his drinking buddy when I was at work. Mandy had become boy crazy and had found some guys in the neighborhood who were happy to exchange booze for sex. I had serious money problems and simply couldn't raise three kids on my income. The psychologist was continually harping on us to forgive the past. Maybe I thought I needed more punishment. I gave in under a mountain of pressure and agreed to give my husband another chance. When released from prison, he took a separate apartment but continued to pursue the idea of reconciliation. I tried to see things from the point of view of the court psychologist and never stopped to think about enabling or codependency behaviors.

"It seemed that imprisonment had drastically changed Milton. I had never seen him cry before, but now he cried easily. He asked for forgiveness. He returned to work and soon showered us with money and goodies. I sensed his compassion for me, yet I was suspicious of him for almost two years.

"Mandy had a lot of problems by that time, and I had reached the end of my rope. I felt lonely and miserable. So one day I gave in and let Milton move back with us. This time he tried to be a real father to the kids, but they all hated it. Our two sons soon found a way to leave home. My oldest son decided to become a minister and said we were too sick for him to be around.

"Mandy had no respect for her father and broke all his rules. So I soon found myself in another trap: parent abuse! She would continually destroy my best dresses, despite my protests. Eventually, most of my belongings were torn apart, even though I double locked them in my room. Mandy insisted that the destruction was Milton's work, but I didn't believe her, because he seemed to have changed. Soon I began to find knives stuck in our furniture, with notes written in handwriting similar to Mandy's, calling me names or threatening to kill me. I felt miserable and was sure Mandy was the culprit because she was upset over her father's return. And whenever I did direct my suspicion toward my husband, I couldn't bear the anxiety it created. I wanted so much to believe he had changed. The cloud of paranoia in our house became unbearable. Most of the time, I simply wanted to die.

Eventually, we detected Mandy's involvement in the cult. Her torture, mutilation and gang rape were too painful for a mother to face. My heart was broken again. Milton suffered from his own guilt and tried to reason with Mandy, but she did not give him any breaks. She wanted to get even with a vengeance, and we felt dizzy and lost. We made several trips to psychiatric hospitals as her drama continued—until the Champ arrived on the scene.

"Perhaps his being black was the magic key to this evolving story. Mandy knew that dating and marrying a black man would hurt her father very deeply. When Tyson showed serious interest in her, I persuaded my husband with all my might to let go of his prejudice and hatred of African-Americans and bless the relationship. To me, the Champ was a ray of light, a hero who had miraculously appeared at our door to release Mandy from her dungeon of trauma.

"I started to call him Champ very soon, as if I wanted to impose the mantle of salvation on his shoulders. He didn't mind. In fact, none of us seemed to worry about the nightmare he was stepping into. Mandy had started to respond to his gentle persuasion and was obviously changing. Even my husband could see the Champ's positive impact on Mandy. She joined Narcotics Anonymous, Adult Children of Alcoholics, and a sexual abuse survivor group, and soon their love for each other blossomed into marriage. The Champ's family were angels, very supportive and loving. Nobody could imagine that within such a short time, their lives would be so bitterly wasted.

"For a few months after their marriage, Mandy and Tyson seemed settled and happy, but the Champ's long hours and involvement with disturbed teens became a sore point. Mandy was jealous and fearful that he may lose interest in her. I think she did everything she could to become pregnant, even though he was not ready to have a child. Mandy had fantasized about having her own child for years, and I thought perhaps a child would bring the two families together and heal some of the old wounds. Tyson and Mandy rented a two-story brick house with a towering door and four huge Spanish style windows. The house was isolated and surrounded by trees, serene and somewhat romantic. But when Mandy moved to her own house, I was deeply disturbed because the destruction of my belongings and knives stuck in the furniture continued.

"Now I was sure it was my husband, and I became terribly paranoid. I was ashamed of myself for having blamed everything on Mandy all those years. I was also incensed and frightened by my husband's craziness. The fragile handwritten notes convinced me that I was the recipient of his rage against his mother and Mandy. Whenever I confronted him, though, he vehemently denied it and that left me at a total loss.

"Several months later, Mandy and Tyson had a son. Our grandson Ricky melted everyone's heart. He is such a beautiful child. You must see him to know what I am talking about. His charm immediately disarms everyone. His presence brought a temporary calm to our stormy relationships. But before long, Mandy went back to her mood swings, drinking, suicide threats, abusive behaviors, and emotional bleeding. She hated everyone but didn't want us to leave her.

"The Champ continued to work with the street kids and spent a lot of time in the south city ghettoes. Mandy did not approve of this and started to despise him. I think he was searching for his own lost adolescence, and she knew it. She wanted a monopoly, and that was unbearable for him. Tyson's dismay with my daughter's relapse and with his own failed efforts, not to mention the daily arguments, caused a deep rift between the two. As for me, I often felt completely helpless and confused. I loved Ricky and the Champ. I didn't want anything to happen to them. I often wished Mandy would die in an accident or something. It is horrible to wish death on your own child, but I felt exhausted and hopeless about her sickness. I didn't want any more tragedies, but I intuitively knew that something horrible was in the making.

"What followed were four suicide attempts by Mandy in the course of three months. She had sensed the Champ's change of heart. She couldn't deal with this loss. Maybe the Champ should have simply let her die in one of these attempts. But, bless his heart, he could not have anyone's blood on his hands. He was too kind-hearted. Each time she tried to kill herself, he took her to the hospital and cared for her and for Ricky. But when she recovered in a few days, she returned to her crazy antics. I can't understand why he just didn't simply take off and disappear.

"Early on that night of ugly destiny, I went to their home for a visit. Mandy was deeply troubled. I didn't do anything. I just wanted to withdraw and run. Perhaps I was acting out on my own crazy need for sacrifice.

"The Champ recounted the events of that night during the court hearings. When he noticed Mandy's desperation when he came home, he had asked her what was wrong. He said her eyes looked so cold and distant that he became alarmed. He had returned home early, since they were predicting a big storm with tornadoes and heavy rain. He was alarmed and asked if he had done anything to upset her. Her silence left him feeling lost in an emotional black hole.

"Reluctantly, she shared her plans to kill the three of them, saying, 'I have tried to end my life several times, but today I mean business. This is the hour of truth. I have suffered enough and can't keep going anymore. I am bitter about my mom not protecting me when I needed her. Your fake love and all the b.s. about courage to heal make me want to throw up. My life started with brutality by my mother, betrayal by my father and then you. Anyone else who showed interest in me just lusted after my body. You seemed different when we met, but you are no different. My misery is at its worst now. I feel dead and numb. I feel like someone buried under tons of dirt. I feel like a demon. If I die, maybe the angel inside of me will be released. Ricky looks so much like you that I can't help it when I dump my rage on him. I have been thinking of offering both of us as a ritual sacrifice. I feel so far away from the real world, it is pathetic. I consider you as the scum of the earth. You are as selfish as any man I have ever known.'

"The Champ tried to reason with Mandy, but she seemed deadly serious. She pulled a gun, talking louder and sounding more vigilant. Tyson felt helpless until a sudden flash of lightening and a clap of thunder brought on a power failure. In the moment of darkness that followed, the Champ tried to disarm Mandy. After a fierce struggle in the dark, Pat explained, two bullets were fired. Mandy's eyes shut forever and the Champ was badly injured.

"He called me at midnight to report the terrible news after he had called the police. They arrested him, and after his wounds healed, he was tried for murder. I took the Champ's side and denied any guilt on his part, but the jury convicted him of manslaughter and sentenced him to three years. He did not appeal. I guess he needed the time to heal.

"My daughter's passion for the forbidden and perverse emerged at young age. She was fascinated with transgression and also with power. Cult activities, drugs and alcohol, chronic abuse and abandonment had all affected her. I wonder if there ever really was any hope for her. She was the product of a cycle of at least three generations of terrible abuse, which no one could bring to an end.

"The court gave us custody of Ricky, since Tyson's parents were too dazed by the course of events and did not want to be part of the turbulence. I plunged into a world of despair, an ocean of guilt for what I didn't do. Flashbacks, ruminations, and sorrow took me over. I lost contact with reality again. But my husband did not hospitalize me. He stayed by me and shared my deep sorrow. This time we cried together. Even though we had Ricky, I couldn't find any meaning in life for a long time.

"The Champ called and wrote often to inquire about his son and that was a great solace to me. Then one day when I came home, my husband very sternly shared some disturbing news. He had taken it upon himself to find out the source of the damage to my clothing. He had hired a detective and installed a hidden camera. It was very shocking to see the films. The culprit was neither Mandy nor he. It was I. I was so ashamed that I wished I could disappear from the face of earth. But I took my husband's advice to return to therapy.

"I found out about my states of dissociation. To me, these living horrors are not imaginary. They are real. I know them. I have joined this group to see if I can finally uncover some of my past forgotten traumas and deal with my grief, once and for all."

Reliving these memories was deeply distressing for Pat, who wept continuously, leaning on a group member sitting by her as she recalled sad memories. At times, her voice became shrill and loud, saying that she wanted to crush her husband without mercy. She had flashbacks of his abuse of Mandy, his two years of imprisonment and the torment of dealing with three emotionally disturbed kids. As she spoke, the memories became a flood, turning her into an explosive container of hate. Toward the end of her story, her words became jumbled and difficult to understand. She seemed to be talking to herself, at times hiding her face from others. When the group encouraged her to cry, she gradually regained her composure.

Facing the family mirror

The reader may feel that Pat's family problems seem so outrageous that nothing in real life experience could compare. Or you may have felt a connection to some of the events in the story. For me, experiencing this woman's pain and struggles, and delivering a eulogy at the funeral of her daughter was like reading a thriller or having a nightmare about it. At times, her family drama overwhelmed me and I had to seek therapy and supervision myself to regain my own composure and remain neutral in her therapy.

Perhaps someone in your own family has had the unconscious role of identified patient,[44] while others felt just as victimized by the patterns of trauma. The fact that you have come this far in this book indicates your interest in grappling with the deep roots, not just the remedies of trauma. Without re-dramatizing family events, you may want to do some soul searching and take a quick inventory of the emotional landscape your own family life provided.

The family is the seat of all negative and positive human expressions, revealing both the bright side and the dark side of the soul. Sometimes families or family members who feel vulnerable to the effects of trauma can be more sensitive to spiritual experiences and transformations. Their calamities may inspire them to embrace the divine. They may come to realize that a great forgiveness can only grow from an act of great pain. They may

---

44   The "identified patient" is a psychological term describing an individual, often a child or teen, in a dysfunctional family, who is either scapegoated and blamed for a family's problems, or who has emotional problems that are not a mental illness, but a normal response to the stress of dealing with an unhealthy family in denial, or who blows the whistle on a dysfunctional family's problems. The phrase originated because family therapists recognized that the child "identified" as the patient is not necessarily the one who is sick.

see that, just as a moonless night reveals hidden stars, the darkness of past trauma accentuates the light. You can take comfort in your own potential as you travel this spiritual journey toward the light, knowing that by developing the bright side of your soul, you can be the one to change the dynamic for your whole family.

The impact of psychological trauma on the family

Fewer and fewer contemporary families have two parents present in the home and have become more transient than ever. For many, the unmet need for intimacy may lead to desertion, isolation, and substance abuse, contributing even further to the weakening of impulse control. Impulsive aggression, in turn, leads to further abuse, creating a vicious cycle of trauma.

My own study of a group of 37 abusive families revealed profound role confusion, immaturity, self-centered attitudes, loss of boundaries, and a multi-generational pattern of deprivation or abandonment (Amanat, 1981). Family members in my research population were mostly intense, violent, suicidal, fearful, and ready to crawl out of their skins. Deception, defiance, panic, guilt, flashbacks, running away, betrayal, foggy memories, out-of-body experiences, reliving past traumas, the inability to differentiate trivial from important stimuli, and poor control of emotions were the norm. Each new generation had faced the same issues, compounding their respective post-traumatic stress. Developmental childhood problems had been transmitted across generations, indicating a kind of psychological inbreeding. Interference with normal development appeared from birth onward and was further complicated by PTSD symptoms. Like many contemporary families, those in my research group had overt psychological dysfunction, albeit more severe and combined with many specific syndromes.

Some incestuous families are classified as being predominantly neurotic, showing symptoms of dissociation, avoidance, rumination, obsession, hysteria, or phobia. Others are diagnosed as paranoid or hypochondriac, with an apparent alienation, numbing, or denial of emotions; still others display alcoholism, substance abuse, personality problems, emotional hemophilia,[45] or infantile and promiscuous behaviors. In some families, outbursts of rage become a way of hiding anxiety, arousal symptoms, depres-

---

45   Some borderline and psychotic individuals and those with severe or complex PTSD are like hemophiliacs: their emotions spill out like an uncontrolled river. See Kreisman, 1991.

sion, and fear of death, paranoia, or self-victimization. A low tolerance for change, multiple conflicts of loyalty, limited emergence of autonomy, bravado cult rituals, problems of intimacy, sibling rivalry, and a number of other behaviors often make these households explosive and perversely indulgent. Yet these expressions of the soul's dark side make them unusually sensitive to spiritual experiences.

In their book on child abuse and neglect, Cicchetti and Toth (1994) have demonstrated the impact of abuse and suffering on developmental organization, regulation of emotion, growth of attachment behaviors, ego systems,[46] on relationships with peers, adaptation to school, and on a number of other functions of the child. State-dependent memories,[47] distortions of reality, lack of integration, increased sensory-motor and decreased explicit memories all add to a need for an identified patient within these families. It seems that soul loss creates such helplessness and self-alienation that it shatters optimal family function. The individual, who has been marked or assigned to be the "sick" family member, then perpetuates the cycle of abuse. These after-effects create a cyclical, inter-generational phenomenon influencing the family system in its totality. Published anecdotes and other literature show that the ghost of trauma can haunt family members for several generations. Children involved in a major disaster, such as a plane crash may initially feel the presence of a ghost in their household. Soon, the ghost experiences become a family and a neighborhood phenomenon, leading to the belief that the house is actually haunted!

In summary, individuals and their family members, who are involved in various forms of trauma, often become inflexible and rigid, making it impossible or immensely difficult for them to assume the risks and hazards of change. Such families function poorly as a unit, often facing multiple crises or new and drastic tragedies. Family members are likely to pay a heavy psychological price in their attempt to ensure family survival. Arrested psychological growth then generates waves of trauma that ebb and flow in a multi-generational process, until someone musters adequate courage to heal and block the repetitive pattern of mutual antagonisms, hate, loss, and

---

46   These refer to defense mechanisms, thought processes, systems of appraising situations, and the sending and receiving of communicative messages.

47   State-dependent memories are those which are normally repressed, but which are recalled in certain states of mind, for example, when a person is sad, outraged, happy, drunk, etc.; they can also be accessed on certain important occasions, or in particularly memorable weather conditions which bring them to mind.

attachments.

A glimpse at the enormous power of family ties gives us a more comprehensive understanding of the complexities behind trauma cycles. Current stresses such as work pressure, abuse and additional traumas are most likely to have a developmental impact. Whenever a family member places more demands for autonomy or separation on the family, the coping devices of the dark side overreact. When the family system is at war with itself, the members, including the traumatized individuals, are caught in contradictory and painful confusion, paralyzing their resources. The impact of separation, death, desertion, and abandonment in these families is often distorted and malignant. Roles within traumatized families are usually skewed, immobilizing individual growth. Often family members feel imprisoned, like captives of rage or depression. In the heat of passion, anger, fear, or guilt, one or more family members may lose control or may have a diminished sense of reality. Such moments may lead to paranoid, suicidal, homicidal, sensual, violent, and/or dissociative activities. Alcohol or substance abuse enhances the breakdown of boundaries, decreasing the taboos against abuse. However a recapturing of the bright side of the soul by any of the family members can completely reverse this tragic cycle and become a new source of growth.

PART II: Remedies for PTSD

Chapter Nine: Treatment and recovery

In this chapter, we will discuss some of the most effective modes of treatment. To help a victim of intense trauma, we need to create a safe environment with opportunities to develop a personal narrative of the trauma history. We need also to assemble as much family and social support as possible, to clarify what actually occurred, investigate the meaning of trauma reactions, process feelings of guilt, abandonment, helplessness, and the individual's coping devices. Some victims need to work on losses and bereavement, while others need to identify triggers for their symptoms and develop new, more effective coping skills.

We may use individual, group or desensitization therapies or stress debriefing. All forms of therapeutic approaches have been used and researched in detail. Some medications have been used for anxiety, depression, insomnia, and hypervigilance.

Narratives as antidotes for PTSD

We have already seen that as the individual re-exposes himself to the pain and suffering of his past experiences, verbalization and sharing of trauma stories decreases their toxicity and eventually brings about a symptomatic relief.

Janet (1889 and 1920) was the first practitioner to describe human memory as an action. He reported that verbalizing trauma memories tends to alleviate the trauma symptoms. Such verbalizations, conducted in a supportive environment, provide healing for the soul.

Modern medical centers are not equipped to attend to the needs of the soul, even though the soul does not need any expensive technologies. If healers can help patients develop and write narratives of their lifelong suffering to share with each other, if we can help one another define our dreams, fantasies and stories, we can tune our ears as caretakers to hear the body's silent speech.

Spiegel (1933) and Grinker (1945), tried to use hypnotism to recover traumatic memory, but they found that shortcuts have no real effect in the treatment of PTSD. As we said earlier, retrieval of memories should be combined with a process of catharsis in a supportive environment, and it should help to integrate the individual in the context of a caring relationship or set of relationships. Meaning, emotions, and feelings are the underlying foundations of such integration. At times, memories of old suffering are distorted and inaccurate. Particularly in victims of rape and atrocities, I have noticed that the victim's memories may not coincide with the memories of other witnesses. This has to do with the phenomenon of state-dependent memory described earlier. The intensity of the individual's terror during the trauma event leads to greater arousal, thus distorting the perception of the actual experience. Over-arousal creates an intense state of learning which then makes the memories unforgettable. We know that in terror states, attention decreases, peripheral details fade, and context changes. These changes lead to perceptual distortions, such as time slowing or amnesia. Under such circumstances, it is helpful to transform explicit memories into a verbal narrative, combining it with the implicit memories of the body.

Clinical predicaments

At this point, the reader may wonder about the difference between generating narratives in group work and having an individual simply relate his or her current concerns to a therapist. A quick look at the down side of therapeutic circles illustrates the challenge. The whole clinical community actually faces its own traumatic dilemma.

Clinical therapy with human beings who have suffered trauma finds parallels with the story of the "Lover's Journey," described in Chapter 13. The stagnation, dissociation and regression caused by suffering, abandonment, and trauma leads to a clinical case of PTSD, bereavement, or victimization. In the depth of suffering, the victim is very much like the hero of "Lover's Journey," initially searching for a cure or recovery in the "marketplace." He or she tries self-control and self-help books or methods, gathers information and consults professionals, but the condition does not change.

This relentless search at times finds the patient in tyrannical encounters and co-dependent bonds with therapists, many of whom perpetuate further victimization. Pain, mistrust, and hostility gradually turn into entrapment, rage, irrational behavior, and chronic relapse. The therapeutic milieu of the contemporary Health Maintenance Organization (HMO) is often hostile or inadequate. Patients in therapy may encounter any or all of the following problems:

- Interference of managed care with therapeutic goals
- Lack of adequate insurance coverage
- Deficient inpatient or outpatient policies
- Bureaucratic peer reviews motivated by cost-effectiveness
- An anti-therapy backlash
- Reliance on and overuse of medications
- Lack of adequate staffing
- Misdiagnosis of PTSD as bipolar disorder
- Prevalence of abandonment, violence, and rage in incomplete treatment schemes, especially in psychiatric hospitals
- Premature discharge and chaotic hospital settings
- Fear of staff layoffs or turnover
- Staff advocates interested in personal power
- Inadequate time to complete diagnostic studies
- Administrative rigidity or insensitivity
- Abuse of patients by the therapists (sometimes playing the role of "the rapist")
- Inappropriate interference of politicians, judges and even the police.

It is not surprising, then, that therapy can be unsupportive. Lack of staff or patient safety can lead to heartbreaking tragedy. A violent patient with PTSD once crushed a fellow psychiatrist's skull with a brick, leaving my colleague disabled with a loss of left-brain function for several years. Another patient assaulted a dedicated nurse, breaking her jaw in a burst of irrational anger. Both cases were due to inadequate HMO psychiatric coverage and the threat of premature discharge.

Achieving a degree of adequate care would require significant changes in our attitude toward trauma and such a prescription may not be available in the current marketplace. Those who suffer from PTSD need a cohesive and powerful survivor community, where the personal knowledge of trauma becomes communal property. These communities institutionalize trauma memories with appropriate spiritual practices, discussions, meditation, and prayer. Group awareness of spirituality in relation to human suffering gradually increases to the extent that memories of trauma are treasured for positive and mutual community growth.

Such a comforting and mirroring environment can provide safety and immunity from impulsive reactions, generate a spirit of hope and develop resolution. Actualization of recovery through deep bonding with fellow victims—who charge no fees—can lead to progress in trauma narratives and a significant reduction of human suffering. A sufferer seldom develops an effective narrative unless he or she feels completely protected in a nurturing and accepting environment.

When such an emotional embrace can indeed occur, exposure forms of therapy (See Chapter 11), help the traumatized individuals better than other methods, but the exposure therapies and flooding must be administered in a uniquely loving and supportive environment with adequate, almost free-flowing time. The psycho-physiological reactivity caused by suffering and trauma often generates such intense arousal levels in traumatized people that they easily withdraw from therapy. They fear that no one can endure their horrors. For this reason, a spiritually protective environment is absolutely essential for therapeutic work.

Patients are generally encouraged to go through the journey of recovery by first plunging to rock bottom in their agony and misery. Knowing that such steps are the best ways of placing pain and suffering in a meaningful context prepares the person for spiritual transcendence. Reenactment of the trauma response may continue for weeks, months, or years within the victimization cycles of traumatized individuals. However, trauma therapy that is carried out in a loving context can make appropriate use of "re-exposure" and help the patient feel that he or she can finally master these horrors.

In the distinctly unspiritual marketplace, abuse of power is very common. Involuntary admissions, chemical pharmaceutical restraint, seclusion and oppressive practices leave many patients bewildered and even more traumatized. I have met many victims, who had been treated with dangerous doses of anti-psychotic medications because their physicians did not have sufficient time to listen and to process trauma memories. Many therapists distance themselves from patients and sometimes even lie to them. When confronted by patients who are acting out, faced with their own lack of resources, or burnout, they try to compensate for their helplessness in therapy by taking a detached clinical inventory, which can lead to further emotional isolation for the patient.

The so-called therapeutic milieu in the marketplace is often fragmented, confusing, and devoid of mutual respect, and so cannot generate health. Nevertheless, those who suffer usually fall into such destructive environments out of a desire for recovery. Many hospitalized ex-patients have bluntly confessed, "The place was so crazy, I thought I should pull myself together and get out of there." When the right moment arrives, the same desire may compel the individual to seek a recovery program with more spiritual themes and concepts.

At this point in the journey toward recovery, the suffering individual often meets a significant ally: a fellow victim, another patient, a sponsor, a teacher or an enlightened therapist. Together they create a mutual bond for search and growth. Like navigators in a small paddleboat, caught on springtime white water, they bravely search for insight, resolution, and transformation. When this happens, the symptoms of illness can evolve into psychological strengths. Integration and closure ensue. In the act of forgiving and making amends, the individual incorporates opposing images in a new creative fashion, beginning a labor of love in guiding fellow sufferers.

The realm of spirituality

In his famous work "Modern Man in Search of a Soul" (1933), Carl Jung foresaw a spiritual revolution by the end of the 20th century. He predicted that humanity would go through labor pains for the creation of this new age, when we would become aware of spiritual needs in the younger generations, and finally synthesize emotion, intuition, and spirituality with reason. Martin Buber (1974) said that human suffering prepares the soul for greater vision.

Despite the implications of these schools of thought, Western cultures have focused primarily on the digital, left-brain perceptions that suppress intuitive and spiritual experience. We are thus afflicted by our own faulty thinking, which separates us from the reality of human existence. Even our language distorts our spiritual nature with time/space expressions: we talk about the future and the past as being "ahead" or "behind" us, as if we could portray time using spatial concepts. Attempting to present spiritual ideas in concrete words, we make grave mistakes about matters which are, in their essence, spiritual.

The spiritually insightful individual uses science in an open, one might say "mystical" way, seeing spiritual experience as a means to feel the grace of God and to reflect the image of the Creator. Suffering can be one of his main tools for growth, directing his mind from the trivial toward the transcendent. With suffering, he approaches perfection, and with perfection, his suffering ends. Divine unity becomes the antidote for pain.

Physicist Niels Bohr (1966) has told us that we all use our perceptual systems to become part of a unified consciousness. In processing reality, the mind uses the neurological apparatus to create partial perceptions. Thus, we are like mapmakers trying to create representations of the world of external reality in our own minds. But these inner maps of reality are influenced heavily by our emotions, love, fear, values, desires, and relationships. They change dramatically with environmental structure, social status and numerous other elements. Nevertheless, the inner maps of the traumatized individual bring about a paradigm shift.

Kuhn, (1962) described such historic paradigm shifts in his radical writings. Today, the most significant shift in human thinking lies in the development of global processes and an awareness of the fundamental unity of mankind. Human beings are now accepting many new paradigms. They are beginning to be able to synthesize multiple views of reality in a more holistic, inclusive, perception of the world.

In her essay "Reflections on David Bohm's Holomovement" (1981), Renee Weber has shown that the multi-paradigm view allows for a different perception of time, space, energy, matter, and the soul. Since our perceptions, through the senses alone, do not conform to a time-space language, we need metaphors and symbolic language.

Ironically, although expensive therapy proves useful for some conditions of conflict and mental illness, it might actually delay the sense of progress or resolution in trauma sufferers. When we use simple talk therapies, we only scratch the surface of psychological pain. Listening to and contemplating spiritual metaphors can help sufferers heal on a deeper level.

The metaphor of the "lover's journey," described in Chapter 13, offers an ideal example, with its symbolic narrative of abandonment, suffering, trauma, and eventual redemption.

Chapter Ten: Scientific and Biological Research

Neuroscience, biology, and pharmacology

During the past 40 years, I have become painfully aware of many significant flaws in psychiatric practice. Appraising the human beings, based purely on their emotional or physical symptoms and pigeonholing (labeling) them into arbitrary diagnostic categories without attending to the underlying causes of these symptoms, grossly misses existential experiences and deeper meaning.

One is tempted to ask the question: which came first, the chicken or the egg—that is, the soul or the brain—in developing an understanding of the true source of the formation of symptoms such as PTSD. There is currently a raging debate about this very question among practitioners and researchers, with some neuroscientists taking the view that the brain, in all its fantastic complexity, is responsible for all human experiences, emotions, self-awareness, and the appraisal of events; many others take the view that a "greater entity," such as the human soul, is the originator of human experiences and self awareness, and that the brain itself is the electro-chemical and biological substrate to the expression of free will, consciousness and spiritual transcendence. Larry Dossey, in his book *Recovering the Soul* (1989) offers a detailed discussion of the soul as a "non-local universal phenomenon" that determines human existence. He cites Austrian theoretical physicist, Erwin Schrödinger, who, among others, was convinced of the existence of a unitary consciousness pervading the universe and wrote of a "mystical union of soul-God."[48]

---

48   Schrödinger, 1969, p. 145.

In the 10th edition of the *Synopsis of Psychiatry*, authors Sadock and Sadock express one side of this ongoing debate:

> The human brain is the organ that is the basis of what persons sense, do, feel, and think; or put in more formal terms, our sensory, behavioral, affective, and cognitive experiences and attributes. It is the organ that perceives and affects the environment and integrates past and present.
>
> By processing external stimuli into neuronal impulses, *sensory systems* create an internal representation of the external world. A separate map is formed for each sensory modality. *Motor systems* enable persons to manipulate their environment and to influence others' behavior through communication. In the brain, sensory input, representing the external world, is integrated with internal drivers, memories, and emotional stimuli in *association units*, which in turn drive the actions of motor units. Although psychiatry is primarily concerned with the brain's association function, an appreciation of the sensory and motor systems' information processing is essential for sorting logical thought from the distortions introduced by psychopathology. [49]

However, the idea that the brain is the seat of human consciousness has been challenged by numerous researchers, including both scientists and philosophers of psychology. After exploring the writings of such researchers as John Horgan (1996), John Eccles (1994), Dean Hamer (2004), Ludwig Binswanger (1963), and the works of many existentialist writers, I am convinced that human spiritual and existential experiences use the brain as a substrate of perception, reaction and growth.

Many researchers have realized now that the region of the hypothalamus in the brain and the system called the HPA axis, are the bridges between the mind and the body. What we refer to as "somatization disorder," the expression of emotions or mental disorders as bodily symptoms, has had a fascinating history throughout the centuries. As early as 2000 years B.C., the Egyptians left illustrative quotations about "hysterical" patients

---

49   Sadock and Sadock (2007), p. 68.

with multiple aches and pains, which, they believed to be caused by the migration of the uterus throughout the body.

In order to treat these patients, they used what we might call "aroma therapy" in two different ways. First, foul-tasting or smelling substances were used to repel the uterus from the upper part of the body, to which it had wandered, and return it to the womb. Then, sweet-smelling substances were used to attract the uterus back to the womb. Greek physicians later accepted the Egyptian healers' views and linked hysteria to new categories of illness. For example, if a woman had a lump in her throat, they called it "globus hystericus," and employed the same Egyptian treatment methods to return the womb to its original place.

This notion of the wandering uterus prevailed until the 17th century, when physicians such as Charles Le Pois, Thomas Sydenham, and later French physicians, Philippe Pinel and Pierre Briquet,[50] developed a different idea about hysteria. In his pioneering research, Briquet realized that of 430 patients with somatization disorder (hysteria), at least half had been exposed to various traumas in childhood or later in life. Briquet clearly demonstrated the relationship of somatization to psychological elements. Later physicians such as Charcot (1887), Freud (1962), Breuer and Freud (1955) and many others studied the relationship between conflict and repressed psychological matters and hysteria.

Modern studies on hysteria drew from the works of Robbins et al. (1984) and Guze (1975), at Washington University. Guze led an extremely productive group of investigators in 1970, who suggested that somatization or hysteria be called Briquette's Syndrome for the pioneering research of Briquette. This was accepted temporarily until 1980, when the third edition of the Diagnostic and Statistical Manual of Mental Disorders attempted to further simplify the diagnosis. They streamlined the criteria for diagnosis to 14 positive lifetime physical symptoms in women and 12 symptoms in men, paring down the original list of 37 physical symptoms caused by psychological influences.

As various researchers recognized the impact of negative emotions on the body, the impact of positive emotions on healing and cure became the target of research. In his book, *The Healing Heart* (1983), Norman Cousins pioneered this work, focusing on the value of optimistic views and creative

---

50   See Smith, 1991, pp. 5–42 and Hales et al., 1994, pp. 596–611.

activities on healing. He documented the role of humor and positive emotions on recovery from a series of serious illnesses. Cousins was convinced that unshakable confidence in the body's ability to recover, coupled with good humor and cheerfulness led to auspicious healing.

Later in the 20th century, research on the effects of the placebo[51] revealed that in clinical medicine, placebos have at least 56 percent of the impact of such drugs as morphine or codeine, clearly demonstrating the powerful influence of the mind and body in terms of pain reduction. The pioneering research of Stella Chess and Alexander Thomas (1984) also revealed that individuals differ greatly in their adaptive behaviors and symptoms. Through research on neurotransmitters completed in the latter part of the 20th century, we became much more aware of the mechanisms that translate psychological information into physiological symptoms.

The most significant developments in mind-body research began with Hans Selye (1976) and his lifetime of groundbreaking research on stress and stress reactions. He showed that as stress affects the brain's limbic system, it, in turn, modulates the functions of the immune system, the endocrine system and the autonomic nervous system affecting the body on numerous levels. When Magoun (1954) later discovered and wrote about the reticular activating system of the brain in 1949, a whole new era of research began on waking-sleep phenomenon, arousal, dreaming, lucid dreaming, and the effects of the activating system on the body. Other researchers focused on the centers for imagination in the brain, on the various memory centers, and on the appraisal systems for all body functions.

State-dependent learning, the impact of hypnosis on the body and its physiology, also warranted investigation, particularly by Braid (1855) Janet (1889) Erickson (1967–1980), and Rossi (1986). These researchers recognized that in certain trances or dissociative conditions, state-dependent memories could reach our conscious awareness, while in other states of the mind we remain unconscious of them. Thus, information acquired in one state of mind perhaps under the influence of alcohol or drugs may be forgotten in the non-drugged state, but recalled again when the individual is under the influence.

---

51   Placebos are simple sugar pills with no medicinal ingredients, given to patients who think that they are being given medication.

The mind/body connection: Science or art?

Recent studies[52] have demonstrated that anywhere from 15 to 20 percent of chronic medical conditions are psychosomatic. This is probably an optimistic estimate, since in specific groups of people, the prevalence increases up to 50–60 percent. Individuals with psychosomatic disorder may have multiple unexplained symptoms that do not meet any ordinary disease criteria, but appear in various medical clinics and create a heavy burden on the health system. Such patients may display a number of physical symptoms. Considering the many variables that may prompt a given symptom, it is clear that well-designed, creative and controlled studies are needed to evaluate somatization as an expression of trauma.

For a pilot research project, I selected two matching groups of adult male patients with the diagnosis of PTSD who suffered from somatization disorder. All had received detailed physical examinations and lab tests, which indicated no organic pathology for the variety of symptoms presented. I investigated their responses to two intervention strategies. Most of these individuals (85 percent) were of Hispanic origin and presented with such symptoms as chest pain, dizziness, diarrhea, carpal tunnel syndrome, gastric or genitourinary problems, and obesity. They had undergone multiple surgeries and exhibited a deep unhappiness with their personal physicians. They thought these doctors had not taken their conditions seriously.

When I detailed the life histories of these individuals, each had suffered a variety of traumatic experiences that affected their souls. Seventy-nine percent of them were separated, divorced, or single. They were evaluated with various PTSD scales, structured interviews, psychological tests, and the Othmer and DeSouza screening index (1985) to evaluate the prevalence of somatization. We collected detailed family and psycho-social histories, including communication deviance, expressed emotion, and other behaviors.

With their consent, the patients were assigned to two treatment strategies based on their availability. The medication group was treated with Sertraline, (Zoloft) 100 to 150 mg daily, as well as brief monthly supportive therapy sessions. All these patients were assigned to one physician, who performed regular physical examinations and discussed every symptom with each patient as a statement of need for care and as a sign of stress. He reassured them that he would follow through with them until the symptoms

---

52   See Smith, 1991.

subsided, taking them seriously and not threatening them with premature abandonment. The patients were encouraged to avoid lab work, surgery, hospitalization, and any other form of treatment until the effects of these medications were fully evaluated. After 24 weeks, the patients were re-evaluated for symptoms of somatization as well as for post-traumatic stress disorder.

I saw the non-medicated patients in groups of four or five twice weekly, combining exposure and desensitization techniques, anger/stress management and spiritual meditation. I encouraged supportive, metaphoric communication for the initial three to four sessions, to build trust and strong bonds. Then I led the group members to retrieve the complete narrative of their memories of traumatic events. I employed various desensitization techniques when focusing on traumatic memories and followed up with a 12-step program designed to help them integrate new emotions and meanings into their experiences. Poetry and metaphors helped patients reframe their suffering, giving new meanings to their conditioned emotional responses. We redefined PTSD as "Peace, Tranquility, Sanity and Dignity." My pilot project revealed not an equal but a much *greater* positive response to group process, desensitization, and spiritual metaphors than to medications.

Neurotransmitters

Recent biological research by Webster (2001) has linked a variety of symptom clusters with a syndrome of serotonin dysfunction. Serotonin is one of the main neurotransmitters dealing with activity, euphoria, and happy feelings. Serotonin has been described as a neurotransmitter for at least 40 years. It coats multiple receptors inside the brain and around the nerve synapses, which are the site of action for drugs such as tranquilizers, anti-depressants, and anti-psychotics.

Disorders related to serotonin dysfunction or other transmitters imbalance include panic, affective problems, sleep, eating, obsessive compulsive, and certain forms of personality disorder. There can be also problems with violence, learning disabilities, phobias, premenstrual syndromes, migraine, irritable bowel syndrome, neuro-dermatitis, sleep apnea, certain forms of psychosis, and suicidal behavior.

A convincing body of evidence now shows that serotonin receptors are spread throughout the mammalian brain and especially in the limbic system. The spread of these receptors makes specific areas of the brain sensitive to various medications. Based purely on physiological formulations, a great number of research projects have used these medications to treat PTSD, somatization, panic, and depression. The relationship of neurotransmitters with love/hate conflicts, impulsiveness, emotional instability, anger, identity problems, boredom, and manic states have all been considered.

Which came first, the chicken or the egg?

Our uncertainty about brain functions raises this age-old question. After evaluating and listening to stories of thousands of people in my clinical practice, I am convinced that existential experiences cause intense changes in brain chemistry. But in the majority of afflicted people, the brain is only the substrate, reacting to these life events. It is not clear whether neurotransmitters and receptors are simply responding to human emotions, or if they actually represent the biological cause of syndromes. Until a few years ago, the prevalence of bipolar mood disorders was around 1 percent of the population, but after the discovery of atypical antipsychotic drugs and under heavy pressure form the pharmaceutical companies, the prevalence suddenly increased to 13 percent. This is undoubtedly due to the fact that physicians do not have time to listen to and explore the life tragedies of their clients.

The current clinical literature is replete with therapeutic interventions to overcome neurotransmitter dysfunction. The use of neuroleptics, mood stabilizers, and atypical anti-psychotics, benzodiazepine tranquilizers, and various antidepressants (particularly the SSRIs) has become quite commonplace. The problem is that physicians use these medications to alleviate symptoms without understanding their true nature. Whenever the patients stop taking the medications, the symptoms resurface. This indicates the possibility that neurotransmitters are simply mediators of human emotions and not the underlying cause of somatization. The overlap of PTSD, depression, and various anxiety disorders makes it very difficult to define a clear cause for somatization. Nevertheless, some researchers report a serotonin dysfunction as a concomitant sign, and, perhaps, a symptom of somatization.

We know that multiple systems are involved in PTSD, creating contradictory data, which are very difficult to interpret. As such, no one biological model can sufficiently describe the problems. It also seems clear that there is not one classical form of PTSD, but that we are dealing with a variety of syndromes, all called by the same name.

The HPA axis and the adrenergic system

The two most widely recognized biological systems involved in PTSD are the HPA axis and the noradrenergic system. The HPA axis is related to the hypothalamic region of the brain, in association with the pituitary and adrenal glands. When a threat to the organism is perceived, several chemicals are released which eventually raise the level of cortisol in the body. Cortisol acts like a break on the noradrenergic system and decreases the levels of noradrenaline in the body. Noradrenaline is the chemical that mediates the fight-flight-freeze response, whenever we are threatened by danger. It causes arousal and hyperactivity, but when the threat is over its levels return to normal. By stimulating the sympathetic nerves, noradrenaline also affects the heart, sleep, the occurrence of nightmares, exaggerated startle reaction, and many other symptoms. Poor regulation of these two biological systems affects the body's reaction to major traumas. However these neurotransmitters must be considered only as mediators and not the main cause of PTSD. The root of all PTSD problems is unbearable suffering and trauma.

Neuro-imaging in PTSD

MRI, fMRI and other imaging techniques of the brain in PTSD patients reveal a decrease in the volume of white and gray matter, particularly in the hippocampus, and in areas related to the appraisal of stimuli. Especially in those having suffered sexual abuse in childhood, the decreased total brain volume is striking. The volume of the hippocampus, which coordinates memory functions, is smaller on the left side of the brain, but this anatomical change is also seen in depressive conditions.

Again in relation to the eternal question of the chicken or the egg, it is not clear if these changes in volume are contributing factors and causes of PTSD, or if they are by-products and symptoms of the condition. It is possible that the imbalance of the two systems mentioned above could actually decrease brain volumes or that these volume changes existed prior to trauma and influenced the individual's response.

The psychopharmacology of PTSD

There are many complicating factors associated with use of medications that influence the outcome of drug therapies. Due to memory problems distractibility or dissociative amnesia, many victims forget to take their medications. Many antidepressant medications initially cause intense anxiety in PTSD sufferers, and some medications used generate drowsiness, dullness, and sleep problems.

Mistrust of authorities may prevent some victims from accepting medication at all, while the persistence of symptoms may cause some physicians to overmedicate or to be more aggressive with medications. Tranquilizers such as benzodiazepines may become addictive. They can also interfere with memory and the creation of trauma narratives, thus postponing recovery. While they do decrease arousal symptoms and may be effective in preventing chronic PTSD conditions, adrenergic blockers, such as Inderal, may cause upset stomach, sleepiness, fatigue, and dizziness.

For these reasons, it is advisable to be cautious with the use of medications and to monitor the response of patients more closely. In general, medications have not proven superior to desensitization or psychotherapy, and only if the victims suffer from other emotional problems co-occuring with PTSD can their use be beneficial.[53]

Memory Research and psychopharmacology

Current neuroscience research shows how we change our memories just by remembering them. This generates a hope that victims of trauma can cure themselves by editing and updating their memories. Memories are highly dynamic and surprisingly vulnerable. In recent years the use of Propranolol, an adrenaline blocker/anti/hypertension medication along with desensitization has opened a new and exciting field of research for treatment and recovery of PTSD sufferers. Researchers at Mount Sinai School of Medicine in New York as well as others in Israel have been using substances such as RU38486 and MDMA and Cortisol to treat PTSD by disrupting and changing trauma memories.

---

53   In his outstanding work *Doing Psychiatry Wrong: A Critical and Prescriptive Look at a Faltering Profession*, Rene Muller (2008) discusses in detail the problems of biological psychiatry.

Chapter Eleven: Desensitization, Exposure, and Cognitive Therapies

Prolonged Exposure Therapy

In this approach, developed by Dr. Edna Foa and her colleagues (Foa, 2002), the individual victim is asked to focus on details of trauma events and report them in the present tense, as if they are happening in the here and now. Active imagining and retelling of traumatic events usually provokes intense states of arousal and the victim's tendency to want to avoid suffering. Exposure is repeated in six to eight one-hour sessions. However, many victims feel hurt and additionally traumatized by this practice. Some 50 percent of individuals drop out of treatment, but those who can tolerate suffering and pain respond very well, and realize that their calamities can become beneficial. Dr. Foa's approach is a form of hardball therapy, not always acceptable by clients and potentially overwhelming.

Eye Movement Desensitization and Reprocessing (EMDR)

The literature on EMDR, developed by Dr. Francine Shapiro and her co-workers (1995) is abundant and well known. Interested readers may find it described in detail on the EMDR Institute Website at: www.emdr.com

Adaptive Rocking Desensitization (ARD)

Background

The information processing system of the brain facilitates mental health and balance in much the same way that the rest of the body heals itself when injured. The perceptual and emotional information resulting from a traumatic event is appraised and processed for resolution and adaptation. Useful information is registered and recorded for future reference along with appropriate emotions.

At times the emotional reaction and arousal resulting from trauma is so intense that it disrupts normal information processing. Consequently, the recording of disturbing images, sensations or beliefs about the trauma are impaired or blocked, leading to arousal, nightmares, flashbacks, intrusive thoughts, and other PTSD symptoms. Certain aspects of traumatic information in these situations are dissociated or compartmentalized. This, of course, prevents the normal integration and resolution of trauma reactions, and leads to PTSD.

Neuro-imaging studies of the brain show that specific structures such as the limbic system, the amygdale, and the hippocampus are involved in this incomplete processing of information. These structures are critical to the function of memory and appraisal of events. The storage of traumatic memories in emotional and compartmentalized forms prevents integration with the verbal and semantic aspects of memory, resulting in the physical and emotional symptoms of PTSD and heightened arousal states.

The process of desensitization helps victims of trauma to integrate the emotional and verbal aspects of trauma response and decreases PTSD symptoms, working as a form of reciprocal inhibition. When the victim is trying to imagine traumatic events and focus on negative beliefs or emotions, rocking movements or other activities such as eye movement, alternative stimulation, or relaxation techniques can inhibit the intense arousal and emotions associated with the trauma. This can help the individual integrate past memories and develop a full narrative of traumatic events. It is for precisely these reasons that I developed and have used for the past 18 years a different desensitization technique, called "Adaptive Rocking Desensitization" or ARD.

The process is as effective as any other desensitization method and is used to decrease the intensity of individual reactions to trauma. I often recommend it as a supplement to group therapy for specific patients. ARD takes advantage of the bi-phasic nature of PTSD to help the sufferer perceive his or her symptoms as prerequisites to mastery and recovery. To achieve this, the individual alternately focuses on and withdraws from trauma images in sequence, with the help of a rocking chair.

This paradoxical approach is basically a homeopathic technique. Like a vaccination, it uses a small dose of trauma to cure a long-term syndrome. It is based on the concept that symptoms are valuable for recovery. At the same time, the use of a rocking or a nursing chair helps to decrease overwhelming emotions or negative outcomes in a process of reciprocal inhibition.

Procedure

1. Individual completes one of the currently available PTSD scales, such as the Mississippi or CAPS, as a baseline tool to determine the intensity of their suffering;

2. Individuals rate their own distress level on a scale of 1 to 10 at the beginning of desensitization,

3. The therapist helps the individual sufferer to create replicas of traumatic events by any artistic means available. Personal creations may be enhanced by images or sound effects borrowed from the media, for dramatization;

4. In the safety of a survivor group or in an individual therapy session, the victim of trauma is exposed to, and alternatively withdrawn from, traumatic images as he or she moves back and forth on a rocking (preferably a nursing) chair. This activity continues for 20 minutes.

5. After 20 minutes of alternative exposure, the patient closes his eyes for ten minutes of relaxation, while the therapist shares carefully selected inspirational stories and metaphors in harmony with the patient's psychology and mindset. To create such therapeutic metaphors, I have relied extensively on the writings of David Gordon (1978), John Grinder and Richard Bandler (1976). Therapeutic metaphors help the victims to reframe and restructure their trauma images.

6. The therapist then encourages the victim to uncover the meaning of his symptoms and to identify the types of recognition needed. Group members if present, can also help him discover what changes he needs to make in order to alleviate his symptoms.

7. The process of alternative exposure to and withdrawal from traumatic images is repeated as many times as necessary to bring the distress level down to one or two units.

Through exposure to ARD, trauma victims soon recognize that understanding the meaning of their emotional symptoms makes them more relaxed and comfortable. Their symptoms gradually change from posing a threat or a nuisance to representing a signal for minor triggers of trauma. The individual may find new strength by increasing his sensitivity to the triggers of trauma and changing his mindset *before* an actual symptom has a chance to manifest itself. Like "visual," "auditory," or "tactile" radar, these triggers can help the individual adapt without undue anxiety.

We can enhance this process by helping the sufferer change the way he uses negative, generalized self-statements (based on guilt, remorse, helplessness and loss of control). We can help him recognize his spiritual station and see how everything he has done throughout his life was in reality a step in the process of growth. We can help him transform his negative self-statements or beliefs into positive ideas and self-respect, in order to foster greater self mastery. As the individual sufferer becomes less anxious, we challenge him to compare the old PTSD symptoms with the new coping styles and transform problems into assets. The life stories of great poets, writers, artists, composers, inventors, entrepreneurs, scientists, religious or political leaders, and even mythological figures may enhance this process during the relaxation phases of alternative imaging.

For most people, flooding and repeated exposure to trauma images gradually change the appearance, content, and progression of trauma events, leading to a clearer narrative and, ultimately, post traumatic growth. The individual replaces anxiety, guilt, rage, or grief with self-acceptance, tranquility, self-love, and dignity.

Adaptive Rocking Desensitization always begins with establishment of communal and spiritual bonding and a therapeutic environment that elicits trust. Only in such an atmosphere can the individual learn that his post-traumatic stress disorder is not a sign of weakness or failure but a path to growth, resolution, and mastery.

Cognitive behavior therapies

These are very effective and powerful treatment methods which most professional therapists are familiar with and use to good effect. Cognitive behavior therapies were developed in the 1960s and 1970s by such practitioners as Albert Ellis and Aaron Beck, and were used initially for treatment of depression. Later researchers applied them to anxiety disorders and PTSD. The salient features of cognitive therapies include the following:

- Self-evaluation of daily functioning and coping mechanisms;

- Identification of deficits in social skills and relating to others;

- Review and appraisal of past trauma and its impact;

- Repetitive false beliefs and thought that dominate the stream of thought and the inner chit-chat;

- Identification of faulty and irrational ideas and thoughts, based on generalization, deletion, and exaggeration of trauma as catastrophe;

- Evaluation of distortions in cognitive process and negative pessimistic thinking;

- Therapeutic attempts to correct faulty thoughts and clarification of the relationship between thoughts, emotions, and the resulting behaviors;

- Separation of old and new traumas to avoid being overwhelmed emotionally.

Modified Cognitive Behavior Therapy

In this approach, developed by Dr. John Briere at the Psychological Trauma Clinic of the University of Southern California (2006), greater attention is paid to regulation and the balancing of emotions, using self-soothing to avoid the sensation of catastrophe.

The therapist regulates the level and duration of exposure in order to avoid states of hyper-arousal and dissociation. Patients are prepared for short-term therapeutic intervention (in 8-16 sessions) after full assessment and an explanation of the treatment details. Patients are reminded that avoiding exposure and truth may decrease anxiety and guilt, but do not lead to healing. For healing to take place, courage is essential.

In this method there is a gradual exploration of memories and exposure is balanced according to the individual's tolerance. Usually there are many traumatic events to process, each one having its own trigger. To expand the individual's narrative of trauma, each of them should be explored. Most victims are hyper-vigilant and perceive danger acutely, so there is a great need for trust and a supportive therapeutic environment. Activation of memories leads to feelings of dread, but since the environment is safe and soothing, the PTSD symptoms are gradually extinguished. This open-ended exploration of trauma memories, coupled with gentle challenging of the patient's desire to avoid therapy, giving support and reassurance, and reframing of symptoms is very effective in reducing the victim's feelings of helplessness and despair. By using spiritual approaches, such as meditation, mindfulness, and relaxation techniques, the effectiveness of modified exposure therapy can be greatly increased.

Trauma processing, exposure, and the gradual exploration of memories are essential features in developing a narrative. But since the number of trauma events is often more than one, it is necessary to achieve therapeutic goals in every session and for each specific trauma event. Victims are often hyper-vigilant and perceive danger to an exaggerated degree. Thus, a very gentle and soothing therapeutic environment is needed to decrease their unusual sensitivity. In this respect, attention to transference reactions is essential, as issues of abandonment and attachment can trigger mistrust. Only the perception of safety can lead to extinction of trauma symptoms. Dr. Briere recommends an open-ended exploration of explicit and hidden memories, with a flexible degree of activation according to the victim's tolerance. He also uses cognitive restructuring after each session, with support, reassurance, reframing, and interpretation to deal with issues of self-blame, helplessness, hopelessness, self-esteem, and overestimation of danger. Emotional regulation training approaches such as relaxation, stress management, meditation, mindfulness, and homework are also used to create narratives and eventual closure. This means coming to terms with overwhelming and horrifying trauma events and eventual acceptance.

Trauma work with children

When working with children, therapists and all caregivers and protection service providers must take care that

- Children's physical safety is ensured;
- Children and their families feel safe and relaxed;
- Basic needs are provided for: food, shelter, and medical services;
- Children and their families are educated about PTSD;
- Symptoms and emotions of all involved family members are considered.

Chapter Twelve: Twelve Steps and Twelve Themes

Preparation for a 12-step program

Before referring an individual with PTSD to a 12-step program, I usually share some symbolic stories to prepare them for the challenge ahead.

The first story is about a holy man sitting under a tree in the middle of the road, eating his lunch. A passerby asks him twice how far it is to the closest town. When he does not get an answer, he leaves disappointed. But after he has walked a few minutes, the holy man calls out to him and says that it would take about two hours of walking to the nearest town. The traveler asks why he did not tell him the first time he asked, to which the holy man replies: "I did not know how fast you walk." The moral is obvious.

Then I share the second tale:

A wise man walks into a city in disarray, in which people are running away in terror, as if their lives are in danger. Wanting to know the cause of their fears, he asks a man, who, pointing a finger towards the west, says there is a mysterious monster on a nearby farm that is frightening all of us. The wise man says he wishes to see the monster and starts immediately to walk in that direction. Some people, curious to see the outcome of his stupidity, follow him until he arrives at the farm. Not seeing any monsters, he asks further questions and, to his surprise, finds out that the assumed monster is a giant watermelon. He starts to laugh and calls the inhabitants fools. Then he approaches the watermelon, cuts a piece of it, and begins to eat. The locals believe that he is definitely the Devil, who is eating a live monster and cannot see that there is blood dripping from his mouth. They attack him and chase him out of town.

A second wise man appears later and the whole story is repeated. But when he faces the watermelon, he starts to shake in terror and tells people that indeed this one is a most dangerous monster. He asks the locals to bring all their building materials and tells them to construct a barricade around the monster. Then he teaches them a prayer and a dance ritual, to protect them from the wrath of the monster. People feel safe with him and ask him to stay in their town as a trusted teacher, to help them learn more. In the first year of his stay, he tells them many stories about monsters and ways of approaching them. In the second year, he teaches them how to read, write, and cultivate a farm. Then in the third year he teaches them how to plant watermelons.

The timeline of this delightful story corresponds to the usual length of various forms of therapy: about three years—very similar, incidentally, to the path of early childhood development.[54]

Following these stories, I discuss the process and the path of 12-step programs and the necessity to listen to numerous stories of traumatized people—including telling their own—go through a set of rituals to become a peer counselor or sponsor, so that they can achieve sufficient mastery and self-confidence to help others recover.

Forming emotional attachments and the concomitant biological release of Oxytocin (the hormone responsible for social recognition and bonding), are the primary means of protection against trauma. Human beings have always used supportive gatherings and social organizations to deal with major challenges. As long as individuals can rely on a stable social support network, they feel protected against catastrophic events. The main task of support groups is to help victims regain a sense of safety and mastery. Fellow victims often provide the most effective form of social support because of shared history and symptoms. Thus, various forms of group therapy have been regarded as the treatment of choice for most trauma victims. I have found the 12-step groups to be unusually effective in the resolution of PTSD, as they enable the members to help each other regain their Peace, Tranquility, Sanity, and Dignity.

54 Children have to gain attachment and complete trust in their care givers with a deep sense of protection and safety. Prayers, rituals, stories, songs, and dance are essential in the first year, for solid attachment. Then they begin the process of separation and independence at about age 2, accompanied by more rituals, pastimes, rules, and advice. In the third year, they incorporate the image of caregivers as a permanent companion, teacher, guide, and model as they proceed to achieve autonomy and self-reliance.

PTSD ANON: Setting up a survivor group

Therapists, like any good teacher, must exercise humility and recognize when the sufferer can benefit from resources beyond those he or she can provide. In this book, I have presented many scenarios in which PTSD sufferers have found relief in the nurturing atmosphere of a therapy or support group. For some individuals, PTSD ANON groups offer a positive framework to supplement traditional therapies.

Dr. Joel Osler Brende (1995) adapted an excellent spiritual guideline for PTSD ANON and graciously allowed me to develop a slightly modified version for my groups. The following brief description may be helpful in setting up a group.

1. Adoption of a Charter

"We are a group of individuals who have suffered psychological traumas and pain. We share our experiences, strengths, hopes, and pain with each other in order to give meaning to our suffering. The only requirement for membership in our anonymous group is a sincere desire to make life better for families, our fellow-sufferers, and ourselves. We are not here to blame, but to understand, grow, and accept responsibility. Our goal is to become more attentive, intelligent, reasonable, and spiritual. We are self-supporting through our own contributions and not interested in any controversial, political, or social issues. The primary purpose of our group is to learn to deal with human suffering more effectively and to develop better survival and coping skills.

2. Serenity prayers

God, grant me the serenity to accept the things I can not change, the courage to change the things I can and the wisdom to know the difference.[55]

---

55   Prayer commonly attributed to theologian Reinhold Niebuhr, but adopted and commonly used by Alcoholics Anonymous and other twelve-step programs.

* * * * * * * * * *

O God! Refresh and gladden my spirit. Purify my heart. Illumine my powers. I lay all my affairs in Thy hands. Thou art my guide and my refuge. I will no longer be sorrowful or grieved. I will be a happy and joyful being. O' God! I will no longer be full of anxiety, nor will I let troubles harass me. I will not dwell on the unpleasant things of life. O God! Thou art more friend to me than I am to myself. I dedicate myself to Thee, O Lord.

> — Abdu'l-Baha

3. 12-steps and 12 themes

All the steps below are important and can be studied separately or in sequence.

Step 1: Understanding power versus victimization:

"We admit to the fact that our lives have become unmanageable because of our psychological suffering and victimization. We have become powerless against the consequences of our traumatic experiences. Even though we have survived physically, we are powerless to win our battle against a new enemy, our memories of trauma, flashbacks of suffering, and reliving of experiences. We have lost our capacity to control our impulses, and we live a life of rage, guilt, suspicion, and fear. It has become impossible or very difficult to love and care for our family and friends, as we tend to isolate ourselves and force others to avoid, dislike, or even hurt us. Our attempts to fight our emotional prison and to free ourselves have been in vain. We find ourselves powerless to control or to advance our psychological health. This step focuses on finding ways to gain power over suffering and trauma, loss of meaning, self doubt, shame, anger, panic, arousal symptoms, isolation, depression, and suicidal thoughts."

No one wishes to admit defeat or powerlessness. But admission to powerlessness is a powerful paradoxical process in spiritual recovery. Humility liberates by helping us let go of illusions of power and find a different level of meaning in life.

People with the most severe forms of post-traumatic stress disorder have a greater chance for recovery through spiritual activities, since they are able to find rock bottom more easily.

Group members are encouraged to meditate on this step for as long as necessary and to write journals, essays, and reports on their own experiences of powerlessness, their illusions of control, and their relapse of symptoms. As they share these with each other, they can learn more about PTSD. We can break the cycle of victimization by

- Acknowledging powerlessness or the destructive use of power;

- Seeking help from God (as individually understood) or other representatives of higher power, individuals, or groups;

- Surrendering symptoms of victimization suffering to God;

- Taking action and ask for help from God to intervene in self-destructive behaviors and restore our sense of power;

- Daily prayer: God, grant me the serenity to accept that I have become powerless over my symptoms of trauma, the courage to change those behaviors I can, and the wisdom to know the difference.

Step 2: Seeking meaning:

"We have come to believe that a power greater than ourselves can restore our sanity and bring meaning to our survival from suffering and trauma. We believe that we have survived for a purpose. Even though we often doubt that survival was better than dying, we seek meaning in our lives in order to overcome our despair. We want to be free from the nagging experiences of grief, guilt, and rage. And we want life to become a privilege rather than a burden."

Many individuals, especially those who have suffered intensely from post-traumatic stress disorder, may resent the concept of a higher power or God. They may have trouble with the idea that God performs miracles in our lives. Some simply become cynical and belligerent. When beliefs and values are shattered by suffering and trauma, the loss of protective shields, and the pain of raw injuries, PTSD sufferers often have a tremendous need to keep their illusions of power and their arrogance against helplessness. But as they join PTSD Anonymous, they gradually realize that developing a new set of beliefs and the emergence of a new lifestyle are not as difficult as they thought. PTSD Anonymous does not ask members to believe in anything if they do not want to. The steps and studies are simply suggestions, helping the individual to gradually enter the path of faith.

Before making any commitment to such acts of devotion, individual need to free themselves from pre-judgments and bias. To investigate the truth, they need a free and open mind, open to the realization that psychology, psychiatry, and pharmacology have not found permanent solutions or cures for human suffering. Victims of violence, rape, incest, torture, combat, or natural disasters continue to suffer from repetitive symptoms of PTSD, even decades after the events that initiated the syndrome. PTSD Anonymous strives to lead affected people to a form of spiritual sobriety and recovery based on love of others and service.

The human soul has almost unlimited capacities, which are now being discussed and tapped by scientists for healing purposes. Ernest Rossi, in his excellent book *The Psychobiology of Mind-Body Healing* (1986) has described the impact of faith and inner spiritual force on human recovery. Anonymous groups apply the concept of higher power on three different levels:

- The higher power within the self;

- The higher power or divinity within the group;

- The higher power as God, our Creator.

The search for meaning requires sharing our experiences with each other, accepting support and understanding, and listening to those who have found meaning in their own suffering. Each member can begin the search for meaning by

- Acknowledging that it is difficult to accept trauma and find meaning in survival;

- Seeking support and direction from God and one's fellow humans;

- Surrendering despair, confusion, and loss of meaning to God;

- Taking action by seeking answers from God and by listening to others, who have survived in spite of emotional pain and found meaning in their lives;

- Daily prayer: God grant me the serenity to seek meaning out of tragedy, to search for an understanding of my survival. Grant me the courage to seek clarity, to free myself from confusion, and give me the wisdom to know the difference.

Step 3: Choosing trust over shame and doubt:

> *Burdened with mistrust, shame and doubt, we made a decision to seek the help of God in order to learn to trust.*

This step is about regaining our ability to trust God, others, organizations, authorities and ourselves. As victims, we may have lost our capacity to trust due to abandonment, betrayal, and faith in illusions of safety, the shattering of our assumptions, or abuse. We can begin to break the cycle of mistrust, shame, and doubt by

- Acknowledging our mistrust in ourselves and others;
- Seeking how we can trust God to resolve doubt, mistrust, and confusion;
- Surrendering our mistrust to God;
- Taking action by putting trust in God and others to test;
- Daily prayer: God grant me the serenity to understand my false pride and to learn how to trust again. Grant me the courage to take the necessary risks in order to gain freedom.

Step 4: Taking a self-inventory and developing self-knowledge:

> *We admit to ourselves, to God and to other fellow humans what we know about ourselves and ask for help in accepting our positive qualities while we change our negative qualities.*

As humans, we are entrusted with such magnificent capacities, that if we rid ourselves of bias and gain self-knowledge, we can almost claim to have achieved the knowledge of God. According to the mystics of India, there exists a network of pearls in the temple of Indra, arranged in such a way that each one reflects all the other pearls, and if you look at them more carefully each pearl reflects the whole universe.

Humans are indeed pearls created in the image of God. Each one can reflect not only all other fellow humans but also the entire creation. We often do not admit to our fears about self-discovery, since the image of God within us has the capacity to resolve any problem, and we find that frightening. When we relinquish our old biases, attachments, prejudices, and clear our minds from time, space, and material attachments, we can become spiritual and reflect the beauty and majesty of our inner divinity. Victims of trauma sometimes carry the lifeless corpse of misery and post-traumatic stress disorder on their backs for many years. In searching for a way out, they have to look inside. This is where they can find the gems of wisdom, along with ugly ogres and frightening experiences of the past.

The experience of many bright trauma survivors has shown that humility and intellect can be compatible. When the jewels of humility and faith are allowed to beautify the intellect, we are reborn as spiritual heroes. The 12 steps of PTSD Anonymous are designed to carry us through this challenging journey of self-discovery toward a new spiritual awakening. This is the stage at which we let go of hypocrisy, self-righteousness, and prejudice, when we can overlook our own limitations, move away from false respectability, and confront the attributes of God within. As victims of trauma, we may have equated self worth with the mastery of frightening situations, repeating victimization patterns or attracting abusers over and over again. We may not have known why we did this. We may have repeatedly punished ourselves due to guilt and shame. A personal inventory can help us learn the truth, accept our positive qualities, and change the negative ones. We can begin our self-inventory by

- Acknowledging that we often do not look at our positive godly attributes and that we have trouble changing the negative ones;

- Seeking to free ourselves from self-destructive, destructive, shameful, and self- condemning attitudes;

- Surrendering our shameful secrets and destructive behaviors to God and accepting help and constructive criticism from others;

- Taking action in receiving feedback and learning about ourselves; and

- Daily prayer: God, grant me the serenity to accept my positive qualities, change those that are harmful to others and myself, and make amends to those I have harmed. Grant me the courage to accept the truth about myself and the wisdom to know the difference between positive and negative qualities.

Step 5: Managing anger:

We seek God's help in understanding anger, controlling its destructiveness, and channeling it in constructive ways.

This step helps us to understand anger or rage and its relation to the triggers of trauma. Rage—and even homicidal thoughts—may have been normal at the time of our traumas or victimization. Anger may be easier to feel than fear, guilt, or grief. In fact, anger may be a cover for other feelings. But anger can become unmanageable, frightening, or destructive. If suppressed, it may block our capacity for self-assertion and transform into bodily symptoms. We can begin to break the victimization cycle of anger by

- Acknowledging that we are powerless to recognize or control outbursts of angry emotions or to channel anger constructively;

- Seeking help from God and others to deal with anger constructively;

- Surrendering our anger and the blocks that keeps us from perceiving it to God;

- Taking action by seeking help in our efforts to reduce intense rage through healthy activities, by expressing anger normally, assertively and constructively;

- Daily prayer: God, grant me the serenity to accept my anger as a normal emotion, even though it may be blocked or may erupt in destructive ways. Grant me the courage to control it when it is unmanageable and to be aware of it when it is blocked.

Step 6: Managing fear:

We seek God's help to relinquish the wall around our emotions and His protective presence during moments of terror and risk.

This step focuses on understanding and coping with fear. Trauma-based panic and fear may be experienced repeatedly, paralyzing our normal functioning. Our trauma fear may have been so overwhelming that we blocked it from our conscious awareness. If so, we may take extreme risks to feel it again in the form of an adrenaline high, and master the fear. The consequences of suppressed fear are the numbing of emotions, isolation, mistrust, and panic attacks. We can free ourselves from the victimization cycle of fear by

- Acknowledging that fear either excessively controls our lives or has been completely blocked, so we take dangerous risks to keep a wall around our emotions;

- Seeking the help of God and others to relinquish the wall around our emotions, to take risks in constructive ways, and learn to depend on God during terrifying emotions;

- Taking action by beginning to let down the wall and accept our fears as normal. Begin to take risks in positive ways and face frightening situations with the help of God and others;

- Daily prayer: God, grant me the serenity to accept fear as a normal emotion. Grant me the courage to relinquish the wall around my emotions and the wisdom to know the difference between normal and abnormal fear.

Step 7: Managing guilt:

> *We seek God's help in facing guilt, to make amends when possible, to accept His forgiveness and to forgive ourselves.*

This step helps us understand guilt and gain relief from its destructive consequences. Survivor guilt can be pervasive and self destructive, particularly if we believe—rightly or wrongly—that we were responsible for the death or injury of others. Guilt may cause unbearable, horrifying and repetitive thoughts, images and dreams, or persistent depression, thoughts of suicide, and physical illness. Conversely, even though we may have no conscious awareness of guilt, its consequences may still be destructive if we engage in abusive or perverse behaviors. We may have been betrayed or abandoned, feel ashamed that we were not in control, or did not act with courage and continue to feel overwhelmed by guilt. We can begin to find freedom from the guilt victimization cycle by

- Acknowledging that while guilt without logical reason is abnormal, it is normal when we were responsible for the suffering or deaths of others, but that continuous self-punishment is destructive;

- Seeking freedom from self-destructive or destructive behaviors, guilty secrets, self-condemning attitudes, and distorted or absent conscience;

- Surrendering to God our guilt and guilty secrets;

- Taking action by asking God and others for help in order to find relief from irrational guilt; accepting God's forgiveness, seeking the forgiveness of others, and forgiving ourselves;

- Daily prayer: God grant me the serenity to regain my sensitivity and make amends to those I have hurt. Forgive me for things I have done or failed to do, particularly if I caused the injury or death of others. Grant me the courage to free myself from guilt, self-punishing, and destructive behaviors, and the wisdom to recognize these behaviors.

Step 8: Accepting grief:

> We seek God's help to grieve for those we have lost, to face our painful memories and emotions, and let our tears heal our sorrow.

In this step, we focus on being able to complete the grieving process. Grief is the normal response to loss, but we may have failed to complete the grief process and remained victims to our emotional pain. We may withdraw, deny that the loss ever happened, intellectualize, or avoid intimate relationships. We may have outbursts of fear or anger, severe depression, intrusive emotions, or obsessions about the object of our loss. We can begin to break the grief victimization cycle by

- Acknowledging that we may be emotionally blocked, unable to grieve losses, and fearful about establishing close relationships;

- Seeking with the help of God to free ourselves of blocked emotions, isolation, and persistent unresolved grief;

- Surrendering our painful memories and losses to God;

- Taking action by saying goodbye to those we have lost, letting down the barriers, feeling sadness and anger, and allowing our tears to flow; and by taking the necessary risks to establish closer relationships, with the help of God and others;

• Daily prayer: God, grant me the serenity to be aware of my losses and to grieve; grant me the courage to change those behaviors that keep me from making close relationships and the wisdom to learn the difference between hanging on out of fear and remembering out of reverence.

Step 9: Choosing life over death:

We reveal to God and those people we trust all remaining self-destructive wishes and, with God's help, we make a commitment to life.

This step helps us to face hopelessness and self-directed anger, which prevent us from embracing life. Hopelessness and persistent despair cause chronic depression, apathy, and thoughts of suicide. Facing death may seem easier than facing life. We can overcome and break the cycle of despair and death by

• Acknowledging that we may be contemplating suicide without taking into full consideration the pain that this would cause for those who survive us;

• Seeking help from God, family members, friends, counselors, and others to resolve self-destructive thoughts, so that we can find life worth living and make a commitment to life;

• Surrendering to God all self-destructive feelings, hopelessness, and plans of suicide;

• Taking action by discussing our feeling with others and asking for God's help; replacing death wishes with a commitment to life, positive thoughts, constructive activities, and relationships

• Daily prayer: God, grant me the serenity to surrender my hopelessness and death wishes to you. Grant me the courage to make a commitment to life and the wisdom to know the difference between selfless love and self-centered hatred.

Step 10: *Valuing justice over personal revenge:*

> *We seek God's help to pursue the cause of justice, gain freedom*
> *from personal feelings of revenge and a desire to be God's channels*
> *of forgiveness to those we once hated.*

This step helps us gain freedom from destructive personal revenge, bitterness, hatred, and the relentless anger that blocks true justice. If life has no other purpose than revenge, it may be easier to live in hatred than in love and peace. There is a difference between justice and revenge. One is personal and the other is social. Justice is the basis for love, peace, and social freedom.

The desire for revenge is the underlying cause of repetitive hatred and war. Although it may bring temporary relief, revenge feeds upon itself and causes further victimization and bondage. If our hatred has become dangerous to others or ourselves, we need help. We can break out of this vicious cycle of victimizing others, violence, and revenge by

- Acknowledging that we are powerless to control hatred, vengeful thoughts, and bitterness that lie deep within us and serve to victimize us, our families and others;

- Seeking help from God to release us from the bondage of personal vengeance;

- Surrendering all our feelings of personal revenge to the care and justice of God;

- Taking action by renewing our daily commitment to God's purpose for our lives, rejuvenating our spiritual strength through the uplifting words of God in sacred scriptures and through shared spiritual activities with friends and others;

- Daily prayer: God, grant me the serenity to surrender myself to you and seek your purpose in my life. Lead me to a creative and fulfilling path of justice. Grant me the courage to commit myself to social justice and give me the wisdom to know the difference between self-centered revenge and your selfless path of justice, love and truth.

Step 11: Finding a purpose:

> *We seek knowledge and direction from God and surrender our-selves to His leadership in order to find a renewed purpose for our lives.*

As victims of trauma, our lives may appear meaningless. At one time, we harbored many destructive emotions: distrust, shame, rage, fear, guilt, grief, isolation, and revenge, which we surrendered to God. Now we must sur-render in new ways by

- Acknowledging that we sometimes slip back into the bondage of meaningless victimization, with all the negative emotions that robbed us of a sense of purpose;

- Seeking to let go of our negative baggage; finding a new relationship with our source, God, and a new sense of purpose;

- Surrender ourselves to God to refresh and gladden our hearts, illumine our powers, and make us joyful and happy beings;

- Take action by talking to others, so we can discover our lofty station and the richness of our soul; renew our daily commitment to seek God's purpose in our lives and renew our spiritual strength through prayer;

- Daily Prayer: God, renew me as I surrender myself to you and seek your purpose for my life; grant me the courage to follow your creative and fulfilling path and the wisdom to differentiate between self-centered quests and your path of justice, love and truth.

Step 12: Finding love and fellowship:

> *We seek God's love in our lives, renew our commitment to the human family, love even those we find difficult to love, and help those who have been victims of oppression and pain as we were.*

This final step helps each member enact the miracle of love. It keeps us free from self-centeredness and meaningless victimization experiences. Having had a spiritual awakening and learning to love and help others, we find it necessary to practice the steps with others. We can remove any blocks to ac-ceptance of love from God and others in order to freely give love. In order to be able to love our fellow men, we have to open ourselves to God's love for us. As described reassuringly in the *Hidden Words*,

> "Veiled in My immemorial being and in the ancient eternity of
> My essence, I knew My love for thee, therefore I created thee, have
> engraved on thee Mine image and revealed to thee My beauty."[56]

Thus, we can renew our commitment to people we have taken for granted, and take joy in the vitality of love and friendships, which we had neglected. With this attitude of love, we can then carry the message of recovery to our fellow humans, sufferers, and victims. We can begin to love others by

- Acknowledging the difficulty of accepting God's love and the love of others and the difficulty of loving those we have taken for granted or found hard to love;

- Seeking openness to God's love and the love of others in our lives. Commit ourselves to family, friends, and humanity and become a channel of God's love for those who are difficult to love;

- Surrendering to the love of God, so that it may flow to and through us;

- Taking action to help those suffering from pain, victimization, and oppression in their lives;

- Daily prayer: God, grant me the serenity to surrender myself to your will and renew your love in me. Grant me the courage to commit myself to the love of humanity, to those I have taken for granted and those who depend on me. God, grant me the wisdom to distinguish between self-centered love and the selfless love that flows from you to all. Help me to bring about the miracle of love in my life and in the lives of others.*

---

56   Bahá'u'lláh, *Hidden Words*, Arabic, No. 3.

* Helping other alcoholics or addicts in AA or NA is a critical part of step 12, shifting the recovering individuals focus from self to others. Providing guidance, encouragement, support and sponsorship dramatically changes the feelings of helplessness to that of being helpful and resilient.

PART III: Spiritual Recovery and Post Traumatic Growth

Chapter Thirteen: Preparing for post traumatic growth

"Love is heaven's kindly light, the Holy Spirit's eternal breath that vivifieth the human soul . . . Love is the most great law, that ruleth this mighty and heavenly cycle, the unique power that binds together the diverse elements of this material world, the supreme magnetic force that directeth the movements of the spheres in the celestial realm..."
— 'Abdu'l-Bahá[57]

The Lover's Journey

The following story, "The Lover's Journey", is a metaphor representing the stages of human spiritual growth. I have many times recited the tale, with great emotional impact, in therapy groups for people of all ages, backgrounds, and degrees of suffering. This journey symbolizes the abdication of fear and the acceptance of love as the essential forces underlying spirituality. The story was first written in poetic form in the 13th century by the great Sufi master Jalaluddin Rumi[58] and later in prose by Bahá'u'lláh[59] as follows:

---

57   'Abdu'l-Bahá, *Selections from the Writings of 'Abdu'l-Bahá*, p. 27.
58   The great epic poem, entitled "Mathnavi," by Rumi, consisted of some 50,000 lines and 424 stories, illustrating man's predicament in his search for God. The first translation into English appeared in 1881. See Nicholson, 1940.
59   Bahá'u'lláh, *The Seven Valleys and the Four Valleys*, written between 1858 and 1862, describes the stages of growth through which man passes in the search for spirituality and knowledge.

There was once a lover who had sighed for long years in separation from his beloved and wasted in the fire of remoteness. From
the rule of love, his heart was empty of patience, and his body
weary of his spirit; he reckoned life without her as a mockery,
and time consumed him away. How many a day he found no rest
in longing for her; how many a night the pain of her kept him
from sleep; his body was worn to a sigh, and his heart's wound
had turned him to a cry of sorrow. He had given a thousand lives
for one taste of the cup of her presence, but it availed him not.
The doctor knew no cure for him, and companions avoided his
company; yea, physicians have no medicine for one sick of love,
unless the favor of the beloved one deliver him.

At last, the tree of his longing yielded the fruit of
despair, and the fire of his hope fell to ashes. Then one night
he could live no more, and he went out of his house and made
for the marketplace. On a sudden, a watchman followed after
him. He broke into a run, with the watchman following; then
other watchmen came together and barred every passage to the
weary one. And the wretched one cried from his heart, and ran
here and there, and moaned to himself: 'Surely this watchman
is 'Izra'il, my angel of death, following so fast upon me; or he is
a tyrant of men, seeking to harm me.' His feet carried him on,
the one bleeding with the arrow of love, and his heart lamented.
Then he came to a garden wall, and with untold pain he scaled
it, for it proved very high; and forgetting his life, he threw himself
down to the garden.

And there he beheld his beloved with a lamp in
her hand, searching for a ring she had lost. When the heart-
surrendered lover looked on his ravishing love, he drew a great
breath and raised up his hands in prayer, crying: "O God! Give
Thou glory to the watchman and riches and long life. For the
watchman was Gabriel, guiding this poor one; or he was Isra'fil,
bringing life to this wretched one!". . .

Indeed, his words were true, for he had found many a
secret justice in this seeming tyranny of the watchman . . . Out of
wrath, the guard had led him who was athirst in love's desert to
the sea of his loved one, and lit up the dark night of absence with
the light of reunion. He had driven the one who was afar into
the garden of nearness, had guided an ailing soul to the heart's
physician.

> Now if the lover could have looked ahead, he would
> have blessed the watchman at the start, and prayed on his behalf,
> and he would have seen that tyranny as justice; but since the end
> was veiled to him, he moaned and made his plaint in the begin-
> ning. Yet those who journey in the garden land of knowledge,
> because they see the end in the beginning, see peace in war and
> friendliness in anger.

I find in this tale a powerful metaphor for re-framing human suffering. Emptying our "selves" from all conventional and borrowed learning is the only way to clear our inner vision. Those who can do so comprehend the close relationship between pain, growth, and meaning. When we stop focus-ing on the real-world problems and see with spiritual eyes, we can shut out suffering and open our vision to the beauty of the beloved.

Trauma alters our perceptions. We respond not only to the traumatic events in our immediate vicinity, but also to the context of the events, their aftermath, and to all similar events in history. Victims of rape, violence, or combat are so preoccupied with intense emotion, that no simple therapeu-tic model can necessarily help them overcome this condition. Yet spiritual metaphors impose an almost holographic meaning on traumatic events. The soothing impact of such metaphors, I believe, contributes to the resolu-tion of the sense of calamity.

Spirituality confronts trauma in depth. The spiritual mind knows the traumatized mind very well. They are similarly transcendent, illogical, and swift. Our peak experiences of spiritual ecstasy and our trauma nightmares are both expressions of the same powerful stuff, the stuff of the human soul. No ordinary language of words can do them justice. Their impact is deep, awe-inspiring, and haunting. The same sense of mystery inherent in trauma also applies to spiritual encounters. Both the mystic deep in meditation and the victim of rape know that no rational mind can understand their feelings.

Mary's story

Mary was diagnosed with paranoid schizophrenia. Hospitalized for several months, she repeatedly stated her delusion that on 13 September 1987, she would miraculously recover and leave the hospital. Someone in the family had told her that they were praying that on that precise date, she would completely recover, with the help of God. She had a deep conviction about her impending recovery on that very day. As professionals in psychiatry, we considered her belief a delusion and part of her illness. Then, early in the morning on the 13th of September, when I entered the hospital lobby, a beautiful, exuberant, elegantly dressed woman was waiting to see me.

"Do you have an appointment?" I asked.

"Not a regular one," she said. "But today is my day to leave the hospital, you remember?"

"Who are you?" I asked. "Do I know you?"

"Look carefully," she said. "Don't you recognize me?"

"Honestly, you don't look familiar to me," I replied.

"Wow, the miracle of makeup!" she said. "I am Mary S. All I did was fix my hair, put on makeup, and get dressed, and you don't even recognize me. Well, today is September 13th. The miracle has happened, and I am leaving the hospital today."

"Well! I am dumbfounded," I said. "I really didn't recognize you. But in order to leave the hospital, you must go through a battery of tests and evaluations. Would you be okay with that?"

She agreed, and comprehensive evaluations failed to reveal any trace of mental illness. She was cured magically on the date prophesied. For many years, I followed her case, out of my own curiosity, but none of her schizophrenic symptoms recurred. Mary told me that after years of misery in numerous failed relationships, she had felt a strong desire to end her isolation, paranoia, and illness. She had asked her family for prayers, so that God could help her achieve this. She had processed some of her childhood traumas with the help of other patients who, at times, were more disturbed than she was. She had learned how to count her blessings. She had revived her innate capacity to love, and she had focused on helping some of the fellow patients by becoming a sponsor. Readiness to leave the world of mental illness had promoted her recovery, along with the intercession of family prayers. Her delusions had evaporated, and she had, indeed, achieved spontaneous recovery.

Evolutionary scientists have shown us the significance of alliances and the way loving bonds can generate miraculous resolutions for suffering. In his Pulitzer Prize- winning masterpiece *Grow or Die: The Unifying Principle of Transformation*, George Ainsworth-Land (1973) described patterns of growth in various organisms, identifying three stages of growth: attraction, bonding, and release. His studies indicate that when an isolated living being achieves a sense of equilibrium or balance, it sooner or later perceives the isolated pattern of life as non-stimulating and inferior. A desire for change is generated within the organism and a growth impulse moves it away from its own autistic boundaries. This shift of emphasis to a higher level of growth is based on attraction to complementary organisms with opposing qualities or, in human beings, with opposing views and behaviors. Initially, they generate a symbiotic togetherness on the basis of replication and imitation. Then, one of the two participants acts as the host and becomes dominant. The other one replicates and imitates. Although powerful, this union is often ambivalent and, as it grows deeper, another important drive pushes them toward release and separation.

Endurance of symbiotic bonds beyond an optimal threshold often leads to hostile dependence and resentment. Readiness for an equal, reciprocal experience naturally ends this imitative growth pattern and releases the living organism for a higher level of autonomy and mutuality. If these imitative bonds are prolonged by force, parasitic dependence results, accompanied by the threat of annihilation, often leading to a struggle to recapture freedom.

In the final phase of development, a series of compromises and accommodations between the two organisms leads to mutual and interdependent growth. Regression, relapse, or other factors may interrupt the advancement of these three cycles of growth.

From a spiritual point of view, when a human being becomes alienated from the core of his being (the "Absolute Reality") and relies on the false images of the "self," he may experience deep trauma and great emotional suffering. Separated from a spiritual source, a person becomes soul sick and laments the pain to other torn individuals, wishing for a reunion, a return to bliss.

When we are free from bondage to the "self" and trust our divine vision, we can experience authentic power. Our goal becomes unity with others and service to mankind. Truth and spirituality have no boundaries. All human beings long for and travel this path of transcendence. Even tyrannical individuals, moving at their own pace, walk a path of spiritual growth. When we achieve our capacity, we can step outside of ourselves and gain mastery over our egos. Exploitation of love is then replaced by detachment and wisdom. The illusions of separation fade away and, like the evolutionary stages of growth, our steps on the spiritual path lead to resolution and freedom.

Like the sleeping beauty in the fairy tale, the self-absorbed dreamer may not be awakened until kissed by a loving prince. In the search of spirituality, when we finally meet our significant ally, our lover, teacher, sponsor, or therapist, we can develop trust, bonding, and mutually transcendence. Maturity and freedom are achieved when we have completed our cycles of growth by returning to our spiritual origins and to union with the Universal Reality.

Love, attachment, and healing

Love suffers long and is kind; love does not envy; love does not parade itself, is not puffed up; does not behave rudely, does not seek its own, is not provoked, thinks no evil; does not rejoice in iniquity, but rejoices in the truth; bears all things, believes all things, hopes all things, endures all things. Love never fails.
— Corinthians 13:4-8

Love as a path of departure

In the course of my work with PTSD sufferers, I have repeatedly witnessed miracles. Regaining one's capacity for faith and relationships transforms trauma into knowledge of human complexity. This leads to greater spiritual power and recovery. Traumatic experiences shake the very foundation of our beliefs about safety and trust. Being so far outside the human expectations, traumatic events at times provoke what may seem unbelievable and crazy reactions. However disturbing or unusual they may be, they are to be expected from sensitive human beings in terrifying events. Actual or threatened death or injury to self or loved ones, accompanied by a sense of horror and helplessness, lead often to a post-traumatic stress reaction that may last for years. Between 15 to 30 percent of traumatized people display such reactions.

For the individual experiencing the typical adaptive responses which help the sufferer to recognize and avoid further danger—the flashbacks, nightmares, arousal, avoidance, anxiety, depression, exaggerated startle or hypervigilance we have been discussing thus far—the path of love and attachment to humanity can help the individual to apprehend an eventual positive outcome.

In Chapter 9, we have seen how modern research has revealed the deep relationship of the body and the soul. When structures in the brain are damaged, any threat to or shattering of the sense of security and human attachment intensifies PTSD symptoms in vulnerable people. When I became more aware of these delicate relationships, I discovered the miraculous impact of returning to love and faith, both for my patients and myself._

As the human soul responds to the symbolic imagery of the heart, hope and a healthier self-image can be restored. Love and therapeutic attachment can make our lives sweeter, richer, and more colorful. This is the essence of the therapeutic alliance and bonding with others. It can occur in therapy or any other form of loving human relationship. An individual who has regained his capacity for loving—that is, who is in touch with his own soul—is able to maintain a balance between pain and pleasure, success and failure, trauma and recovery. Such a person does not perceive the dark side of life as an unnecessary burden or an evil imposed from without, but rather as another stage in growth.

Other practitioners have also discovered the idea that traumatic experiences can represent a positive pathway for growth. In his book *Authentic Happiness*, Seligman (2002) puts forward the concept of positive psychology and demonstrates the way a positive life experience can be born of trauma experience, otherwise known as post-traumatic growth or the PTG phenomenon. Thus, it is beginning to be better understood that trauma brings into focus the value of love in human relationships as one of our most essential intrinsic human strengths.

Suffering and spirituality

*History despite its wrenching pain can not be unlived, but, if faced with courage,
need not be lived again.*
　— Maya Angelou

Suffering in society

The collapse of the World Trade Center towers revealed the impulse for destruction in a few souls, but in many others, it revealed devotion to the pres-
ervation of life. As the towers began to collapse, complete strangers stopped
to comfort those with injuries, held the hand of frightened co-workers
racing down floor after floor, or threw themselves over a passing mother's
newborn infant on the street. The sheer numbers of heroic stories—as compared to the ugly profiles of the 19 hijackers—prove the compassionate side
of human nature and outshine the dark ones. More recent events in Iraq
and Afghanistan, as well as the human responses to tsunamis, earthquakes,
floods, and other natural disasters, prove the same point.

We have always needed social support for the protection of the helpless.
Humanitarian assistance has always helped survivors of trauma find some
shred of meaning in their tragedies. Social support represents a fundamental
aspect of the human attachment phenomenon, requiring a capacity for trust
and empathy. Fortunately, these qualities seem to be hardwired in the human
soul. During such disasters as terrorist attacks, combat, and other mass traumas, human relationships solidify and people help each other with an amazing
spirit of self-sacrifice and heroism.

The World Trade Center and Pentagon attacks are certainly not the
only recent examples. We witnessed this phenomenon during the genocide
of World War II and in many areas of political conflict around the world
since that time. In my own life, I encountered many such acts of compassion
during the years of persecution of the Baha'is in my country. Religious conviction often shields humans against trauma by re-framing calamities as a test of
God in the path of growth. It can turn a tragic incident into an exercise that
deepens the potential for coping. Shifting from the concepts of "self", "ego" or
"identity" to spiritual experiences of unity and cooperation removes the borrowed and deceptive imagery of the ego as a true entity and helps us to avoid
comparison, labeling, and prejudice.

Shortly after the 9/11 attack, authorities inaccurately accused several men of association with the terrorists, because of their suspicious sounding Middle Eastern names, their coincidental flight arrangements, or other unfortunate connections. These accusations were all based on stereotypes and the process of labeling. Many individuals with strong faith, whether Muslim, Jew, or Christian prayerfully endured interrogation without resenting their accusers. They knew their temporary incarceration was a small trial compared to the grief of those who had lost family members in the disaster. They said that all things happen for a reason and felt that this test could make them stronger.

The sacred writings of many religions present adversity and tribulation as God's providence. Trauma increases the depth of meaning in experiences of danger, betrayal, and death. It promotes spiritual growth and a rejection of egocentricity. Meaningless trauma seems devastating, but social context can strongly influence the way in which the trauma is interpreted. Yet, whenever conflicting individual values confuse the social meaning of trauma, blaming the victim becomes a temptation. Many women over the years have chosen not to pursue rape charges because of the likelihood that they would be blamed themselves—a common practice. When acts of war do not seem justified or do not find popular support, the soldiers who have been involved in the conflict may suffer deeper trauma scars.

In his book *The Broken Connection*, Lifton (1983) states that both society and the victim prefer to deny any accountability for trauma, since acceptance of responsibility reveals how fragile and vulnerable both individuals and the social system really are. The images incorporated in the self-identity, create a deceptive and unreal image of reality. Just as Narcissus fell in love with his own image in the pond and drowned when he dove in to capture the ideal image of himself, human beings develop unreal or deceptive self images, which they then fall in love with, leading them to deny responsibility for, or blame, their victims. The tendency, then, is to disavow or discredit the trauma. Victims typically do not express their emotions or memories correctly, making it even easier to blame them for the trauma. In Iran, where I grew up, whenever the government executed members of the Bahá'í Faith, the family had to pay for the bullets used to kill the person and take possession of their loved one's body for burial. Followers of the Baha'i Faith were and still are guilty of being "heretics," and "unclean spreaders of corruption" therefore, deserving greater punishment and degradation..

This same effect often holds true for many traumatized war veterans. Their loved ones, acquaintances, and society at large often suppresses their stories, and when they become agitated, despondent, or cruel, the victims are blamed for the undoing of their own character.

Justice is another major issue related to trauma. We often cling to the illusion of benevolence in our societies. Yet when massive numbers of people become victims of war or tragedy, we challenge the concept of justice. Responsibility for trauma becomes a dubious enterprise for the individual and for the society. Societies spend money to treat trauma victims, in order to suppress communal feelings of guilt, but resentment for these expenses reinforces the transfer of blame to the victims.

Chapter Fourteen: Transcending Trauma

You gain strength, courage and confidence with every experience in which you really stop to look fear in the face... You must do the thing you can not do.
    — Eleanor Roosevelt

Faith in human nature does not come easily for some, who usually point to the prevalence of war and violence throughout history as proof of the innate aggressiveness of man and the hopelessness of the human condition. They remind us that it is easy to show altruism and love for our families, but less common and more laborious to display loving altruism toward the entire human race. People struggle to accept foreigners, to trust strangers, or to avoid the exclusivity of us vs. them.

These nay-sayers have a good point. During the 20th century, somewhere between 110 and 240 million people died as a direct or indirect result of war and violence. The number of *civilian* casualties of war exceeded the loss of military personnel six times over.[60] Many of those who engaged in battle aspired to become heroes, to thwart their enemies and make their own people victorious and proud—that is, as defined by those who believe that human beings are innately aggressive.

Where does this perception come from? How can we find a more spiritual definition of heroism today, after witnessing the carnage left by so many wars? How can we turn trauma into transcendence and cynicism into hope? To answer these questions, we must first understand the side of human nature that fosters enemies in the first place.

---

60   Brzezinski, 1993.

In his pioneering work on child development, Rene Spitz (1959) recognized that the initial task of a human infant is to make distinctions between self and others, and between animate and inanimate objects. Any defect in the process of attachment and bonding between the human infant and its caregivers might impair the nurturing environment that teaches socialization. Instead, the child may develop a sense of abandonment and loss or may begin to protest, to make aggressive demands, or to become violent.

The initial community of two (the mother and the infant) helps the child incorporate a certain internal structure into his personality. Later social experiences solidify this inner structure. Initially, the child has a very limited sense of his own existence or boundaries. Gradually he recognizes that his pain and pleasure are strongly related to his mother's availability or distance. When a mother is available to meet her infant's needs, the child feels pleasure and comfort. Without her closeness, the child feels pain and anguish. Gradually, two inner images (a good and a bad mother) evolve. The unavailable mother is perceived as hateful, and the child's primitive feelings of hatred begin to expand to include the notion of an enemy or a danger. This process underlies the defense mechanisms of splitting and dissociation.

Separation sickness and loss of faith

As mentioned earlier, Western psychology attributes "separation sickness" to the loss of attachment and inadequate bonding with one's mother or primary caregiver (Cassidy and Shaver, 1999). Researchers studying comparative human and animal behaviors (Bowlby, 1965; Mahler, 1968) recognized that after a period of initial attraction to the mother, a symbiotic bond or coexistence develops. The child then gradually separates from his mother (at around age three), and when he has incorporated a complete inner representation of her, the process of separation-individuation evolves.

Premature separation from the mother or the mothering image during these formative years may create a "separation sickness" or anxiety/protest reaction called *reactive attachment disorder*. It may take the form of aggression, depression, sadness, grief, apprehension, addiction, or personality disorders such as narcissism. Not surprisingly, the Taliban's terrorist movement against the West employed young men who received their many years of training as orphans and refugees living in a military school. One of the pilots of the plane that first struck the World Trade towers could not even remember having a mother.

When a child is unable to experience trust, moments of pain make him feel utterly helpless. He may then project his agony onto others, taking on the role of victim and creating enemies in his mind. Violence is often a consequence of limitations or rigidity of possibilities. Under such conditions a person has to deal with environmental circumstances or threats with limited emotional capacities or options. The individual may regress to childhood paranoia and fears of violence. George Lucas created a metaphor for this concept in his epic Star Wars, revealing Darth Vader (the dark invader of the soul) as father to the hero, Luke.

The tendency to classify and compartmentalize teaches us to create enemies in our minds. Looking at humankind existentially, we find a more widely occurring form of "separation sickness"—some call it alienation—when the individual separates from his spiritual core. Erich Fromm, in his classic work *The Art of Loving*, considers the separation from such natural qualities to be the core of all human anxieties. A human being separated from his true nature cannot connect with his natural spiritual life. Having lost his childhood paradise, he feels alienated from other humans. He is lonely, helpless, and imprisoned in isolation. He tries to overcome his separation sickness with a variety of futile soothing behaviors. Spiritual splitting creates such a deep state of estrangement that it cannot be cured or treated with sensual experiences, alcohol, drugs, dependent relationships, conformity, or authoritarian behaviors. It responds only to a divine love and a devotion to God.

Spirituality can mean boundless freedom. To engage with one's spiritual identity is to loosen the power of religious institutions and take charge of your "self." It can open one's mind to the immensity of the bounties of the human soul. Contemplating spiritual reality brings a regeneration of hope and faith, as it allows one to contemplate how the divine and the human can flow together perfectly. It means seeing God as the source of love and life, as the essence of perfection. A person who is able to contemplate spiritual reality is in his best and deepest state of mind.

Spiritual people use limitations and suffering not to create enemies but as opportunities to help others. I learned this again and again when dealing with abused children and trauma survivors. I saw despair transformed into optimistic hope, and understood how time could become pregnant with new and exciting possibilities in the minds of these victims. No matter how horrible the trauma, hope moved the majority of victims toward virtue and greater contentment.

On October 7, 2001, the day the United States began retaliations for the terrorist attacks on New York and Washington, the *Los Angeles Times* featured an article, later published as *Positive effects of Terrorism and Posttraumatic Growth*[61] and a spate of studies showing the tendency of many trauma sufferers to enhance their lives after enduring painful experiences. The article quoted Richard Tedeschi, co-author of *Post Traumatic Growth*, as saying that two-thirds of the victims he studied showed growth in several ways, developing

- A greater appreciation for life
- Deeper spiritual beliefs
- A sense of strength and effectiveness
- Closer relationships with others
- Pursuit of unexpected paths.

Spirituality serves as the healing dimension that moves us toward growth. This capacity is unique to human beings. However, the regeneration of hope may require hard work and guidance from "spiritual" teachers who can help us to transcend absorption with self. The poet Rumi describes this absorption with a Sufi tale:

> A lover knocks on his lover's door.
>
> She asks, 'Who is it?'
>
> He responds, 'It is me, beloved.'
>
> To which she answers, 'There isn't sufficient room for both of us here.' She doesn't let him in.
>
> A year later he knocks again.
>
> 'Who is this?' she says.
>
> 'It is you,' he answers.
>
> And she replies: 'Come in.'

This capacity for feeling the oneness of a loving existence—the striving for transcendence—is actually hardwired in human nature and is so powerful that it can dominate our instincts. Perhaps the highest level of such loving devotion lies in the human capacity to love God. Human love for the Creator allows us to contemplate the will of God. It means being receptive to, submitting to, beseeching, devoting oneself to, or depending on, God's mercy, grace, and compassion.

---

61   Vasquez et al. 2007.

Some circles within Western culture portray this act of love for God in a negative light. They consider dependence on anything or anyone—including God—to be a form of psychological weakness. Despite the vast body of literature showing the clear and obvious relationship between unmet dependency needs and personality disorders, shame, anxiety, and madness, Western culture persists in valuing self-reliance above all.

Some Eastern cultures see love for God as the foundation of community and extended family. This kind of love generates a powerful spirit of cooperation, while lack of reliance on spiritual love and attendant moral values has led to our maddening struggle for independence and self-reliance. Fortunately, group therapy settings allow for the practice of family or community love and foster a kind of "maternal," nonjudgmental, accepting love.

Behind the act of love for God lies an incredible regenerative force that leads to a feeling of atonement and unity with others and with the universe. This unity becomes the antidote to alienation. Reliance on God ends separation sickness, thus limiting the scope and reach of emotional illness.

Approaching God

I have written this section for those who believe in God. For those who claim to be non- believers, I have no way to scientifically prove the existence of God. God is an unknowable essence or the foundation of being. Modern physics tells us that in the so-called Planck epoch (10^{-43} of the first second after the Big Bang),[62] all the major laws of physics were operational. If there was the minutest change in these laws and equations (10^{123}), there would be no universe!

In his brilliant essay *One Cosmos under God*, the philosopher psychologist Robert Godwin (2004) has presented excellent arguments for the existence of God, the "ultimate source of being," citing physics, evolution, Big Bang theory, anthropology, and mathematics. His views are corroborated

---

62   In physical cosmology, the Planck epoch—named after physicist Max Planck—is the earliest period of time in the history of the universe, from zero to approximately 10^{-43} seconds (one Planck time), during which quantum effects of gravity were significant. It could also be described as the earliest moment in time, as the Planck time is perhaps the shortest possible interval of time, and the Planck epoch lasted only this brief instant. At this point approximately 1.37×10^{10} years ago the force of gravity is believed to have been as strong as the other fundamental forces, which hints at the possibility that all the forces were unified.

by biologist Ludwig von Bertalanffy, the author of *General Systems Theory* (1975) who described the creator of the universe as a source of vast information and knowledge (Logos), leading the cosmos towards negative entropy and growth. A great number of modern scientists in the fields of biology, mathematics, physics, and cosmology agree with these authors that creation is not accidental but the product of a supreme intelligence.

Frames of reference and devotion

Before we discuss the processes of prayer and meditation it is necessary to clarify some important points. Human social structures function on the basis of two distinct frames of reference: one is scientific, focused on discovering and explaining the cause and effect aspects of reality, relationships, or activities of objects and living beings; the other is a devotional mindset that generates a sense of love, direction, and altruism, regardless of scientific judgments. The latter is the foundation of faith and religion—meaning "that which binds together"—in its pure form, as brought by the great Messengers of God, founders of the world's religions. It is now clear that these two frames of references must function in harmony in order to prevent superstition and prejudice, as well as aggressive, destructive, and evil actions.

Moreover, it is important to differentiate between the words "modern," "modernism" and "modernity" to avoid any confusion about our discussion of prayer and meditation. "Modern" refers to a new process or attitude as distinct from an old process, whether material or mental. No modern societies can take advantage of modern scientific knowledge and the physical products of such science and remain trapped in pre-modern prejudices and superstitions. But true modernity or modernism has to do with new and modern beliefs and practices. The age of enlightenment in Europe and later America triggered these modern behaviors, which revolve around the notions of individuality, the right and responsibility of the individual to search for truth independently, humanism, human nobility, rationalism, altruism, and moral responsibility.

The modern world view rejects many ancient concepts such as original sin and has concluded that the myths and legends in ancient religious texts are purely symbolic, not to be taken literally. Thus, the modern human family needs a frame of devotion in a religious system that accepts the harmony of science and faith. This system is cleansed of pre-judgments about others, and proclaims unity in diversity, justice, and moderation.

The reader may find it helpful to think of the sacred in terms of a new frame of devotion, in which God is understood as an "unknowable essence." In this understanding, prayer becomes a direct discourse with the Creator, open to all, and burning away all obstacles in the path of unity with God. Prayer goes far beyond the simple request for benefits. It consists of the recognition of our essential aloneness in God's presence and tapping into our deepest spiritual nature. Prayer helps mere mortals achieve harmony and integrity and allows unrelated thoughts and feelings to interact and regroup. Spiritual meditation in solitude also helps our brains to function at their highest potential.

Mindfulness and meditation: Buddha and Freud

Sati, Vipassana, or *mindfulness* is an experience of meditation that cannot be expressed in words or mental images. Sati is a pre-symbolic and spiritual experience, which demands that we suspend our mental faculties and thought processes. It is a form of healing silence.

Mindfulness is an ancient practice of transcendental self knowledge akin to modern free association, which tries to access the innate, intuitive, divine, archetypal and spiritual system of wisdom. Full awareness of experience, here and now, leads to exploration and discovery of hidden emotions, indicators of distress, symptoms, unspeakable truths, metaphors, themes and triggers of encoded or implied information, not available to the conscious stream of thought.

Robert Langs (1991) presents a dual system of human mind, which includes a conscious faculty for adaptation to reality and an unconscious system comprising of a fear/guilt complex and another deep system of wisdom inherently perceptive and knowledgeable. The defensive fear/guilt system raises a tireless voice of opposition to the search for truth. The deep wisdom system on the other hand according to Langs indicates "thinking carried out without awareness". This system deals with encoded, symbolic, derivative and poetic or metaphoric language. It can be accessed by daily practice of free association/mindfulness with an attempt to decode metaphoric symbols and their triggers.

I wish to add Rumi's metaphor of four birds of prey, to explain the four trouble making aspects of the ego to Lang's fear/guilt system. Those aspects include greed for power and wealth(The duck who searches for food incessantly), (The Rooster) for lust, (The Peacock) for vanity and (The Crow) for narcissism. According to Rumi and other Sufi sages the human accusing self (superego), creates guilt/shame and fear emotions as defensive mechanisms against these instinctual drives.

The symbols, images, and words used in everyday life and conscious thought are arbitrary and secondary processes, taught by our parents, educators, and the society around us. They often serve to disconnect us from the core of our being, and keep us tied to the mundane aspects of material life. Our existential core however is like a spiritual ray of light from the Creator connecting us to the world of spirit. Once again, Rumi expresses this idea beautifully, when he tells us:

I was a heavenly bird who did not see the mud below; now I am a bird of this world caught in the mud and unable to fly.

Falling from our innate unconscious and spiritual wisdom system to superficial and arbitrary conscious experiences, indeed symbolizes a fall from paradise.

Bahá'u'lláh used this same analogy of the bird in a slightly different way, saying:

O SON OF BEING!

The bird seeketh its nest; the nightingale the charm of the rose; whilst those birds, the hearts of men, content with transient dust, have strayed far from their eternal nest, and with eyes turned towards the slough of heedlessness are bereft of the glory of the divine presence. Alas! How strange and pitiful; for a mere cupful, they have turned away from the billowing seas of the Most High, and remained far from the most effulgent horizon.[63]

Everyday thought processes can be described as "colors" that envelop our transluscent spiritual nature, imposing invented roles, life scripts, beliefs, and preoccupations that keep our material life empty, futile, and often ugly. Even a cursory glance at the world around us today shows the destructive impact of these worthless secondary and borrowed values. It is as if our mundane thoughts become prisons for our souls, preventing spiritual progress and distracting us from love, unity, and true happiness. What we

---

63   Bahá'u'lláh, *The Hidden Words*, Persian, No. 2.

call consciousness is, in reality, a form of slumber to avoid dealing with our souls. Rumi, tells us that "those apparently awake, are indeed in deep sleep and tangled in delusion."

Rather than accepting the unity and wholeness of the soul, we divide our minds into compartments such as ego, superego, or id and give them a variety of deceptive names, as if they were real. The by-products of these mundane preoccupations are greed, the need for power, lust, vanity, and narcissism. These illusions cloud our minds and prevent us from engaging with reality and that which is truly meaningful.

The spiritual teachers of China, India, Iran, and some of western mystics now agree that daily meditation, mindfulness and free association, are healthy exercises that help to free us from the illusions of our very thought processes. When we are released from this imposed or borrowed self-identity, a new birth can take place and enable us to experience the divine.

The essence of the human being is spiritual wisdom called the holistic wisdom by Rumi and that which our minds conceive of as material reality is actually only a vague image or shadow— something like a holographic image—of a much greater reality. To leave this illusory world and arrive at spiritual truth, the Buddha, 2500 years ago, presented Vipassana or mindfulness as a pathway to spiritual life. He was aware that our first impressions of an event or entity— before our minds divide it into categories of appraisal—are pure and untainted by the conscious thought process. During these initial fleeting moments, we perceive everything in a state of unity with the cosmos and our mind has not yet identified "dog" or "chair." We perceive the dog or the chair without a name and as a non-entity, as part of world unity. Our awareness in these brief moments is deep and spiritual. Unfortunately, we begin, immediately, to appraise, classify, and categorize what we see into separate realities.

The main purpose of Vipassana is to extend these brief moments of deep awareness, to change our experience of life and move from mental illusions to spiritual reality and deep wisdom. Mindfulness enables us to create a mirror image of reality and move away from the conscious mental processes of the ego. In a state of mindfulness, one does not judge, appraise or categorize. One is not surprised, does not criticize, and perceives the world as a mirror of universal consciousness. Sadness, joy, hope, fear, anger, and other emotions are experienced naturally and do not lead to shame, guilt, fear, pride, or prestige. There are no opposites, no deception, and no denial.

One is mentally naked and cleansed of memories, beliefs, or thoughts. This is a state of "inner vision," not bound by the limitations of time and space. There is no more a "self," and one remains a simple viewer of change, birth, and death as they happen in a show of life. There are no prejudgments, but only pure detachment and transcendence. One becomes fully aware of the infinite wisdom within and is in touch with the suffering related to material attachments.

Hundreds of studies in both the East and the West, show that prayer and meditation relax the brain, as demonstrated on an EEG. Very much like biofeedback, it balances the entire autonomic nervous system, the heart, the pulse, the breathing, the blood pressure, the muscle tone, and even the body temperature. Increasing the alpha waves in the brain, it assists the processes of overcoming addiction, stress, overeating, negative emotions, and even cancer. Prayer makes us more alert, empathic, serene, secure, and self-confident.

Yoga or *yoke* means connection with God. As we practice meditation, depending on our individual capacity, these moments of "yoga" increase and soon we are able to have longer and longer periods of spiritual unity, along with deep relaxation and serenity. There are literally hundreds of books and special training centers for the practice of mindfulness and the reader has a wide choice of schools to attend and study. In my daily practice of meditation, I select a sacred, inspiring passage or mantra, and imagine my favorite vocalist chanting this mantra as I listen in my imagination. My mind will continue to distract me from my inner chant, but I don't resist. I allow any thought, image or emotion that comes to follow its course to the end as I am mindful of it. But whenever I catch myself distracted, I simply return to my inner chant.

The human soul with its capacity for awareness and consciousness of God is akin to a deep ocean, hiding within the walls of physical temple. This incredible spiritual capacity, can make us self-subsisting and independent of all else but God. The soul's relation to our body is almost like a mighty sun contained in an atom. The same way that we can not contain an ocean in a jar, we can not hold this incredible spiritual power in the frame of our physical bodies. Recognizing our capacity for God-consciousness shines the mirror of our hearts to such extent that we can understand the truth of God's creation.

Rumi's story of "Two Painters" is a wonderful metaphor in this regard. The Chinese artist who has asked for dyes, pigments and brushes creates a beautiful mural in his compartment of the hall. The Greek artisan, who has requested cleaning and shining materials, transforms his compartment to a hall of mirrors. When they pull the curtains between the two compartments, the Chinese mural appears far more glorious in the neighboring hall of mirrors.

We can free ourselves from physical attachments through meditative reflection and approach the realm of magnificence and meanings. The world of meaning is absolutely cohesive having no differentiations, comparisons, classes, differences, diversities or dualities. It is a holographic unity.

The only possible way of arriving at this form of meaning is through volition, meditation, patience, love, knowledge, responsibility, action, sacrifice and detachment. Yes a soul like a mirror cleansed off the dust of Ego defenses can reflect the world of spirit with much greater radiance.

As human beings we have free will and can decide personally to go for this ultimate search for God-consciousness. Spiritual progress is the work of the soul. It can only be acquired with love and without regards for space-time limitations. The reality of man is his capacity for awareness of unity with the creator (Yoga).

The scientific research referred to has shown the equal effectiveness of this mindfulness practice with other approaches to meditation, such as Chican, Kundalini, autogenic training, Morita, and Zikr.

During mindfulness we are in loving communion with our creator without awareness of our ego, personal identity, or conscious thought. We become aware of our emotionally charged triggers for behavior, decode our dreams, metaphoric expressions, associations and all encoded feelings or fantasies. We extract and become fully aware of their themes, search for their triggers and achieve knowledge. We connect with our inner deep wisdom system and grow.

The sacred literature of all the world's great religions prescribes prayer and meditation as the foundation of man's ability to know the will and purpose of God. Even the mention of God serves as a healing balm for all of the ills of man. The Koran symbolizes prayer as a ladder to heaven. Indeed, the holiest moments of life occur during loving, personal dialogue with the Creator. We soar on the wings of the soul to the divine presence of God. Enlightened and full of joy, the soul catches fire. Worshipping its Beloved without fear or desire and with complete detachment, it blossoms in the gentle rain of grace.

Prayer in action

Prayer enhances our capacity to respond consciously and thoughtfully, rather than instinctively, to what is happening in our environment. Prayer strengthens the capacity to delay response and to meditate on the consequences of an action, a capacity unique to humans among all living beings. The focus on communion with God transforms us into intelligent beings not immediately at the mercy of our instincts. In a prayer state, we overcome the barriers between the individual and the Absolute. We enter a mystical state and experience a deep oneness with the cosmos.__

People around the world pray in innumerable ways. A heartfelt conversation with God is only one form of prayer. Beautiful melodious prayers with music nourish the soul, generating a devotional attitude. Prayer based on inspirational verses and sacred writings lead to immense serenity, as one becomes mindful of life and the meaning of creation. Like a receiver free from all background noise, prayer invites contact with the divine. It allows us to retreat from the distractions of daily life and cares and an enormous freedom from the self.

The other form of prayer lies in action, specifically, in acts of love and attachment. A television documentary showcased the life of a soldier in Vietnam who had saved as many as 40 or 50 lives in one night on the battlefield, before giving up his own life under enemy fire. The program focused not so much on his story, but on the stories of those he saved: the children and grandchildren they had later raised, and what their lives had become in the 32 years since the event. The concluding remarks pointed out that perhaps many doctors, musicians, and other people who enlighten and nurture the world are alive today because of the heroism of this one 21-year old young man. As Nelson Mandela once said, "We are born to manifest the glory of God that is within us. It's not just in some of us; it's in everyone".

Recognition and development of our inner capacities and "gems" brings to life the pearls of beauty in the entire creation. The material and physical imperfections then lose their importance. We become spiritually free, not interested in controlling or manipulating others. We release others, letting everyone be him or herself. Loving becomes powerful and unlimited. We see no one as an untouchable. Everyone can share the beauty of life with us. All human beings appear as beautiful flowers in the human garden.

When we are spiritually free, we don't play with other people's emotions. We do not fear suffering and pain or feel troubled by death. There is no intolerable pain, as we submit our will to the will of God. We see everyone emerging in our lives as destined to help us grow. Spiritual relationships then become free and dynamic. They instill in us a sense of intense moral responsibility. Considering every human as equal and valuable, we act to end hunger and disease, crime and injustice, destruction of the environment, and all evil. We focus our energies on developing human perfections and capacities, walking with God and using every crisis to enhance our spiritual growth and freedom.

As illustrated in the "Lover's Journey," pain becomes the paramount and distinguishing feature of spiritual freedom and universal love. Depression, sadness, and grief are precursors of this spiritual freedom. They pull us away from superficial questions to deeper spiritual issues. As Thomas Moore stated in his book *Care of the Soul* (1992), they move us toward deeper reflection on how we relate to others and on how we can become instruments for service to humanity. Acceptance of our spiritual unity with others disengages us from our egos, and helps to generate true faith. We become aware of the unlimited and the miraculous. We can release our nightmares and awaken to a world of serenity and beauty. It is in this frame of mind that virtue, love, and morality become our main interests.

We are the recipients of a mighty culture of mysticism and spirituality from scholars and saints of the East and West. They all assure us there are no limits or boundaries to the human spiritual experience. We can confirm their claim by taking a few minutes to visit the continents of our soul and, in the process, witnessing incredible vistas that will leave us truly astonished.

When we immerse ourselves in this timeless, space-less world, our concentration and desire transform. The passing of time does not affect us anymore. We do not age. We shine in a new world of power, strength, and beauty. We feel privy to an awareness that nothing in this material world is more beautiful than truth. We can then fully realize this truth by finding our own unique approach to the divine and by seeking a vision of how our lives can become heroic instruments for good.

Spiritual heroism can bring the contenders of life and death together as enduring companions. That explains why we have witnessed a revolution of spirituality and meaning among the survivors of the Holocaust, the wars, and the epidemic of abuse and violence, which makes these people the heroes of modern times. A shift of emphasis in our spiritual experience can lead to transformation. Thus, the happy endings of mythological stories about the human soul lie not in merely accepting the contradictions of our spirits but in seeing our spiritual resilience as evidence of our capacity to transcend tragedy.

The contemporary traumatized and spiritual hero has to face a long period of obscurity during his time of greatest danger, setbacks, and tribulation. He is thrown inward, to his own depths, almost by force, and outward to the unknown. Like the characters in Mozart's "Magic Flute," he endures unexplored darkness on the path to transcendence. His guide may be an oppressive tyrant, or a helpful, loving friend leading him to revival and rebirth. To survive such experiences, the hero needs extraordinary patience and wisdom.

Serving humanity and adopting the spirit of sacrifice leads the traumatized hero to the status of moral leader. He or she can indeed become a saint. Endowed with pure understanding, self-restraint, firmness, and, having turned away from hatred, greed, and domination, he or she becomes worthy of unity with the imperishable. The traumatized hero is not frightened of death, as death serves as yet another step in the process of human transformation.

Mahatma Gandhi says:"The best way to find yourself is to loose yourself in the service of others". Individuals such as Somali Mam in Cambodia, Aung San Suu Kyi in Burma, Nelson Mandela in South Africa and Opra Winfrey in the U.S., are wonderful examples of traumatized heroes living among us.

Trauma work shows us that numbness and apathy do not stem from ignorance but from self-protection. We subconsciously fear reliving the despair that trauma situations arouse. Society compounds the problem by insisting on repression and creating taboos against the expression of anguish. The refusal to feel takes a heavy toll on the human soul. It hampers our capacity to process and respond. Those who would become heroes must learn that despair, grief, and rage can be confronted and creatively challenged.

The spiritual heroes of today are not manipulative, paternalistic authoritarians who know all. They do not approve of dictatorship or partisan politics, which are essentially divisive. They realize the deficiencies of power politics, narcissism, domination, and control of others, and of the selfish drive for status. Their orientation is fundamentally service to the common good, personal transformation, belief in the nobility of human beings, and spiritual transcendence. They believe in leadership through service, development of their own latent potential, and in their capacity to contribute to the advancement of human civilization. Their moral responsibilities include the search for truth and the application of that truth to daily life.

Chapter Fifteen: Freedom from the Self

Hundreds of authors have books and conducted research on the topic of the "self"—a never-ending scientific and spiritual debate. One excellent example come from Roy Mendelsohn, in his work *The Synthesis of Self* (1987), in which he discusses the "I" of consciousness. Another is found in *The Mind's I: Fantasies and Reflections on Self and Soul*, by Hofstadter and Dennett, who write in detail about the fantasies and reflections of the self and soul, in their quest to understand the essence of the human mind.

Heinz Kohut's 1971 book *Analysis of Self* took the field of psychoanalysis by storm and led to an explosion of research on the topics of self and narcissism. Kohut initially proposed a bipolar self comprised of two systems of narcissistic perfection: a) self ambitions and b) self ideals. He called the first the *narcissistic self*–later, the *grandiose self*–and the second *idealized parental images*. According to Kohut, these poles of the self represent natural stages in the psychic development of infants and toddlers. His ideas about "selfhood" or complete autonomy lie at the foundation of the prevalent Western approach to psychology and his models are used by many practitioners of psychotherapy and self help.

Many contemporary researchers argue that the preoccupation with independence is harmful, because it creates racial, sexual, and national division. The very notion of selfhood is being attacked because it is seen as necessary for the functioning of advanced capitalism. Psychology is today employed as a technology that allows humans to buy into an invented and arguably false sense of self. Such freedom may assist governments and industry to exploit the population as a whole. Some even go so far as to say that for an individual to talk about, explain, understand or judge oneself is linguistically impossible, since it requires the self to understand *itself*—a psychological impossibility. Moreover, this is seen as being philosophically invalid, since it is self-referential, implying that the self can explain the self.

Modern neuroscience has utilized a variety of technologies, such as the MRI and brain scans to prove that the self is a byproduct of brain function. There is some validity to this idea. The human brain consists of tens of billions of neurons and other cells, amazingly organized and interconnected with thousands of electro-chemical bonds, synapses, transmitters, peptides and hormones. A brief glance at the anatomy of the human brain shows that all inner and outer perceptions are registered on three levels: memory, recall, and recognition. We have billions of neurons involved in vast areas of the brain which deal with visual, auditory, tactile, motor, balance, taste, and smell memories—all connected to each other, in addition to those systems which handle appraisal, emotional reactions, language, the imagination, etc. These cells each function like living computer chips, all recording in a coordinated way unimaginably vast bits of information.

Every one of these information centers competes for our attention or thinking, depending on the strength of emotions attached to them and various inner or environmental triggers. So, in everyday life, our minds are like a battleground for these often contradictory thoughts, each one taking its turn and fading away as it is overwhelmed by other thoughts.

From the time we are born, most of us receive frequent messages from our care givers that we are unique and better than other children. We are told we deserve to be greater, that we were not meant to have unskilled or tedious jobs, and that such work is beneath our dignity. We must try to achieve distinction, become eminent, and leave the humble and demeaning jobs for others less worthy than ourselves.

But since most of us never achieve such a high station, we begin to feel inadequate or inferior. We seldom realize that our parents, teachers, and cultural guides were not interested in our spiritual qualities. Rather, their main concern was with our social roles and identities. They were teaching us how to play our part in the programmed family or social script.

Eckhart Tolle's writings on the topics of spirituality, self and flowering of human consciousness have created a revolution of awareness, very similar to metaphoric stories of Rumi in terms of human identification with the ego. Both Rumi and Tolle have tried to direct their readers from identification with perishable "forms" to imperishable "meaning" of life

Without reliance on our spiritual nature, we continue to compare, classify and infer. We admire or condemn. We show great interest—even esteem—for heroes and celebrities, chase after medals, standings and being "number one." We long for praise and adulation and feel satisfied when we achieve even minutes of fame. That kind of false "self" is enamored of authority figures and likes to follow them. It is terrified of and escapes from freedom. Not knowing what to do with liberty, it searches for anything that has the stamp of approval from external authorities in order to feel real.

The self, being, and existentialism

Our friend Rumi has a story about a man afflicted with *pica*—a medical disorder characterized by eating normally inedible substances—who is buying sugar in a grocery store. He realizes that the grocer's measuring weight is made of mud. He eats some of it on the sly, thinking he is clever. Yet he is losing his purchased sugar for cheap mud. We too, often exchange valuable objects for trash and our souls for gold.

Many of the so-called authorities whom we admire are afflicted with the same condition of *pica*: they seek our applause and not our freedom. They are indeed enemies, not friends. Rumi uses mud as a symbol of man's vanity and all that strengthens the "ego" or self-identity. The "self"—what he calls *nafs*—does not seek originality or meaning. It looks for games, scripts, and vain show. It wishes to obscure reality. It craves substitutes, not awakening.

The soul—in reality a mystery of God—does not experience inferiority, greed, fear, aggression, or annoyance. It is creative, loving, compassionate, curious, secure, and fashioned in the image of God. The soul is the deepest reality of our existence, and is what enables us to have virtue, to be imbued life with purpose and meaning, and to be of service to our fellow humans.

The "self" on the other hand appraises, deduces, admires, or labels to keep itself busy. It creates imaginary borders, norms, limitations, and walls. Nevertheless, the bulwark and fortifications of the "self" are insecure and shaky.

Approaching the soul through shared experience

Many authors have tried to explain the soul. I agree with author Larry Dossey (1989) that the human soul is not matter, energy, force, light, wave or particle, but, rather, an immaterial entity, which does not occupy space or time. Since the soul is a mystery, whose reality we cannot grasp, we have had no choice throughout history but to use symbols to try to define it. I like to think of the soul as an emanation from the boundless ocean of God's knowledge, working in harmony with the body, or, to use an analogy, what some might describe as a bird in a cage. Contemporary writers[64] on spiritual themes have attempted to describe the soul, using concepts, such as: "the zero point field," "the universal consciousness," "the force," "the depth experience," "the universal holomovement," etc. But most these descriptions are vague and unconvincing.

Spiritually speaking, the trauma sufferer has to bargain with meaning. Suffering transforms our mental functions to holographic processes. It enables the individual to abandon literalism and approach mystery. Literalism narrows the ambiguity of truth while symbolism, condensation, displacement, and imagery promote deeper penetration of reality and meaning.

Trauma victims may feel haunted or possessed by the ghosts and demons of fear, which contribute to their recurrent symptoms and contagion of their trauma emotions. Ordinary forms of endurance do not seem adequate to overcome such emotions. The trauma victim may respond better to therapy when it is combined with spiritual awareness. As we have already discussed, spiritually oriented survivor communities provide healing environments that create metaphors to memorialize trauma. They offer an atmosphere of security and a powerful "holding or supportive, environment."[65] In an atmosphere of humble, service-oriented individuals, other forms of therapy may also prove beneficial. Eventually the traumatized individual must create a commonality with fellow humans, which helps integrate PTSD symptoms as a growth enhancing phenomena.

---

64   See Mc Taggart (2008); Dyer (2001); Chopra (2004); Walsh (1998); Peck (1985); Penrose (1994); and Hillman (1996).

65   A "holding environment" is described as a nurturing, responsive atmosphere ; in therapy it refers to a milieu of psychological safety, which prevents the patient from acting out.

From the self to the soul

Once as a child I asked my father about the meaning of "soul." He said he didn't know how to explain the soul in words. "You know our blind neighbor Mr. H.," he said. "He was born blind. He has never experienced color or the light of the sun or the moon. There is no way I can explain color or light for him with words. When you lose a personal item such as a key or your school bag, I am sure you get nervous and begin right a way to search until you find it. Surprise! Surprise! Few of us humans search for our "soul" or "true self," which we often lose in the bustle of our everyday activities, desires, and attachments. As long as we feel comfortable and secure, we forget about the soul. If you want to learn about the soul you must use your inner vision. It is only the light in your heart that can appreciate the mystery. No one can help you do that. You are on your own. Now go and think about this. You will understand."

Years later, when I read the works of Carl Jung and Karen Horney, I realized that burial of the human being in the dark prison of the "self"—called the "cage" by the mystics—is an ancient human problem. The "self" somehow obscures and hides the "soul." Like smearing mud on a mirror, it blocks out the reflection of the shining sun. As humans we are not capable of fighting or defeating our "self- perceptions," since our conscious thoughts do not clearly understand what the "self" is.My grandfather, a Hassidic rabbi and well versed in the Kabbalah, often explained to us that before we can become spiritual beings we should break the vessel of our minds and prepare for salvation. He believed that all creation is a reflection of the glory of God and thus, at its core, spiritual. To make his point, he told us a Hassidic tale about the necessity of "self" deconstruction:

> There was once a glorious civilization of highly advanced people, living in a heavenly city and enjoying unsurpassed beauty.
>
> Due to certain natural disasters, these people had to be evacuated and placed temporarily in a desolate island close by. Their senses were deliberately dulled by the Creator, so that they would not suffer too much, since in their new abode, the only available food was cabbage.
>
> The first generation of people remembered the beauty of their homeland and longed for a speedy return. They had no choice but to adapt to their new desolate habitat. Their real world was destroyed and they could not recreate it.

The second generation started to doubt the existence of such a homeland and satisfied themselves with the only food available: cabbage. The third and fourth generations avoided talking about the possibility of such a homeland, while future generations prohibited such discussions altogether, and charged fines, and levied prison terms, even sentenced people to death for even talking about it!

Many years later, a messenger from the homeland arrived to announce the glad tiding that the promised "paradise" was now ready, that people could return and capture the glory of their past lives.

The messenger was captured, imprisoned, and sentenced to death for his crime. A few people who had become his disciples and who had been greatly moved by his sacrifice and love, decided to take the risk of swimming across the bay towards the Promised Land.

But some followers had doubts about the messenger's sincerity, and, fearing starvation, decided each to carry a big bag of cabbage with them on the journey, just in case. They all drowned in the sea and the rest of inhabitants remained captive in their island prison.

My grandfather insisted that this story illustrates our condition as human beings. Separated from our soul or spiritual core, we feel impotent to free ourselves from the base conditions we have accepted as reality. We do not know, what reality is, since our inner vision is blocked. We mistake our illusions, images, and maps of reality for absolute truth. We are incapable of breaking our vessel of selfishness in order to approach our souls.

I am convinced that we need a radical and revolutionary vision of human psychology as the supreme discipline of the soul. At the heart of this new vision, we need to accept the principle of the fundamental and spiritual unity of mankind. We need to develop an understanding not only of the individual "soul," but also of the "soul of the world." A return to the soul should, I believe, be considered as the central core of human life and psychology.

Contemporary assumptions about the healthy "self" or "self-actualization" are impossible strivings without a spiritual vision. Separated from our divinely given spiritual nature and mental and emotional slaves to everyday material existence, we do not understand much about the "cage" we live in, or how to deconstruct or renounce it.

As we look around at the world today, we can see that humanity is drowning in a swamp of pollution, war, death, hunger, abuse, violence, and misery. We protect ourselves from this ugly reality by drawing beautiful pictures of love as a sublimation defense of the ego.

To overcome this predicament, we need to suspend our conscious thoughts by meditation and prayer. Cleansing the "conscious self" does not mean rejecting our material lives. We can achieve freedom from the "self" through our actions by service to humanity and assumption of moral responsibility.

As I mentioned earlier, Rumi has yet another wonderful tale about cleansing the "self":

> Two painters, Chinese and Greek, each boast that he is the greatest artist in the world. To test their claims, people divide a big hall into two compartments separated by a tall curtain. The Chinese artist asks for brushes, paints, pigments, and dyes and draws a beautiful mural. The Greek artist asks only for cleaning materials. When each is finished with his "creation," the judges first visit the Chinese compartment and view the magnificent mural. But when they draw aside the curtain and see what the Greek artist has done, they find are in awe. For he has polished the walls of his compartment so that they gleam like mirrors, reflecting the beauty of the Chinese mural even more magnificently!

The recognition of our material limitations helps us understand the limitless infinity of the spiritual world. Death makes us aware of our primary human responsibility to make moral choices and for determining our destiny.

Ultimately, the language of the soul is poetic, symbolic, and mystical. It is beyond analysis and reflection. The very process of interpretation based on ego functions and defense mechanisms is suspect. Those interpretations from the colored glass of ego rob the potential mystery of the soul. The soul, being unrecognizable through the faculty of reason alone, needs spiritual interpretation for its symbols. Only communion with the Divine, through meditation and prayer, can achieve this. The soul, like the mythical phoenix, grows through adversity and afflictions, to enter the depths of spiritual experience and humility and prepare itself for an even more majestic rebirth.

Self identity

Psychological identity is an invention of the mind, its qualities all calculated on the basis of assigned or assumed social roles. Whereas the "self" (ego) deals in pretend maps and images of reality, the natural function of the mind is to acquire true knowledge.

Karen Horney, the author of Self Analysis (1968), compares the self with a prison and tries cleverly to shed light on all the corners of the prison of self. She does not realize however, that the prison of self is a dream created by the mind and not a true reality. Horney failed to appreciate that the inventions, interpretations, appraisals, and comparisons of the mind do not represent the reality of the mind. We cannot know our true and natural selves using only the yardstick of the mind or the ego.

Like many other analysts, Horney did not realize that without letting go of the self or suspension of our conscious thoughts, true insight is impossible. Insight can come about only when we shut our eyes to the self and open them to our inner vision.

In short, the "ego-self," is an addictive disease filled with splits, labels, classifications, comparisons, authoritarianism, prejudgments, and narcissism. Our true soul is often damaged by these deceptive images of the self, but we ignore the disaster and revert to our mundane, illusory song and dance. Freedom from the self can come only when we recognize the trickery of the mind and the dangers of imposed or borrowed social roles. The need for return to spontaneity and to our divine roots means that we must avoid being deceived by false conceptions. Mindfulness meditation has been proven by numerous researchers to increase human resilience as well as altruism.

The founders of the world's great religions all encourage us to free the bird of our souls from the cage of the "self." This same idea has been forcefully/clearly presented by Abraham Maslow in his The Farther Reaches of Human Nature (1971), devotes much attention to people he calls "transcenders" and "peakers," who model themselves on the saints, sages and prophets. In many of the world's sacred writings—as, indeed, in most languages and cultures—spiritual concepts are often referred to as feminine: the Bible refers to the "Bride of God;" nature is often called "Mother Earth;" the Gnostic traditions have an invocation to the "Holy Mother" or "bride of God;" Sophia is regarded by the Eastern Orthodox as the soul of the world; in ancient Greece, the soul was called psyche, or anima, a feminine entity. As a feminine symbol, the soul is bonded to the concepts of love, union, intimacy, communion, creativity, imagination, and mysticism. It is capable of miraculous healing when aided by faith.

To know the soul, we must open our eyes to reverence. We must absorb the metaphors that describe the soul as a source of imagery, poetry, art, music, and symbolism. The soul can be felt and touched, but not defined. The human spirit has a capacity for expansion and union with the universal consciousness. It evolves through the practice of knowledge, love, and will (conscious choice). It is attracted to beauty, harmony, and growth. It searches for the infinite, for truth and strives for true service, sacrifice, peace, and moral discipline. To this extent, it is a reflection of the Creator. The reader may find it helpful to refer to Spiritual Being, A User's Guide (1997), by Happy Dobbs, who discusses in great detail the relationship between spirituality and detachment, sacrifice, happiness, faith, love, service, virtues, and unity.

In the following passage, Bahá'u'lláh offers us a blueprint for the practice of spirituality:

> Be generous in prosperity, and thankful in adversity. Be worthy of the trust of thy neighbor, and look upon him with a bright and friendly face. Be a treasure to the poor, an admonisher to the rich, an answerer of the cry of the needy, a preserver of the sanctity of thy pledge. Be fair in thy judgment, and guarded in thy speech. Be unjust to no man, and show all meekness to all men. Be as a lamp unto them that walk in darkness, a joy to the sorrowful, a sea for the thirsty, a haven for the distressed, an upholder and defender of the victim of oppression. Let integrity and uprightness distinguish all thine acts. Be a home for the stranger, a balm to the suffering, a tower of strength for the fugitive. Be eyes to the blind, and a guiding light unto the feet of the erring. Be an ornament to the countenance of truth, a crown to the brow of fidelity, a pillar of the temple of righteousness, a breath of life to the body of mankind, an ensign of the hosts of justice, a luminary above the horizon of virtue, a dew to the soil of the human heart, an ark on the ocean of knowledge, a sun in the heaven of bounty, a gem on the diadem of wisdom, a shining light in the firmament of thy generation, a fruit upon the tree of humility.[66]

---

66   Bahá'u'lláh, *Epistle to the Son of the Wolf*, p. 93.

Chapter Sixteen: Conclusion—From Post-Traumatic Stress Disorder to Post-Traumatic Growth

Recognizing myself as a "wounded healer" in the field of psychiatry, and reflecting on my own trauma-crisis memories, I realized that I, too, had experienced a major transformation in my life, with multiple positive changes, especially during the years in medical school. My perspective had expanded and my sense of responsibility intensified. I felt more liberated and fulfilled, with a deepened sense of humor and resilience. I became more creative, and began to write poetry, prose, and many papers, and books. I also took a keener interest in social reform, women's rights, racism, and the ever-present abuse of children. These were all new fields of interest for me, truly manifestations of "post traumatic growth," or PTG.

Over the past few years, attention to this new field of trauma studies has grown significantly, and a plethora of research papers and books have emerged. Tedeschi and Calhoun (1998) have written extensively on this topic especially on the issues of prevalence, correlation with PTSD, and the main factors related to growth. The American Psychological Association Help Center website has a screening device (PTG Inventory), assisting individuals to assess their own post-trauma growth behaviors and attitudes. Items included in the inventory are:

- Changed life priorities
- Greater appreciation of the value of life
- Development of new interests
- Greater self reliance
- Better understanding of spiritual matters

- New life paths
- Greater capacity for intimacy
- Greater expression of emotions
- Exploration of new opportunities
- Greater compassion
- Stronger faith

PTG is fairly common, occurring in some 60 to 70 percent of traumatized people, and manifesting particularly as positive changes in self-perception, relationships, philosophy of life, and empathy. Patricia Frazier and her colleagues at the University of Minnesota completed a longitudinal research project on sexual abuse victims to assess the prevalence of PTG. They investigated coping strategies and perceived sense of control. In a population of 174 female sexual assault survivors, they found PTG in 46 to 80 percent of cases, depending on the time elapsed between the traumatic events and the period of growth. Similar studies on individuals with PTSD and substance abuse revealed greater maturation and responsibility, increased perspective and self-awareness, a sense of liberation, fulfillment, and contentment.

During my years of service to war veterans in Los Angeles, I noticed that some felt their lives to have been enlarged by the sufferings of war. One of the Gulf War veterans discussed his harrowing story, which led to the loss of one leg and tremendous suffering. But he reported feeling richer, wiser, more compassionate, and more appreciative of life. Asked whether he would endure it all again, he replied, "The guys I served with were awesome. . . I would go through it again for the guys I served with. Yes, absolutely. I wouldn't change it for the world."

The potential of combat to inflict psychic wounds has been known since the time of the ancient Greeks, but if we contemplate each of the heroes and heroines in all the cultures of the world, each had to face his or her own dragon. Most people by now have some knowledge of the symptoms and agonies of PTSD. However, PTG or post-traumatic *growth* is the experience or expression of positive life change as an outcome of calamities, adversities, or life crisis, the proverbial "silver lining" on the dark cloud. Dr. Mark Chesler and his colleagues studied survivors of childhood cancer and came to the conclusion that PTG is different from simple resilience. They consider resilience to be the process of bouncing back, but PTG to be a form of thriving and reaching higher levels of functioning. PTSD and PTG can exist together in the same individual, but the ability to integrate trauma memories and the details of suffering into one's life and yet thrive is essential features of PTG.

Conceptual models of post-traumatic growth (PTG)

As discussed in greater detail in chapter 3, Jannof-Bulman's research in 1992 shed further light on the concept of shattered assumptions in PTSD. It seems that a form of spiritual-cognitive processing moves individual victims of trauma in the opposite direction, towards psychological thriving. It may come as a surprise to some to realize that PTG, as an outcome of human attempts to cope with adversities, is far more prevalent than PTSD, although some overlap may occur.

Historically, Hebrews, Greeks, Hindus, Christians, and Muslims knew the essence of PTG long ago, that "calamity" can be "providential."[67] The transformative effect of calamity was observed after the crucifixion of Jesus and the millennia of holocausts against the Jewish people and others. A metaphor related to this phenomenon of growth is the attack of anteaters on ant colonies. Usually within a few days after attack the size of colonies and their organization multiplies with stronger soldiers, food gatherers, and reproduction. In Islam, suffering and the death of the self is the main goal of God for man in reaching spiritual transcendence.

The 20th century has seen an explosion of psychological writing on growth, self-actualization, and the search for meaning. Some of these writers such as Frankl, Maslow, Yalom, and Kaplan became something akin to folk heroes and gurus themselves. However, systematic research on PTG began in 1990 with populations of cancer patients, transplant receivers, accident and sexual assault victims, casualties of war, refugees, and hostages.

Tedeschi and Calhoun first used the phrase posttraumatic growth in 1996, but earlier researchers had used similar concepts, such as "stress related growth," "flourishing," "search for meaning," "thriving," and "transformational coping," to express the same idea. These concepts were generally linked with resilience, optimism, and hardiness.

PTG occurs mostly in adults and teen-agers, not children. However,

---

67   Bahá'u'lláh, *The Hidden Words*, Arabic, No. 51: "My calamity is My providence, outwardly it is fire and vengeance, but inwardly it is light and mercy. . ."

during the St. Louis resilience studies, Anthony and Cohler (1987) reported a number of "super kids" displaying many of the characteristics of PTG.

Stages of PTG

1. Initially a traumatic event destroys the individual's assumptions about benevolence and safety, with attendant devastation of predictability, control, safety, decency, identity, and faith;

2. Traumatized individuals then search for new paradigms of security; according to Tedeschi and Calhoun, they struggle with new realities caused by trauma, as in the aftermath of an earthquake;

3. Later on, a process of cognitive re-structuring and re-framing takes place, resulting in new mental constructs, which are shock resistant and robust.

The lessons learned from adversity and disaster can be both emotional and rational. They change the personality structure, and lead to greater courage and new value systems. Nevertheless the memories of trauma events may persist, causing distress and anxiety. The PTG inventory (PTGI) developed by Tedeschi and Calhoun surveys several domains of growth and include among the 21 items issues such as greater appreciation of life, new sense of priorities, greater empathy and more intimate relations, feelings of personal strength, recognition of new opportunities, and spiritual/existential growth.

My own earlier research (1984) on rape trauma victims identified two major personal characteristics in individuals who tended to recover quickly and move on: a) a positive approach and greater sense of autonomy and b) a greater ability to seek out others for help, coupled with behaviors that elicit caring impulses in others. Other researchers in the field referred to learned optimism, resulting in greater openness to new experiences and advancement.

As we have seen earlier, disclosure of trauma memories to others especially within a supportive survivor group and positive contemplation of the past eventually leads to the formation of a complete narrative. This is the ultimate antidote to PTSD and has been faithfully practiced for centuries by Jewish people around the world. Such coping behaviors are transformational in nature; create new meanings, new goals, and a tendency to work through trauma effects. The individual moves from homeostasis and balance to heterostasis and change. Self-regulation improves and there is a realization that old viewpoints and habits of life were only meaningful before the trauma events. Now, the time has come to change them. Perhaps these traumas were the most important happenings, waking people up to the need to change their life style. In this sense, then, the traumatic events become triggers for wisdom and new insight.

An interesting extension of this topic relates to positive events such as childbirth, marriage, religious, or other peak experiences, identification with important movements, ideas or people at an opportune time, all of which work as a mental mutation to cause spiritual growth. After all, is not wisdom, in and of itself, the by-product of positive or negative events which gradually lead to mastery, greater competence, and the development of new resources for coping?

Major traumas create a state of limbo, as formerly established life scripts and roles shatter and the person become de-individualized. The necessity for change then leads to new scripts and roles in which the world is perceived from a more "selfless" position. Prejudgments, prejudices, and pastime schedules are shed, as trauma removes the veil of self like a Zen *kōan*.[68] According to Janoff-Bulman, (1992) cognitive re-processing leads to greater mental preparedness, existential re-evaluation, and emotional strength. The self, transformed in this way, understands narrative much better and the use of culturally meaningful metaphors helps the individual find a positive and coherent conclusion to suffering.

This form of growth should not be mistaken for situations of denial, dissociation, or lying for secondary gain. After all is said and done, we cannot expect all trauma victims to display post-traumatic growth, much less blame them for having PTSD. The community would prefer to ignore or deny the pain of PTSD. Thus, the concept of PTG should not be used to generate false hopes or to blame victims for not having "normal" personalities. This negative response can be dangerous, tempting us to be complacent about the existence of PTG in some individuals, and discount the significance of the evil, pain, and suffering which caused the PTSD in the first place.

---

68   A koan is a story, dialogue, question, or statement in the history and lore of Zen Buddhism, generally containing aspects that are inaccessible to rational understanding, yet may be accessible to intuition. A famous koan is: "Two hands clap and there is a sound; what is the sound of one hand?"

Post-traumatic growth and well-being

Dr. Martin Seligman (2002), one of the gurus of positive psychology, expressed concern that 60 years of effort and $30 billion of expense lavished on making dysfunctional people "functional" had not generated any greater sense of happiness. He felt the time had arrived for psychology to move towards more positive aspects of life and the issue of well-being. He presented a happiness equation as: $H=S+C+V$, where "H" represents enduring happiness, "S" genetic and inherited qualities, "C" life and environmental circumstances, and "V" voluntary control. He believes that we do not have much influence over "S" and "C", but we do have the ability to increase our overall well-being and happiness by 40 percent through voluntary activities such as sensory enjoyment, full absorption in various daily tasks, and meaningful service to others. These are some of the positive characteristics that we observe in people with PTG.

Individuals with PTG experience a deeper sense of contentment and satisfaction, hope, and optimism about future, as well as a higher capacity for love. They are brave, forgiving, and spiritual, and are able to enjoy vocations, appreciate beauty, capitalize on their talents, display wisdom, and possess good social skills. Human strengths achieved through the experience of adversity act as buffers against emotional illness, making the person more virtuous. We see in PTG a resurgence of faith, an improved work ethic, honesty, hope, perseverance, insight, and world-mindedness. Self-determination leads to greater competence, feelings of belonging, as well as personal autonomy.

In order to be helpful to the victims of trauma, it is important to explore spirituality, creativity, peak experiences, and wisdom, as is highly prized in all cultures. Wisdom is the cumulative result of organizing knowledge in the pursuit of excellence, in other words, expert knowledge about the fundamental and pragmatic issues of existence. How amazing it is that so many individuals, possessing great wisdom, were exposed to unusually adverse situations in their lives. These experiences enhanced their creativity and enjoyment of life, long-term happiness, authenticity, sense of realism, and, ultimately, their well-being.

A final word to my readers

This book has been written in response to requests from several hundred of my patients who had shared their journey of recovery with me. Perhaps there was a conscious wish on their part to have a concise reference to the course of their suffering and final arrival at a new definition of PTSD: Peace, Tranquility, Serenity, and Dignity. Some might also have need of a transitional "object"—such as this book—to make our bond symbolically permanent.

I wish to extend my deepest thanks to all those individuals and families who have been in treatment with me, and who have been my greatest teachers in the practice of my craft. I earnestly hope that my readers will find this book helpful.

Ebrahim Amanat, MD

References

'Abdu'l-Bahá, *Paris Talks*, London, Bahá'í Publishing Trust, 1969.

—— *Selections from the Writings of 'Abdu'l-Bahá*, Wilmette, IL, Bahá'í Publishing Trust, 1982.

—— *The Promulgation of Universal Peace*, Wilmette, IL, Bahá'í Publishing Trust, 1982.

Ainsworth-Land, G., *Grow or Die: The Unifying Principle of Transformation*, New York, John Wiley and Sons, Inc. 1986.

Alexander, F., *Psychosomatic Medicine: Its Principles and Applications*, New York, W. W. Norton, 1950.

Amanat, E., "Borderline psychopathology and incest," in Anthony and Gilpin, (Eds.) *Three further clinical faces of childhood* (1981), pp. 36–73.

—— "Rape Trauma Syndrome: Developmental Variations," in Stuart and Greer, *Victims*, 1984, pp. 36–56.

Andersen, H. C., *The True Story of My Life*. London, Longman, Brown, Green, Longman, 1847.

Anthony, E. J., "Risk, Vulnerability, and Resilience," in Anthony and Cohler, *The Invulnerable Child*.

Anthony, E. J. and B. J. Cohler, *The Invulnerable Child*, (St. Louis Risk Research Project), New York, The Guilford Press, 1987.

Anthony, E. J. and D. C. Gilpin, (eds.), *Three Further Clinical Faces of Childhood*, New York, SP Medical and Scientific books, 1981.

Arnold, M., *Emotion and Personality*, Vols. 1 and 2, New York, Columbia University Press, 1960.

—— *Feelings and Emotions*, The Loyola Symposium, New York, Academic Press, 1970.

Attar, F-D., *The Conference of the Birds*, New York, Penguin Classics, 1984.

Bahá'í Prayers, Wilmette, IL, Bahá'í Publishing Trust, 1988.

Bahá'u'lláh, *Epistle to the Son of the Wolf*, Wilmette, IL, Bahá'í Publishing Trust, 1988.

—— *Gleanings from the Writings of Bahá'u'lláh*, Wilmette, IL, Bahá'í Publishing Trust, 1983.

—— *The Hidden Words*, (Arabic and Persian), Wilmette, IL, Bahá'í Publishing Trust, 1982.

—— *Selected Writings of Bahá'u'lláh*, Wilmette, IL, Bahá'í Publishing Trust, 1979.

—— *The Seven Valleys and The Four Valleys*, Hofheim-Langenhain, Baha'i-Verlag GmbH, 1988.

—— *Tablets of Bahá'u'lláh*, Haifa, Israel, Baha'i World Center, 1978.

Banquet, J. P., "Spectral analysis of the EEG in meditation," *Electroencephalographic Clinical Neurophysiology* 35:143–151, 1973.

Barlow, H., *Dead for Good: Martyrdom and the Rise of Suicide Bomber*, Boulder, CO, Paradigm Publishers, 2007.

Benson, H., *Timeless Healing*, New York, Fireside Press, 1996.

Berne, E., *Sex in Human Loving*, New York, Pocket Books, 1976.

von Bertelanffy, L., *General Systems Theory: Foundations, Development, Applications*, New York, George Braziller, 1975.

Binswanger, L. *Being in the World*, New York, Harper and Row, 1963.

Bloom, Mia, *Dying to Kill*, New York, Columbia University Press, 2005.

Bohm, D., *Wholeness and the Implicate Order*, London, Routledge and Kegan Paul, 1980.

Bohr, N., *Atomic Physics and Human Knowledge*, New York, Vantage Press, 1966.

Bowlby, J., *Maternal care and mental health*, Columbia University Press, 1951. (Reprinted and abridged as *Child Care and the Growth of Love*, New York, Penguin Books, 1965.

Braid, J., *The physiology of fascination (Part 1) and The critics criticized (Part II)*, Manchester, UK, Grant and Co., 1855.

Brende, J. O., "Twelve Themes and Spiritual Steps," in Everly, G. S. Jr. and J. M. Lating (eds.), *Psychotraumatology*, New York, Plenum Press, 1995.

Briere, J. and C. Scott, *Principles of Trauma Therapy*, Thousand Oaks, CA, Sage Publications, 2006.

Briquet, P., *Traité clinique et thérapeutique de l'hystérie* [Clinical and therapeutic treatise on hysteria], Paris: Ballière, 1859.

Breuer, J. and S. Freud, *Studies on hysteria*, Standard edition 2, London, Hogarth Press, 1955.

Brzezinski, Z., *Out of Control: Global Turmoil on the Eve of the 21st Century*, New York, Touchstone Press, 1993.

Buber, M, *I and Thou*, New York, Macmillan Publishing Company, 1974.

Burgess, A. W. and Holstrum, L., "Rape Trauma Syndrome," *American Journal of Psychiatry* 131:981–986, 1974.

—— "Adaptive Strategies and recovery from rape," *American Journal of Psychiatry* 136:1278- 82, 1979.

Byman, D. *The Five Front War*, New York, Wiley and Sons, 2008.

Byrd, R. C., "Positive therapeutic effects of intercessory prayer in a coronary care unit population," *Southern Medical Journal* 1 (7), July 1988.

Calhoun, L. G. and R. G. Tedeschi, *Handbook of Post Traumatic Growth*, Lawrence Earlman Associates, 2006.

Campbell, J., *The Hero With a Thousand Faces*, Bollingen Series XVII, 2nd ed., Princeton, NJ, Princeton University Press, 1968.

—— *The Masks of God: Oriental Mythology*, New York, Penguin Books, 1976.

Camus, A.: The Stranger, Knopf, New York, 1954.

Cassidy, J. S. and P. R. Shaver (eds.), *Handbook of Attachment: Theory, Research and Clinical Application*, New York, Guildford Press, 1999.

Change, Watzlawick, P. and Weakland, J.: New York, Norton 1974.

Charcot, J. M., "Lessons on the illnesses of the nervous system held at the Salpêtrière," in Delahaye, A. and E. Lecrosnie, *Progrès Médical*, Paris, 1887.

Chess, S. and A. Thomas, *Origins and Evolution of Behavior Disorders*, New York, Brunner/Mazel, 1984.

Chopra, D., *The Book of Secrets*, New York, Random House, 2004.

Cicchetti, D. and S. Toth, Child Maltreatment: Theory and Research on the Causes and Consequences of Child Abuse, Cambridge University Press, 1998.

—— (eds.), *Rochester Symposium on Developmental Psychopathology: Disorders and Dysfunctions of the Self*, New York, University of Rochester Press, 1994.

Cloninger, C. R. and S. B. Guze, "Hysteria and Parental Psychiatric Illness," *Psychological Medicine* 5, 1975.

Cloninger, C. R., R. L. Martin, S. B. Guze, and P. J. Clayton, "A Prospective Follow up and Family Study of Somatization in Men and Women," *American Journal of Psychiatry* 143: 873–878, 1986.

Cousins, N., *The Healing Heart*, New York, Norton, 1983.

Danieli, Y., "Differing Adaptational Styles in Families of Survivors of the Nazi Holocaust," *Children Today* 10:6–10, 1981.

Das, N. and Gastaut, H., «Variations de l'activité électrique du cerveau, du cœur et des muscles squélettiques à la cour de la méditation et de "l'extase" yoguique,» *Electroencephalographic clinical neurophysiology* 5, 1956.

Davis, P., *God and the New Physics*, New York, Simon and Schuster, 1983.

—— *Reagan's America*, New York, Institute for Psychohistory, 1984.

—— "The History of Child Abuse," *The Journal of Psychohistory* 25(3), 1998.

—— *Emotional Life of Nations*, New York, Other Press, 2002.

Diagnostic and Statistical Manual of Mental Disorders, First Ed., Washington, DC, American Psychiatric Association. 1952.

Dobbs, H., *Spiritual Being: A User's Guide*, Oxford, George Ronald, 1997.

Dolin, R. and Bolton, P., *Race, Religion and Ethnicity in Disaster Recovery*, Boulder, Colorado, University of Colorado Press, 1986.

Dossey, L., *Recovering the Soul*. New York, Bantam Books, 1989.

Douki, S., F. Nacef, A. Belhadj, A. Bouasker, and R. Ghachem, "Violence Against Women in Arab and Islamic Countries," Archives of Women's Mental Health, 6(3):165–171, August, 2003.

Dyer, W., *There's a Spiritual Solution for Every Problem*, New York, Harper Collins, 2001.

Eccles, J., *How the Self Controls Its Brain*, New York, Springer-Verlag, 1994.

Eliot, T. S., *Waste Land and Other Poems*. London, Faber and Faber, 1973.

Elkins, D. N., L. J. Headstrum, L. L. Hughes, J. A. Leaf, and C. Saunders, "Towards a Humanistic Phenomenological Spirituality," *Journal of Humanistic Psychology* 28(4), 1988.

Elkins, D., "Psychotherapy and Spirituality: Towards a Theory of the Soul," *Journal of Humanistic Psychology* 35, 1995.

Ellis, E. M., B. M. Atkeson, and K. S. Calhoun, "An assessment of Long-Term Reaction to Rape," *Journal of Abnormal Psychology* 90, 1981.

Erickson, M. H., "Further experimental investigation of hypnosis: Hypnotic and non-hypnotic realities," in E. Rossi (ed.), *The Collected Papers of Milton H. Erickson on Hypnosis. I. The Nature of Hypnosis and Suggestion*, New York, Irvington, 1967–1980.

Esslemont, J. E., *Baha'u'llah and the New Era*, Wilmette, Bahá'í Publishing, 2006.

Fenwick, P. B. C., S. Donaldson, L. Gillis, J. Bushman, G. W. Fenton, and I. P. Tilsley, "Metabolic and EEG Changes during Transcendental Meditation: An Explanation," *Biological Psychology* 5, 1977.

Foa, E. B., *Effective Treatments for PTSD*, New York, Guilford, 2002.

Frankl, V. E., *Man's Search for Meaning*, New York, Washington Square, 1963.

Frazer, Sir J. G., The Golden Bough,

Freud, S., *On the Physical Mechanisms of Hysterical Phenomena*. Standard Edition, London, Hogarth Press, 1962.

—— "The Etiology of Hysteria," in J. Strachey (Ed. and trans.) *Standard edition of the complete psychological works of Sigmund Freud*, Vol.15, London, Hogarth Press 1962.

Fromm, E., *The Art of Loving*, New York, Bantam Books, 1968.

—— *The Heart of Man*, New York, Harper and Row, 1971.

—— *Anatomy of Human Destructiveness*, New York, Henry Holt and Co., 1991.

Galbraith, J. K., *The Affluent Society*, New York, Haughton Mifflin and Co. 1998.

al-Ghazzali, Abu Hamid Mohammad, in *Kitab-i Kimiay-i-Seadat* [The Alchemy of Happiness], Teheran, Markazi Booksellers, 1973. (Original Persian text)

Godwin, R., *One Cosmos under God: The Unification of Matter, Life, Mind and Spirit*, St. Paul, MN, Paragon House, 2004.

Goertzel, V. and M. G. Goertzel, *Cradles of Eminence*, Boston, Little Brown, 1962.

Goldberg, A., *The Evolution of Self Psychology*, New York, Routledge, 1991.

Gordon, D., *Therapeutic Metaphors: Helping Others Through the Looking Glass*, Cupertino, CA, Meta Publications, 1978.

Grinder J. and R. Bandler, *The Structure of Magic*, Palo Alto, CA, Science and Behavior Books, Inc., 1976.

Grinder, R. R. and J. P. Spiegel, *Men under Stress*, Philadelphia, PA, Blakiston, 1945.

Griset, P. L. and S. Mahan, *Terrorism in Perspective*, Thousand Oaks, CA, Sage Publications, 2003.

Guze, S. B., "The Validity and Significance of the Clinical Diagnosis of Hysteria (Briquet's Syndrome)," *American Journal of Psychiatry* 132:138–141, 1975.

Hales, R., S. C. Yudofsky, and J. Talbot, *American Psychiatric Press textbook of Psychiatry*, 2nd ed., Washington, D.C., 1994.

Hamer, D., *The God Gene*, New York, Doubleday, 2004.

Hamilton, Edith, *Mythology: Timeless Tales of Gods and Heroes*, Boston, Mentor Books, 1942.

Hatcher, J. S., *The Arc of Ascent*, Oxford, George Ronald, 1994.

Hepburn, S. and R. J. Simon, *Women's Roles and Statuses the World Over*, New York, Springer, 2006.

Herman, J. L., "Complex PTSD," *Journal of Traumatic Stress* 5(3), 1992.

Hillman, J., *The Soul's Code*, New York, Warner Books, 1997.

—— A *Terrible Love of War*, New York, Penguin Press, 2004.

Hofstadter, D. and D. C. Dennett, *The Mind's I: Fantasies and Reflections on Self and Soul*, New York, Bantam, 1981.

Holmes, M. R. and J. S. St. Lawrence, "Treatment of Rape Induced Trauma," *Clinical Psychology Review* 3, 1983.

Hooley, J. M., "The Nature and Origins of Expressed Emotion," in Hahlweg K. and M. J. Goldstien (eds.) *Understanding Major Mental Disorders: The Contribution of Family Interaction Research*, New York, Family Process Press, 1987.

Horgan, J., *The End of Science: Facing the Limits of Science in the Twilight of the Scientific Age*, New York, Broadway Books, 1996.

Horney, K., *Self Analysis*, New York, W. W. Norton, 1968.

—— *Neurosis and Human Growth*, New York, W.W. Norton and Co., 1970.

Horowitz, M. J, *Stress Response Syndrome*, Northvale, NJ, Jason Aronson Inc.1986.

James, W., *The Varieties of Religious Experience*, Cambridge, MA, Harvard University Press, 1985.

Janet, P., *L'automatisme psychologique*, Paris, Felix Alcan, 1889.

—— The Mental State of Hystericals, Paris, Alcan, 1911.

—— The Major Symptoms of Hysteria, New York, Hafner, 1920.

Janoff-Bulman, R., *Shattered Assumptions: Towards a New Psychology of Trauma*, New York, Free Press, 1992.

Jung, C. G., *Modern Man in Search of a Soul*. New York, Harcourt Brace, 1933.

—— *Memories, Dreams and Reflections*, New York, Vintage Press, 1989.

Kafka, F., *I Am a Memory Come Alive*, New York, Schocken Books, 1974.

Kaplan, H. I., and B. J. Sadock, *Synopsis of Psychiatry: Behavioral Sciences/Clinical Psychiatry*, 10th ed., Philadelphia, Lippincott Williams and Wilkins, 2008.

Kaplan, L. J., *Oneness and Separateness: From Infant to Individual*, New York, Simon and Schuster, 1978.

Kardiner, A. and H. Spiegel, *War Stress and Neurotic Illness*, New York, Hoeber, 1947.

Kardiner, A., *The Traumatic Neuroses of War*, New York, Hoeber Books, 1941.

Keane, T. M., "Post-Traumatic Stress Disorder: Current Status and Future Directions," *Behavior Therapy* 20, 1989.

Keats, J., "Ode to a Nightingale," in Jack Stillinger (ed.), *John Keats: Complete Poems*, Cambridge, Mass., Harvard University Press, 1982.

Kilpatrick, D. G. and L. J. Veronen, "Treatment for Rape-Related Problems," in L. H. Cohen, W. L. Claiborn, and G. A. Specter (eds.), *Crisis Intervention*, New York, Human Services Press, 1983.

Kilpatrick, D. G., C. L. Best, and L. J. Veronen, "Factors Predicting Psychological Distress among Rape Victims," in C. R. Figley (ed.), *Trauma and Its Wake*, New York, Bruner Mazel, 1985.

Kohut, H., *The Analysis of the Self*, New York, International University Press, 1971.

van der Kolk, B.A., *Psychological Trauma*, Washington, American Psychiatric Press, 1987.

van der Kolk, B.A., A. C. McFarlane, and L. Weisaeth, *Traumatic Stress*, New York, The Guilford Press, 1996.

Kopp, S., *If You Meet the Buddha on the Road, Kill Him*, New York, Bantam New Age Books, 1976.

—— *Raise Your Right hand Against Fear: Extend the Other in Compassion*, Minneapolis, MN, CompCare Publishers, 1988.

—— *The Pickpocket and the Saint: Free Play of the Imagination*, New York, Bantam New Age Books, 1983.

Kreisman, J. and H. Straus, *I hate You, Don't leave me!* New York, Avon, 1991.

Krystal, H. (ed.), *Massive Psychic Trauma*, New York, International Universities Press, 1968.

—— "Integration and Self-Healing in PTSD," *Journal of General Psychiatry*, 14(2), 1981.

—— *Integration and Self-Healing: Affect, Trauma, Alexithymia*, Hillsdale, NJ, Analytic Press, 1988.

Kuhn, T. H., *The Structure of Scientific Revolutions*, Chicago, University of Chicago Press, 1962.

Kulka, R. A., W. E. Schelenger, J. A. Fairbank, R. L., B. K. Jordan, and C. R. Marmar, *The National Vietnam Veteran's Readjustment Study*, New York, Bruner/Mazel, 1990.

Langs, R., *Psychotherapy: A Basic Text*, New York, Jason Aronson, 1982.

_____ "Take Charge of Your Emotional Life" Self-Analysis Day by Day, New York, Henry Holt and Company, 1991

Levi, H., *History of Jews in Iran*, Los Angeles, Mazda Publishers, 1999.

Lia, B., *Architect of Global Jihad*, New York, Columbia University Press, 2008.

Lifton, R. J., "Psychological Effects of the Atomic Bomb in Hiroshima: The Theme of Death," *Daedalus* 92, 1963.

—— *The Broken Connection*, New York, Basic Books, 1983.

—— *Death in Life: Survivors of Hiroshima*, Random House, New York, 1967.

—— *Home from War*, New York, Simon and Schuster, 1973.

Lutherville, M. D., (ed.) *Dissociative Disorders: A Clinical Review*, Baltimore, Sidran Press, 1993.

MacLean, P. D., "Psychosomatic Disease and the Visceral Brain," *Psychosomatic Medicine* 11, 1949.

Magoun, H. W., "The Ascending Reticular System and Wakefulness," in J. F. Delafresnaye (ed.), *Brain Mechanisms and Consciousness*, Springfield, IL, Thomas, 1954.

Mahler, M., *On Human Symbiosis and the Vicissitudes of Individuation*, New York, International Universities Press, 1968.

—— "Symbiosis and Individuation: The Psychological Birth of the Human Infant," *The Psychoanalytic Study of the Child* 29: 89–106, Yale University Press, New Haven, 1974.

Mai, F. M. and H. Merskey, "Briquet's Treatise on Hysteria: A Synopsis and Commentary," *Archives of General Psychiatry* 37, 1980.

Maslow, A., *The Farther Reaches of Human Nature*, New York, Viking Press, 1971.

Matsakis, A., *Post Traumatic Stress Disorder: A Complete Treatment Guide*, Oakland, New Harbringer Publications, Inc., 1994.

deMause, L. *Foundations of Psychohistory*, New York, Creative Roots, Inc., 1982.

McFarlane, A., B. van der Kolk and L. Weisaeth (Eds.), *Traumatic Stress: The Effects of Overwhelming Experience on Mind, Body, and Society*, New York, The Guilford Press, 1966.

McTaggart, L., *The Field Updated*, New York, Harper Collins, 2008.

Mendelsohn, R. M., *The Synthesis of Self*, New York, Plenum Medical Book Co., 1987.

Moore, T., *Care of the Soul*, New York: Harper Perennial, 1992.

—— *The Re-Enchantment of Everyday Life*, New York, Harper Perennial, 1996.

Muller, R. J., *Doing Psychiatry Wrong: A Critical and Prescriptive Look at a Faltering Profession*, New York, The Analytic Press/Taylor & Francis Group. 2008.

Murphy, L.B. and Moriarty, A. E., *Vulnerability, Coping and Growth*. New Haven, CT, Yale University Press, 1976.

Nadelson, C. C., M. T. Notman, H. Zackson, and J. Gornick, "A Follow-up Study of Rape Victims," *American Journal of Psychiatry* 139:1266-1270, 1982.

Nasiri, O., *Inside Jihad*, New York, Basic Books, 2006.

The New Testament of the Jerusalem Bible, Reader's Edition, New York, Image Books, 1969.

Nicholson, R. A. (ed.), *The Mathnavi of Jalalu'ddin Rumi*, Leiden, E. J. Brill, 1940.

Olds, J., *Drives and Reinforcements*, New York, Raven, 1977.

Othmer, E. and C. DeSouza, "A Screening Test for Somatization Disorder (hysteria)," *American Journal of Psychiatry* 142:1146-49, 1985.

Oyle, I. and S. Jean, *The Wisdom Within*. Tiboron, CA, H.J. Kramer Inc. 1992.

Pape, R., *Dying to Win: The Strategic Logic of Suicide Terrorism*, New York, Random House, 2005.

Papez, J., "A Proposed Mechanism of Emotion," *Archives of Neurology and Physiology* 38, 1937.

Peck, M. S., *The Road Less Traveled and Beyond*, New York, Simon and Schuster, 1997.

Penrose, R., *Shadows of the Mind*, New York, Oxford University Press, 1994.

Peterson, K. C., M. F. Prout, and R. A. Schwarz, *Post Traumatic Stress Disorder: A Clinician's Guide*, New York, Plenum Press, 1991.

Pribram, K., Languages of the Brain, Experimental Paradoxes and Principles in Neuropsychology, Englewood Cliffs, NJ, Prentice-Hall, 1977.

Putnam, J. J., "On the Etiology and Pathogenesis of the Post-traumatic Psychoses and Neuroses." *Journal of Nervous and Mental Disease* 25, 1898.

Reagan, R., *Where is the Rest of Me?* New York, Duell, Sloan and Pierce, 1965.

Reuter, C., *My Life is a Weapon: A Modern History of Suicide Bombing*, New Jersey, Princeton University Press, 2004.

Robbins, L. N., J. E. Helzer, M. M. Weissman, H. Orvaschel, E. Gruenberg, J. D. Burke Jr. and D.A. Regier, "Lifetime Prevalence of Specific Psychiatric Disorders in Three Sites." *Archives of General Psychiatry* 41:1687–92, 1984.

Rosen, D. M. *Armies of Young: Child Soldiers War and Terrorism*, New Jersey, Rutgers University Press, 2005.

Rossi, E. L., *Dreams and the Growth of Personality: Expanding Awareness in Psychotherapy*, New York, Brunner/Mazel, 1985.

—— *The Psychobiology of Mind-Body Healing*, New York, W. W. Norton and Company, Inc. 1986.

Russell, B., *The Autobiography of Bertrand Russell*, Vol.1, Boston, Little-Brown, 1967.

Russell, D. E. H., *Sexual Exploitation: Rape, Child Sexual Abuse and Workplace Harassment*, Beverly Hills, CA, Sage, 1984.

Sadock, B. J. and V. A. Sadock, "Obsessive-compulsive disorder" in Kaplan and Sadock (eds.) *Synopsis of Psychiatry*, 2007, pp. 604–612.

Schrödinger, E., *What is Life?* London, Cambridge Press, 1969.

Sears, W., *Thief in the Night*, Oxford, George Ronald Publishers, 1961.

Seligman, M., *Learned Optimism*, New York, Pocket Books, 1998.

—— *Authentic Happiness*, New York, Simon and Schuster, 2002.

Selye, H., *The Stress of Life*, New York, McGraw-Hill, 1976.

Shah, Idries, *Tales of Dervishes*, Oxfordshire, Pergamon Press, 1967.

Shakespeare, *Henry the IV, Part One*, London, Oxford University Press.

Shapiro, F., *Eye Movement Desensitization and Reprocessing*, New York, The Guilford Press, 1995.

Shay, J., *Achilles in Vietnam: Combat Trauma and the Undoing of Character*. New York, Touchstone, 1994.

Shoghi Effendi: The Promised Day Is Come, Wilmette, IL, Bahá'í Publishing Trust, 1967.

Smith, G. R., "Somatization Disorder in a Medical Setting," APA Publishing Trust, 1991.

Spiegel, D., "Dissociation and Trauma," in Lutherville, M. D., (ed.) *Dissociative Disorders: A Clinical Review*, Baltimore, Sidran Press, 1993.

Spitz, R. A., *A Genetic Field Theory of Ego Formation*. New York, International Universities Press, Inc.,1959.

Strachey, J., (ed. and trans.), *The Standard Edition of the Complete Psychological Works of Sigmund Freud*, Vol. 15, London, Hogarth Press, 1962.

Stuart, I. R. and J. G. Greer (eds.), *Victims of Sexual Aggression: Treatment of Children, Women, and Men*. New York: Van Nostrand Reinhold Co., 1984.

Swift, J., *Gulliver's Travels*, London, Oxford University Press, 1998.

Talbot, M., *The Holographic Universe*, New York, Harper Perennial, 1991.

Tedeschi, R. G. and L. G. Calhoun, *Post-Traumatic Growth*, Philadelphia, PA, Lawrence Erlbaum Associates, 1998.

Thoreau, H. D., *Walden*, New York, The Library of America, 1985.

Tolle, E., A New Earth: Awakening to Your Life's Purpose, Dutton, 2005

Toynbee, A., *A Study of History*, New York, McGraw-Hill, 1972.

United States Department of Health and Human Services Administration on Children, Youth and Families, Washington, DC, Government Printing Office, 2006. Available at: http://www..acf.dhhs.Gov.Program/cb

United States Criminal Justice Statistical Analysis Center, *Official Reports of Domestic Violence Victimization*, 2000 to 2005.

Vasquez, C., P. Pérez-Sales, and G. Hervás, *Positive effects of Terrorism and Posttraumatic Growth: An Individual and Community Perspective*, New York, Lawrence Erlbaum Publishers, 2007.

Wallace, R. K., "Physiological effects of transcendental meditation," *Science*

167, 1970, pp. 1751–1754.

Walsh, N. D., *Conversations with God*, Charlottesville, NC, Hampton Roads Publishers, 1998.

Watts, C. and C. Zimmerman, "Violence against Women: A Global Burden," *The Lancet* 359(9313):1172–1172, 2002.

Watzlawick, P. *The Language of Change*, New York, Basic Books, Inc. 1987.

Weber, R., "Reflections on David Bohm's Holomovement: A Physicist's Model of Cosmos and Consciousness," in Valle, R. S. and R. von Eckartsberg (eds.), *The Metaphors of Consciousness*, New York, Plenum Press, 1981.

Webster, R., *Neurotransmitters, Drugs and Brain Function*, New York, Wiley and Sons, 2001.

Williamson, M., *A Return to Love*, New York, Harper Collins, 1990.

Woolf. V., *Moments of Being*, New York, Harcourt, Brace, Jovanovich, 1977.

World Health Organization, *Bulletin* 6:401–480, 2005.

Yehuda, R., *Treating Trauma Survivors with PTSD*, Washington, DC, APA Publishing Trust, 2002.

Zeig, J. (ed.), *A teaching Seminar with Milton H. Erickson*, New York, Brunner/ Mazel, Publishers, 1980.

Zimmer, H., *The King and the Corpse*, New York, Bollingen Series, 1948.

Zonderman, S., *A Study of Volunteer Rape Crisis Counselors*, Smith College Studies in Social Work, 1975.

About the author

Dr. Ebrahim Amanat is currently Clinical Associate Professor of Psychiatry at Keck School of Medicine, at the University of Southern California and Child/Adolescent Psychiatry Consultant with the Los Angeles County Department of Mental Health. He is a writer, lecturer, and educator, having taught in various university settings for the past 40 years, and a life fellow of the American Psychiatric Association. Dr. Amanat is the author of several books, including *Depression and Suicide* (1967), *Specific Learning Disabilities* (1968), *Riddle of Dreams* (2003), *A Return to Respect* (2006), and *The Troubled Adolescent: A Practical Guide* (ed. with Jean Beck 1984). He is the author of several monographs on creative parenting, anger and grief, and various pathologies. His professional papers have been published in such journals as the *American Journal of Orthopsychiatry, Journal of Adolescence, Res. Medica,* the *Journal of Child Psychiatry and* Human Development as well as Journal of Family Therapy.

Dr. Amanat is the recipient of awards from both the American Medical Association and the American Psychiatric Association for his contributions to the field of psychiatry and a Congressional Citation for his services to victims of trauma. He received the Hands on Hearts Medal from the Veterans' Administration, and a Special Recognition Award from the Los Angeles Vet Center.

After receiving his first medical degree from the University of Tehran, Iran in 1960, Dr. Amanat came to the United States, where he received further training in adult, child, and adolescent psychiatry, and later in dynamic psychiatry, communicative therapies, Ericksonian approaches, and the use of spiritual metaphors. He returned to Iran for three years to teach and immigrated to United States in 1970.

For the past 30 years, he has been active in the field of trauma desensitization and 12-step programs in California and Missouri.

Dr. Amanat lives in California with his wife Mahin Mashhood Amanat, MD.

Breinigsville, PA USA
08 December 2010
250913BV00005B/135/P